EDUCATION FOR DALITS

EDUCATION FOR DALITS

By

L. Venkateswara Reddy
M.A. M.Ed. (Ph.D.)
Vice-Principal
Chaitanya College of Education
Markapur
Prakasam Distt., A.P.

M. Lakshmi Narayana
M.Sc., M.Ed.
Lecturer
Vinukonda B.Ed., College
Vinukonda, Narasaraopet
Guntur Distt., A.P.

General Editor
Dr. Digumarti Bhaskara Rao
M.Sc., M.A., M.A., M.Ed., Ph.D.
Reader
R.V.R. College of Education
Srinivasa Nagar Colony
Guntur–522 006
Andhra Pradesh
India

DISCOVERY PUBLISHING HOUSE
NEW DELHI-110002

First Published-2004
Reprinted: 2013
ISBN 81-7141-872-4

Published by

DISCOVERY PUBLISHING HOUSE
4831/24, Ansari Road, Prahlad Street,
Darya Ganj, New Delhi-110002 (India)
Phone: 23279245 • Fax: 91-11-23253475
E-mail:dphtemp@indiatimes.com

Printed at: Dynamic printers,

Contents

Preface

Despite all sloganeering and tall claims, very little has practically been done for the empowerment and upliftment of the downtrodden in our society — the Dalits.

No doubt Dalits have been receiving education and training for last many decades now. They are also recruited in services in a fixed number — thanks to reservation. Yet, the educated, advanced and emancipated among the Dalits are far less than other classes and groups in our social fabric, if their ratio in population is taken into account.

The fact is that, Dalits need all encouragement in the field of education and deserve to be emancipated in academic vocations.

In order to focus on the core issues and practical problems, this author has presented this research-based work for the benefit of scholars, teachers and students, engaged in the field of education. The undersigned hopes to be encouraged and appreciated for this effort in an area, where remains a dearth for good books.

Author

1 Introduction

In India, the Scheduled Castes are a stigmatised lot and on this account they suffer from a number of disabilities that are buttressed by religion. Some of their disabilities are "untouchability", segregation, low economic status, politically less powerful, low level of education and little chances of mobilization. All these factors, reinforce each other mutually only to worsen the lot of Scheduled Castes. Though legally or constitutionally they are no longer "untouchables", in practice many of them still bear that stigma.

In the beginning of the last century Scheduled Castes were also called harijans[1] (children of God). Many of the "untouchable" leaders wondered as to why they had been singled out as `children of God'? Were not others also the children of God? If not, whose children are they after all? They saw through in this division another attempt of subtle segregation from the rest of the Hindus. The "untouchables" were also called *avarna, pariah,* and out-caste, because they had been keptout of *chaturvarna* scheme of social stratification and are below the line of pollution and considered inferior to the "twice born". They were also known as *panchamas* because they supposedly came after the *chaturvarna*. Their touch and some times their shadow and even their voice are believed to pollute caste Hindus. There may be a regional variations in the form and content; "untouchability" may range from the notion of pollution by sight or hearing or proximity in the south, to pollution by direct physical contact in the north. But this affirmation remained with us from times immemorial.

For the purpose of present study the term dalit has been used to include all those people of different communities among the Scheduled Castes who were traditionally subjected to invidious discriminations on grounds of "untouchability" and categorised as "untouchables", downtrodden, exterior castes, ex-untouchables, Depressed classes or *Dalits*. This study was deciphered with special reference to Andhra.

As far as the Census reports are concerned, there are 59 *Dalit communities* (sub-castes) in Andhra. *Madigas* constitute the largest number, i.e., about 15.94 per cent of total population and their percentage in total Scheduled Caste population is 45.8. They are followed by *Malas* constituting 37.9 per cent and *Adi-Andhras* 6.8 per cent. These three subcastes form bulk of total *Dalit* population in Andhra accounting for as much as 90.6 per cent. The share of rest of the 56 communities is mere 9.5 per cent. Due to this dearth of information and historical evidence, in this chapter only two major communities, i.e., *Malas* and *Madigas* have taken up for detailed examination.

The chapter comprises three parts. Firstly, an attempt has been made to study educational development among dalits. And the role of various agencies/organisations which led the dalits and formed their ideologies in their effort to challenge an exploitative tradition of the society. We shall examine the attitude and influence of the British officials, the effect of Missionary activities on local dalit communities, and the growing realization among the "untouchables" that in education lay the key to future development. Secondly, we shall study how educational development resulted in the rise and growth of dalit movement to build their own identity in the Indian socio-political fabric. Between 1920-1940 they gained much importance in the game of numbers in Census reports. Thirdly, we shall examine how the process of identity formation culminated in the emergence of "Adi" ideology.

It has become one of the truisms of the historical procession that the peasants of traditional societies are the 'Silent Actors' of history. If this is true, the same way applied to an even greater degree to dalit communities of India. When we attempt to trace the rise of an educational movement among dalits, we face an acute shortage of direct evidence about the realities of dalit social life even for most of the nineteenth century. Unfortunately, neither official nor non-official sources or statistics are detailed and sophisticated enough to be put together a comprehensive picture of dalits. Till recently, their origins are obscure and difficult to trace their development and their presence was neglected. In standard history work on India, dalits were treated either as marginal people without a history of their own or as objects rather than subjects. Often these works do not mention these "untouchables". Even if a sentence or a paragraph was, written about them, certainly it would be of rules which spoke on how to avoid of how to punish "untouchables". Fortunately, recent decades have witnessed a group of socially concerned scholars (mostly foreign scholars) and a growing number of dalit intellectuals seeking directions for the future through a better understanding of the dalit past.

The Indian system of education in the past was non-universalist, parochial and partisan. Though the content might appear to have universal appeal at first sight, ancient Indian education was, after all, the product of Indian outlook on knowledge and corresponding scheme of life and values. In ancient India, the traditional Hindu social structure seemed to have evolved a system of allocation of rewards relating to prestige, power and wealth in a manner that each of the three "higher" *varnas* (dwijas) could get one of these. The Brahmin received the highest prestige in the society, the *Kshatriya* the greatest power, and the *Vaishya*, the largest share of wealth. The remaining sections of the society, broadly called *Shudras* (occupational or manufacturing castes) rendered services of a personal nature and were engaged in growing food and in manufacturing articles of necessity and comfort. To the extent religion provided the basis for this social stratification, inequality had been a structural features of the traditional Hindu value system. An inequitable division of function was legitimated by religion and a social structure based on caste endogamy ensured its continuity. Maintaining such an order necessitated a value system, thought and logic, which the educational pattern and content facilitated education was a preserve of only few privileged sections through i.e. until the nineteenth century when western education was introduced. Education in such a society was meant essentially to the perpetuation of a new generation to take the place of the previous one. As such the education imposes cultural values and interests of the "upper" castes/privileged classes. The reproduction of culture through education is shown to play a key role in the reproduction of the whole social system. It served as a potent means of social control. Thus education since times immemorial till the end of nineteenth century was limited only to a few privileged castes. In pre-British Indian society had a religious content and theological causation was supreme. In contrast, the modern education system introduced by the British was theoretically open to all and its contents were secular.

Instructions in formal education or for that matter in any kind of education for more than one reason was seen necessary and more or less limited only to the dwijas ("twice-born") castes.[15] The Brahmin, who was engaged with the classical religious texts interpreted and communicated them to the illiterate masses in their local dialects. The *Kshatriyas* has to learn to rule and get aquinted with weapons, state crafts and organizational matters and some schooling for this purpose was necessary. The *Vaishyas* required the knowledge of arthmetic for transcating business, keeping records and maintaining accounts. While some sort of skills necessary for carrying on the crafts at the domestic level could well be acquired within home, i.e., the artisan groups or Shudras. So the "untouchables" were the only section of the society left out with no accessibility to education of any kind. The ancient law giver Manu, prescribed that education of Shudra children was an offence and this doctrine was in very much practice till the fag end of nineteenth century. Denial of education to the dalits perpetuated their social humiliation, economic exploitation, political marginalization and cultural subordination.

The initiative for modern education in early modern Europe created new techniques evolved for building radically new institutions for "mass", "national" even "popular" education inspired by apocalyptic dreams and millenarian vision. The movement, inspired and advanced by August Hermann Francke

(1663-1727) of Halle University, spread to the royal houses of Denmark and Honouer and the Court of St. James helped generate the Society for Promoting Knowledge (SPCK), which in turn promoted educational work in India. By 1780s, schools run by Christian Friedrich Schwartz and his associates were attracted by many non-Christian students especially Brahmins and other "upper" castes who hoped that the new learning would better qualify them for positions within rapidly expanding establishments of the Company.

By the first half of the nineteenth century some more new developments had taken place in the educational history of Madras presidency. Sir Thomas Munroo, Governor of Madras (1820-1827) introduced a comprehensive and farsighted scheme, after realising the fact that literacy was confined to Brahmins, merchants, village lords and "principal ryots". Although Munro had no wish to interfere with the existing indigenous educational pattern and held the view that the people should be left to manage their schools in their own way, he ordered a general survey of "complete list of schools in each district showing the number of scholars and teachers, castes to which they belonged books and the materials they used and the sources of funding for these institutions. The results of this survey, along with an estimation of Census data provides a fascinating view on education of 1820s, more precisely in 1823-25. Madras Presidency as a whole, there were 12,498 schools and 188,000 students in population of 12,850,941 roughtly 1 school per 1000 persons and 1 student per 67 persons. Education was under the control of Brahmins and religious in content and the medium being Sanskrit and Telugu. Brahmins comprised 60 to 75 per cent of all pupils for out numbering "clean" non-Brahmin, mercantile communities and former-warrior lords of villages. The books used in these institutions were either directly derived from the *Vedas* and various *Shastras, Puranas* or from the other epic literature, and the teachers were none others but a brahimns.

One shocking aspect of the report of the survey was, the virtual exclusion of "untouchable" communities from education. The category "pariah" or "unclean" Shudra invariably found in other Census reports is conspicuously absent here. While significantly, the number of Brahminial (Aryan or Sanskrit) social categories the *kshatriyas* being a notable omission: Moreover, survey figures themselves reveal that Brahmins and *Vaishyas* made up an average of 34.5 per cent of all pupils in village schools. The "untouchable" communities, whether it was "pariahs" and "Pallars" (of Tamil speaking areas) or "Malas" and "Madigas" (of Telugu speaking areas) or any other of the servile communities, who made up half of the population, were not counted. The reasons being that the Brahmins made up the forms and then done much of the actual work so there is less possibility that one could expect them to enter to *dalit wadas* (Dalit hamlets) to get an actual report or state of their affairs. The whole efforts of Munro to patronize popular education was heroic but short-lived. It was heroic because while the Governments of Bengal and Bombay were getting confused between oriental and western learning for the higher classes, Munro made a herculean attempt to foster popular education of masses through the vernaculars with a vision of improving the lot of Indians. It was short-lived because although Munro weathered all storms in his effort to introduce vernacular education to masses from 1822, his elaborate schemes were reversed immediately after his death in 1830, in favour of English education. This reversal seems paradoxical because of the adherence to the filtration theory appeared stronger in Madras presidency than elsewhere.

The Charter Act of 1813, realised the importance and permitted the missionaries to work in the Indian territories of the Company for the education and proselytization of the Indian masses, a fertile ground for proselytization. Later in 1823 the General Committee on Public Instruction was set up to give a shape to government policies. In 1837 English was made the language of administration and a Government Resolution of 1844 threw subordinate positions open to Indians. Therefore, the English education attracted Indians and rapid expansions of English education were taking place. The famous Wood's Despatch of 1854, realised the need of educating the masses not only through English but through the vernacular as well.

After the Despatch of 1854, the Director of Public Instruction took charge of the Department of Education. In spite of innumerable subjects "Rate Schools" which were novel to the presidency and unique to Andhra especially Godavari district. The rate schools were the schools started in the district of Godavari, under the enthusiastic scheme, the villagers were to contribute for the education of their children. The ryots voluntarily subjected themselves to a rate or subscription to maintain schools in their villages. As per the system of rate schools it was directly connected only with the land-holding classes, who could contribute for their maintenance along with their regular revenue payments. Since the "untouchable" communities constituted the bulk of agricultural labourers with the absence of land they could not benefit from these rate school system. This scheme of voluntary rate lost its voluntary aspect and had to be legalised with the Madras Education Act of 1863.

The above mentioned discussion shows that there was no provisions for education of "untouchables" in the indigenous educational system. Munro's enquiries also throws a good deal of light that there were a few backward class pupils but none from "untouchables". As a result of the dominance of filtration theory and the fear of offending the caste Hindu people, the British Government in India made no efforts till the end of nineteenth century to make a provision for the education of "untouchables". But the official apathy was compensated by the pioneering efforts of missionaries to educate deprived communities in general and "untouchables" in particular.

It has been found in the annals of modern missionaries that the new branch of missionary activities called "Educational Mission" owes its inception to Alexander Duff of the Free Church of Scotland. He intented that western education and values imparted by missionaries through their English medium schools be used as an effective instrument of evangelicism. The Association of Christian Missionaries with Telugu speaking people dates back to the 15th century, when two Jesuit Fathers and a Brother worked their way to Chandragiri in Chittoor district. The missionaries took the initiative for imparting education and to prepare the "untouchables" for higher walks of life. By working for the welfare of the deprived communities the missionaries succeeded in luring thousands of them to the fold of Christianity. In Madras presidency both Telugu and Tamil speaking regions during and after the appalling famine of 1876-1879, in which the missionaries rendred to the famine stricken people, the "untouchables" saw the contrast between Hinduism which marginalised them and Christianity that helped them in distress went into the fold of Christianity.

With the yeomen service extended by Christian missionaries, dalits realised that they cannot depend upon their own countrymen. Either in social recognition or in economic benefits at the need of the hour, one like during the famines, missionaries came forward and stretched their helping hands but not the Hindus. Slowly and gradually dalit converts increased in number.

The Christian missionaries believed that caste was the strongest obstacle to the spread of the Christian faith. Hence they adopted a new strategy to change the way of life by establishing schools, bringing social reform etc. which helped the deprived communities. Though, proselytization continued to remain throughout as the ultimate aim their yeoman service in the other fields gained recognition and popularity among the "untouchables" of Andhra.

By the end of nineteenth century nearly twenty Mission Societies were established and started their emancipation work in Telugu speaking areas of erstwhile Madras presidency. In 1700 A.D. Karnatic Mission was established at Nellore and later, extended their branches to Cuddapah and Krishna districts. Roman Catholic Mission established at Cuddapah in 1735, London Missionary Society at Visakhapatnam and extended to Bellary, Anantapuram and Vizianagaram areas. These were again followed by Society De Missions Strangers was established by French in Krishna district, Vikar of Apostolic Mission established in 1832 later expanded to Nellore, Cuddapah, Anantaputam and Krishna. American Baptist Mission was established in 1840 and expanded to Udayagiri, Ongole, Bapatla, Khambam and Kurnool areas. American Lutheran Mission came in 1842 was later on expanded to Gantur, Repalle, Bapatla, Palnadu, Vinukonda, Bandaru and Rajahmundry.

The Protestant Mission commenced its operations from 1843

in and around areas of Nellore, Guntur and Blandaru. They established many educational institutions, with Nobel College in Machilipatnam being one of them. The Free Church of Scotland was established at Nellore in 1848, and English Church Missionary Society in 1865. They worked in the districts of Krishna, Godavari,Kurnool and Cuddaph and extended its branches in all possible towns including Nandyala, Mutyala Padu, Bandaru, Eluru, Bezawada etc. Later on in 1890, the Canadian Baptist Mission established branches at Kakinada, Bheeminipatnam, Srikakulam, Baptist Mission established branches at Kakinada, Bheeminipatnam, Srikakulam, Bobbili and Tuni. These were followed by Basel Evangelican Missionary, Chelwing Hostein Luthern Mission, and St. Francis of Sales Mission.

Aş part of their philanthropic work they established schools and colleges attached to the Churches and did a good deal for the upliftment of the oppressed sections, and through this process, missions introduced the humanistic element of the western civilization to the natives.

Missionaries by providing education, Medical and other social service activities not only benefited them in terms of conversion or proselytization, but also opened the eyes of the Caste-Hindus about the marginalisation of these unfortunate masses. Starting from second half of the nineteenth century to early decades of twentieth century many "Untouchables" perhaps also compromised with proselytization because they resented the rigid customs and ill-treatment of Caste Hindus, which were product of Chaturvarna scheme, buttressed by Hindu religion and were saddled with various forms of discrimination. Conversion not only changed the life style of "untouchables" but also influenced a lot of caste Hindus, later to follow the lives of the "untouchables."

The Mass conversion Movements in Andhra, particularly among the "Untouchables" in favour of Christianity gained currency and continued remaining well in to the early decades of twentieth century. According to 1931 Census it is estimated that nearly 20 per cent of depressed classes (then untouchables were counted under this phrase) in West Godavari, 32 per cent in Krishna and 57 per cent in Guntur district had been converted to

Christianity. In some areas there were converts of each and every "untouchable" of the hamlet. Malas and Madigas had been ordained in increasing numbers and by early twentieth century, the casual observer might well have been excused for thinking that Churches existed solely to serve the needs of the deprived and the outcastes. The missionary contribution had helped by providing literacy to illiterate uplifting the Dalits instituting western ideals and principles and cultivating a feeling of nationalism among Indians.

The work of Christian missionaries were benefitted by different communities in different ways. "Untouchables" took this in two ways. Firstly, those who got converted to Christianity, got a new standing in it and they felt that this was certainly better than suffering under Hinduism. Secondly, those who still remained in the fold of Hinduism started realising that the dogma of 'untouchability' which for so long had justified their miserable condition was false and the same was not held by the missionaries.

The caste-Hindus who witnessed the amelioration work of missionaries and who were exposed to the western education and knowledge started loosing faith in Hinduism and caste. However, neither all the educated Hindus became totally indifferent to Hinduism, nor even those who lost faith in Hinduism went to the fold of Christianity. Surprisingly they stopped at 'half way houses' like Brahma Samaj. Both groups of neo-orthodox (western educated) and the traditional orthodox (non-western educated) Hindus tried to organize Hinduism such Brahmos in Bengal, Arya Samajists in Punjab. Theosophilical society in South India. The basic tenets of all these were not only unopposing Hinduism but were very much interested in bringing out all sects of Hindus into one, to reform Hinduism. The activists later on known as reformers of modern times either religious or social. Another aspect of missionaries worth mentioning here is, they stimulated the Hindu socio-religious reformers to bring about social developments and education among Dalits so as to reform Hinduism and to prevent them from embracing other religions like Christianity and Islam.

The impact of western humanitarian, liberal and rationalist ideas stirred several Hindu reformist movements, beginning about the middle of the nineteenth century. The social reformers of the nineteenth century perceived "Caste system" as morally and ethnically abhorrent, socially debating and politically devisive. From second half of nineteenth century to early decades of twentieth century the reform movement worked on humanitarian grounds, were as after 1920 it took a political form. Education occupied a cardinal place in the programme of social reform movement in Andhra. In addition to reform Hinduism other equally strong motivation being their fervent attempt to formulate and implement an alternative based on science and mass education through the medium of vernacular languages to counter the educational enterprise of the government, either primary or university education (which) was always within the confines of the colonial needs and interests. So also the social reforms of Andhra realized and recognized the need to develop vernaculars to spread reformist ideal among ignorant masses.

The two outstanding individual reformers of Andhra were Telugu brahmins, Kandukuri Vireslingam (1948-1919) and Raghupati Venkataratnam Naidu (1862-1939). Viresalingam centred his activities in and around Rajahmundry and northern circars, while Venkataratnam concentrated in the vicinities of Kakinada and Machilipatnam. They appealed for the eradication of caste distraction and advocated sympathy towards "untouchables". These two were followed by many such as Unnava Laxminarayana, (a brahmin writer), Tripuraneui Ramaswamy Choudhary (a Khamma, poet) etc. All these reformers considered education as an instrument to bring about the amelioration of untouchables.

A few enlightened members provided education for "untouchables" Andhra Deena Sangham was founded at Machilipatnam in 1907 to attend of the social economic and spiritual aspects of the ameliorative work. It gave a good deal of concern to education and by 1924, they could open 12 night schools, day schools and one part-time school for girls in and around Machilipatnam. Handicrafts such as tailoring, drawing, tape-weaving were taught in these schools to help "untouchables" to lead an independent life.

Philanthropic-minded caste-Hindus played a major role in uplifting the "untouchables". Vireslingam started a school and admitted `untouchables' children and gave them free education with the help of his highness the Maharaja of Pithapuram. The Maharaja of Pithapuram motivated by reformist ideas undertook number of welfare oriented activities for the "untouchables". He not only provided admission for dalits in their high school at Kakinada, but also established two separate hostels for Dalit boys and girls and the other hostel called Ram Mohun Roy hostel at Kakinada for dalits who were pursuing college education. Infact, most of the first generation of Dalit intellectuals of Andhra were products of these educational institutions sponsored by the charitable assistance of his highness the Maharaja.

Though R. Venkataratnam Naidu began his reformist activities in late 1880s, but constructive work for dalit education was possible only after he became Principal of Pithapuram Rajah College (1905-1919). He also presided over many anti-untouchability Conferences in the presidency. Ram Mohan Roy School for dalits at Rajahmundry was started by Chilakamarti Laxminarasimham in 1909, with English as well as Telugu as medium of instruction. He also offered free tutions to the dalit children.

Religious and revivalist organizations like Prathana Samaj, Brahmo Samaj and Arya Samaj vehemently criticized the evils of caste system and pleaded for education of untouchability but did nothing concrete in this area. While Prathana Samaj was more on humanitarian lines, that of Arya Samaj was for cultural domination and Hindu consolidation. The members of Manya Sangam and Adi-Andhra Society showed an inclination towards brahmoism for its rejection of the authority of Vedas and discording of Yagnopaneeta (*Jandyam* or the "sacred" thread). But soon they realized that the "untouchable" converts to Arya Samaj did not receive any kind of respectful treatment like any other caste Hindu convert.

Later developments, which severed dalits connection with Arya Samaj, confirmed the deep-rooted prejudices of the caste Hindus. It betrayed their conviction that by becoming Arya

Samajists, the heart of the Hindus would change and that they would reform the "untouchable" communities, and raise them to their level of enlightenment. Exemplifying this, there was an incident in 1914, at the Arya Samaj Anniversary at Bengampet Vaidik Ashram. A competition was conducted among the pupils of schools to receive vedmanthras with their meaning, which was also participated by Adi-Hindu Primary Schools. When a dalit student stood first and gained the applause of the audience, the Secretary of the Vaidik Ashram felt jealous since a Brahmin student could not compete and made a rude and vulgar remark to the dalit student. He said that a *Chandal* (an "untouchable") do not deserve such a honour, and finally the prize was not given to the dalit student. Consequently, dalits severed their connections with the Arya Samaj and gardually they withdrew themselves from the cobweb of the reformers.

By the second decade of the twentieth century the social reform movements, initiated by Kandukuri Viresalingam and his fellow members had come to an end. This was partly due to death of Viresalingam (1919) and increasing popularity and mass political agitations of Indian National Congress and emergence of numerous caste associations were said to have been reasons for the decline of social reform in Andhra. But this was countered by saying that "from 1920s social reform acquired wider dimension and a new orientations:". What are those forms and orientations? On the one hand Gandhian concensus model of reform. "internal reform and self purification" did nothing constructively but only tried to integrate the dalits and to solidify Hinduism. At another level nationalist press, focussed on the evil practice of untouchability, and much of sympathetic literature was produced in all possible forms, such as songs, pamphlets, novels and short-stories. But the question is when there was no scope for education for Dalits, how could they read the literature? Every one became writer and speaker, but none was there to follow or listen. So the whole efforts of caste-Hindu writings did not make much sense. But, by 1920s Government realised their biased attitude towards Dalit education, but for long they were hesitant to implement their policies for the upliftment of "untouchables" with the fear of offending the caste-

Hindus. The efforts taken by the colonial agencies toward Dalit education is also worth mentioning here.

The policy of protective discrimination developed in stages since the Woods Despatch of 1854. The lower castes had been excluded from higher education 1854 in accordance with downward filtration theory which advocated higher education to the "higher" caste alone. The then Board of Directors of Education felt that until the prejudices of the people in this respect were overcome, what was intended to enlighten the great mass of people might otherwise, from their prejudices degenerate into a boon to the lowest classes alone. The reply of the government to the letter of the Court Directors of May 5, 1854, stated that nobody should be refused admission to a government school or a College merely on the ground of Caste. The woods Despatch of 1854 threw open education to all classes and the despatch of 1857 discouraged the idea of separate schools for the lower castes.

However, the opposition of the high castes to the admission of students from the depressed classes in public schools was very strong in the Madras presidency. The government considered its earlir decision and the Education Commission Report of 1883 recommended the establishment of separate schools wherever necessary. In 1891, approving the institution of separate schools, the Hindu wrote that it is impossible to expect caste-Hindu children and these classes to study together in the same schools. Nor can much be expected from local boards... Government is perfectly justified in showing special consideration to a class, whose conditions must be a blot on any civilized social system.

In 1893, the Madras government sanctioned a series of proposals, which were widely hailed as the Magna Carta of *panchama* education. Among the measures recommended by it were: special training schools with a higher stipend for *panchama* students and teacher trainees: establishment of special schools by local boards and municipalities for *panchamas* in all villages, wherever they were in large numbers; grant of *poromboke* lands for *panchama* schools; Night schools, for which suited the labouring classes: non-claiming of refund of building grants if the buildings were used for school purposes for six years etc.

However, there were difficulties in conducting even separate schools because of the caste prejudices of the officer. Most of the inspecting staff belonging to 'higher' caste, were reluctant to enter Dalit colonies and inspect their schools. An Indian Christian Missionary Society true to its mission brought to the notice of the government in 1905, that the caste consciousness inspector declined to enter Dalit villages and called up the school well beyond the village and examined even written answers of the pupils from a distance not less than ten feet and wished to get away from there as soon as he could. Even Government of India had confessed that the officials of educational departments were displaying a hostile attitude towards the educational matters of the lower classes.

Apart from these separate schools for Dalits, Board of Revenue recommend the appointment of a special agency for the promotion of the interests of those classes. It observed that however liberal might be the attitude of the government towards them and whatever might be the facilities created for the improvement of their conditions, the effect desired could not be produced as long as there was no separate agency to carry out the policy of the government in this respect. Along with an agency the government felt the need of "a special officer with a suitable staff under him should be appointed as protector of the depressed classes" remarked the Board of Revenue. The functions of this officer were to study the economic conditions of these classes and submit proposals to the government for improving it, to see the philanthropic bodies working in the field received such help from the government as they required, and to promote education and other better living facilities. Among the important measures adopted under this agency were the admission of students from these castes to public managed schools, and stoppage of grants to private schools which excluded them, and financial assistance through fellowships and remission of fees etc.

As a result, the new special agency was termed as the Labour Department, not as the name may suggest for the benefit of industrial workers, but for the upliftment of depressed classes. C.F. Paddison, a senior ICS officer as the first special officer designated as the Commissioner of Labour, and a Deputy

Commissioner of Labour was appointed in 1920. A Labour Advisory Board comprised of one European, one Brahmin, and one Adi-Dravaida (Member of an "untouchable") was also constituted in the same year. A district labour office was also constituted in 1922 and in the districts there special works had also been commenced.

The labour department started its work in Godavari District in 1920 and grew fast in size and scope. Between 1921 and 1924 extensive activities on a gradual increasing scale were undertaken in Krishna and Guntur districts. Promotion of elementary education was a primary concern of labour department, which started separate primary schools for the depressed classes called "labour schools". The number of these schools increased with the general expansion of the activities of the department.

The admission of "untouchable" children increased slowly. In 1918-1919, subsidies were sanctioned to local bodies, for opening of 82 additional elementary schools for the benefit of these classes. The Board elementary schools at Veeravasaram (Peddapuram Taluk), Kapieswarapuram, Sankatayapalem (Ramachandrapuram Taluk) admitted "untouchable" children in their schools and an "untouchable" teacher was appointed at Veeravasaram.

In spite of the welfare measures and special efforts taken by the government, the progress of the educational development of "untouchables" was very low and slow. In the municipal areas of Ankapalli, Tenali Narasaraopet, Hindupur and Tirupati the numbers of depressed classes admitted into schools was nil. In Ganjam, Nellore, Ballery regions the increase was not appreciable. In Krishna district of 671 caste-Hindu schools under taluk Boards, only in 28 schools, the children of depressed classes were admitted. The only exception being Godavari district, there were 62 schools with 2414 boys and 34 girls of "untouchables" along with 43 night schools by 1922.

In spite of government orders to the district Boards to admit "untouchables" without any discrimination caste-prejudices against them unabated. The Assistant Labour Commissioner asked all the teachers to admit "untouchable" children and warned if they did not carry out government's policy, they would lose subsidies. The Director of Public Instruction also asked the local boards and Municipalities should work to remove the caste prejudices by admitting all castes. But caste-Hindu fundamentalists seemed least bothered about the government orders and warnings.

Exemplifying this, the Amalapuram Taluk Board passed a Resolution in 1920, on the collective petition of the villagers of Sakurru, Indupalli etc. that the admission of *panchamas* in public schools was undesirable. In northern Circara districts, caused some unpleasantness among the Caste-Hindus, due to their children were made to sit side by side with "untouchables". In Dharmavaram, Chandragiri, Narsapur, Gobichettiyapalayam, Pavancha taluks, caste-Hindu children were withdrawn on the admission of *panchama* children in to the schools.

Below given table shows the rise and growth of Dalit education along with caste-wise breakup from 1891 to 1931. Initial inspiration of missionary activities was followed by Philanthropic efforts, and encouraged by colonial government, but the "untouchable" education couldn't progress considerably.

As the table shows, the certain "upper" castes like Brahmin, *Komati* or *Chittiyar, Kapu* and *Reddy* were the highest educated communities. Even middle other occupational communities like *Kamsali, Balija, Mangali* were considerably better placed. Whereas the least educated communities were none other than *Malas* and *Madigas* ("Untouchables").

Again in 1931 when the Government decided to admit "exterior" castes (as Dalits were called then) pupils in all aided schools, which resulted in the closing down of many schools and from a many other schools the Caste-Hindus withdrew their children. Notwithstanding facilities provided by the Government literacy rate among Dalits was mere one per cent beyond primary stage. Before 1901 they were less than one per cent literates, and by 1931 the figure had risen slightly.

In the later parts of 1930s after the formation of popular ministries, further impetus was given to the educational programme of Dalits including scholarships and hostel facilities. Government Ordinances of the ministry period shows the steps taken for the educational development of the period. The Dalit students admitted to primary schools (labour schools) increased throughout the period. Below mentioned period demonstrates this.

The above given table reveals the manner in which the Dalit education developed in the presidency. On the one hand, the government was alotting new schools and at the same time they were closing down the schools in more numbers than they started except during 1937-38. But most of the time, these ameliorative programmes were only on the paper and no stern implementation measures were taken.

Notwithstanding special measures of the growth of Dalit education was very low in comparison with the literacy level of general population. Apart from Caste-Hindu prejudices and their non-cooperation with colonial policies, the socio-economic conditions of Dalits were also held responsible for the fall in their educational growth. Coupled with the fear of oppression by the Caste-Hindus, the maximum drop out rate reveals the fact that poverty was their constant companion, and they withdraw their children during the agricultural seasons and they force lack of availability of economic incentives. Besides the overt discrimination mented out to them by caste-Hindus, most of the Dalits come short of money for tutions, conducive environment to study. Thus, the economic backwardness in apart from social disabilities and consequent fear of oppression by the Caste-Hindus, were major impediments in the progress of Dalit education in Andhra Pradesh.

It is noticeable that educational development was very nominal because there was no room for earlier education. The earlier generation of educated Dalits, received quality education at the mercy of missionaries, philanthropic-minded reformers' efforts and help from the British government's agencies. In this way, from the first few drops of soccer of learning the fell among the parched "untouchables" by the turn of the last century resulted in trickling of educational opportunities, which began to widen into a small stream. Out of it emerged the first generation of educated untouchables. The first teachers, the first to take the few places opened to them in government services, like Military and Railways. By 1920 and 1930s more "untouchables" children followed their foot prints into schools. Those elders, still only a handful of individuals took their part in the political struggle in the congress movement and Gandhi's campaigns against British.

Growth of Dalit Education in Madras Presidency (1936-39)
(Table showing the Labour Schools and Students)

Year	*No. of Schools at the beginning of the year*	*No. of Schools Newly Started during the year*	*No. of Schools closed during the year*	*Night Schools Working*	*Total Schools working*	*Total Students*
1936-37	1006	031	59	5	0978	39,226
1937-38	0978	238	26	3	1190	48,203
1938-39	1190	036	48	3	1178	48,947

Source: Proceedings of the Labour Department, Administrative Report of Madras Presidency, G.O. 2623, Dated November 26, 1937; G.O. 2196, Dated June 11, 1938 G.O. No. 2109 dated August 25, 1939.

In the economic front, after the major irrigation schemes launching on Krishna and Godavari rivers during 19th century, started the basic intensive cultivation of rice and other cash crops for growing market. Large scale commercialization of agriculture had taken place by early parts of 20th century. This process, also eliminated traditional Caste and *Jajamani* ties which had bound the Dalit labourers, and aided in development of a mobile labour force opportunities for many Dalits to move ahead. Thousands of Dalit labourers used to travel every year from the east coast of Indian in search of work on the docks at Rangoon in Burma. This Burmese factor also played a significant role in development of their economic side of lifestyle and some of them even invested for education of their brethren back home.

During 1930s, Dalit uplift was influenced by two diversified strong currents and ended up in dividing the united Dalit movement. One is that of Gandhians, and the other is communists. Congress 'Harijan' organizing began with the formation of the Andhra branch of the Harijan Sevak Sangh at Vijayawada in November 1932. The Caste-Hindu reformers, K. Negeswara Rao and M. Bapineedu were its President and General Secretary respectively. Two Dalits, Vemula Kurmayya, (Krishna district) and Naralasetti Devendrudu (West Godavari district) were its joint secretaries. These two played a major role in organizing the Adi-Andhra conferences and educated and influenced many Dalit rural populace. Gradually the larger section of Dalit intellectuals got absorbed into the congress with its 'Harijan' technology and its reiteration of Hindu identity. Thus, it followed a cautious and a limited method of philosophy.

The other major factor, during 1930s was the emergence of communists. Communist movement entered into Dalit colonies as a working class movement and it entered more forcefully than any other movements in 1930s and 40s. They organized the rural poor, workers and agricultural labourers. As a whole, the communist movement certainly played a significant role in raising the wages of Dalit labourers, organized them from a scattered un-organized labourers into a strong force of labour unions, and educated them with socialism and marxism. Active participation of Dalits in communist movement, created a consciousness of unity and fight for their rights. At political level, though the congress claims that it was responsible for bringing the Minimum Wages Act, which benefitted Dalits more than any other section, the communist mobilization of Dalits was responsible for a constant upgradation of minimum wages; as the movement was "economic determinist".

But the communist party articulated only the questions and took a good deal of care to examine that the Dalits did not develop into an independent identity by transmigration of Ambedkarism in marxism. They did not even develop a paradigm of their own to tackle the disfigured identity of Dalits. A careful examination of communist literature of the period, even till 1970s shows that the communists addressed the Dalits as 'Harijan's while claiming themselves to be Anti-Gandhians. The mechanical application of dialectical materialism was obvious that only wage and land, they thought, would undo the Brahminical past. Nowhere a sembalance of critiquing of Brahminical tradition was found in the communist theoretical discourse.

A conscious effort was put in by Dalit intelligentsia to develop a theory of exploitation to build up a strong unity. For them, education was a weapon, with a dual purpose. Firstly, installing reform to change their living habits and superstitious practices and secondly to arouse in them a consciousness of the oppression and exploitation by the Caste-Hindus and to organize them for gaining a respectful place in the society. They realized the limitations of both the philanthropic as well as the government. It was the first generation of educated Dalits, inspired by ideas of reform and the notion of equality they took the initiative of organizing the educational activities for their communities.

Dalit intelligentsia criticized the existing educational methods and expressed their grievances. Gurram Jashua, powerful and a popular Dalit poet felt that:

> Our books are as meaningless as the crops of our forefathers
> if we confine reading to these books
> And the posterity will be as learned as the trained bull
> That snakes or nods its head to the prompting of its master
> Thrust such decadent books on the heads of people
> And the tree of knowledge will never flower

Bhagya Reddi Verma (1888-1939), a Dalit intellectual, and social reformer from Hyderabad, he felt that education was essential for an all-round progress and uplift of untouchables. To begin with, his educational activities, a lower primary school was opened at Jagan Mitra Mandali office at Easamiah Bazar in 1910 followed by one at Lingampalli and the third at Bogul Kunta. Later on, four more schools at Chanchalguda, Sultan shahi,Dhulpet and Gonfoundry were opened. Thus, at the first stage seven schools were started and run with public funds.

By the early years of 1903s these Adi-Hindu primary schools grew up to 26 and about 2500 Dalit children were its beneficiaries. To run these schools, finance became the main problem. In 1993, the government (of Nizam) came out with a proposal to take over these schools. When they asked for adequate grant to run these schools, the proposal was agreed to with certain specific conditions with regard to medium of instruction to be in the mother tongue of the pupil but not Urdu as it was compulsory in government schools in those days. And secondly to introduce some handicrafts in the schools.

Against the background of illiteracy, and ignorance with the influence of neighbouring state Hyderabad Dalit leaders started their educational activities for Dalits in coastal Andhra Dalits established Schools and Hostels for Dalit Children. Here the Burma factor is conspicuous and played a major role in helping to establish schools and hostels. Vundru Tatayya (1850-1930) was one of the Burma returned Dalit reformer who earned early 300 acres of land in Burma and another 150 areas of land in ponnamanda, his native place in Rajolu Taluk of East Godavari district. Every year he used to go to Burma to collect money for Dalit education in Andhra, alongwith other reformers. In 1920s he established a school at ponnamanda, and funded for the construction of some other schools. He gave the financial assistance to the buildings at Anaravaram, Allavaram and Modalukuduru villages. Tatayya not only did the yeomen service for Dalit education but also influenced many Dalit Leaders including Golla Chondrayya Kusuma Tatayya. Tadiswamy, Pamula Reddy, Kona Venkanua etc. for uplifting the Dalits.

With regard to the hostels for dalit pupils, many were established by the Dalit activist, functioned even without grants from governments. In 1928 at Rajahmundry, two separate hostels for Dalit boys and girls were established by Jala Rangaswamy. In 1930s Eali Vadapalli (1911-1972) established school and a hostel at Mandapet. He also established Laxmi Industrial Training School at Ramachandra Puram. He begged in order to feed the students, as there was no funding at all. In 1936, another hostel was established by Gollachandrayya (1818-1972) at Rajolu. In 1937, Bapuji Harijan Hostel was established by Pandu Laxmanaswamy (1892-1960).

In addition to education, Dalit intellectuals also established many journals and newspapers to impart awareness among the

Dalit Masses. In the process of these awareness programmes of *Bhajan Mandalis,* and other cultural activities played a major role in identity formation. The educated Dalits, though very few but they were much enough to make their presence felt and in creating a socio-political and cultural consciousness among Dalit masses.

By 1920s an emerging non-Brahmin Movement in Madras presidency challenged the Brahmin dominance, and laid the basis for many of the themes influencing dalit movements, including a non-Aryan or Dravidian identity. During the same time a new generation of literate and militant dalits were vigorously rejecting both *Panchama* and the *Harijan* identity and were organising themselves as *Adi-Andhra.* The original sons of the soil. Similar situation can be found all over India. In Punjab, it is called Adi-Dharma Movement, in Madras it is called Adi-Dravida Movment. and in U.P. it is called Adi-Hindu Movement. For Andhra, the decisive year was 1917. Madari Bhagyareddi Varma and Chairman Reception Committee respectively organized conference labelled a Andhra Desa First Panchama Conference at Bezawada in (4-6 November 1917). Brahmin and Caste-Hindus also attended this conferences including Gudur Ramachandra Rao. Ayyadevera Kaleswara Rao, Vemuri Ramji Rao etc. In his Presidential address Bhagyareddi Varma while narrating the atrocities of Caste-Hindus on "untouchables" and their miserable plight, argued that term *panchama* was nowhere found in the *Puranas* or other Hindu scriptures and the so-called *panchamas* were the original sons of the soil and they were the rulers of the country. The delegates then rejected this term *panchama* and constituted themselves as Andhra Desa First Adi-Andhra Conference. All together they passed 18 resolutions, relatively non-controversial. Such as appealing to the government to nominate Adi-Andhras to local bodies and legislative council, to establish separate schools and wells. And they were against the temple entry, saying that it was a futile agitation and unwanted thing as it was no way beneficial to the untouchables. But caste tension showed up for three days of the conference, the famous Kanaka Durga temple was closed for fear of an attempted entry.

After this Andhra conferences were held every year starting form village, taluk, district and regional levels. Their constant passing of resolutions in all the conferences, urging the government to label them as Adi-Andhras, Adi-Dravidas, as per the linguistic areas, forced the Madras legislative council adopt the resolution.

1. That this council recommended to the Government that the term "panchama" or "paraya" used to designate the Ancient Dravidian community in Southern India should be deleted from Government records etc., and the term "Adi Dravida" in the Tamil and 'Adi-Andhra' in Telugu Districts be substituted instead".
2. On Behalf of the government an undertaking was given the government would have no objection to call the members of this community. 'Adi-Dravida' in Tamil, 'Adi-Andhra' in Telugu districts and particular members of the community 'Dravidas', if they prefer to be so called, but it would not be possible to re-edit old records. The government accordingly direct that the following terms shall in future be adopted in place of 'panchama' or 'paraya' or similar terms in all official documents:

The Adi-ideology, and the Adi-Andhra consciousness intensified as the very spread of conferences in 1920s and 1930s throughout the districts indicates a broad rural level consciousness in identity formation. So does the fact that by 1931 census indicated 838,000 people listing as *Malas* 612,000 as *Madigas* and 665,000 as Adi-Andhras in Madras presidency alone.

The nineteenth century social reform movement was preoccupied more with the evils associated with women and religion: education, supposed by as a means of enlightenment and progress was limited to the "twice born". Later on at the close of nineteenth century same feeble efforts were made to extend education to women and untouchables. Until then, the ideological basis for educating untouchables was built mostly by missionaries and later on by Dalits. Social reforms counted Dalits only as a marginalised Hindus. This was in reaction to Christian intrusion to proselytise them and the assertion of Muslim identity. The little that the reformers did ameliorate and educate untouchables practically failed until 1920s and 30s. Schools became an institutional form of reiterating the Dalit's under-privileged and unequal status.

Missionaries treatment towards untouchables was tempered by humanism and a zeal to solve their problems and satisfy their immediate needs. Such an attitude was pathetically lacking in the fragile efforts made by the reformers.

Education and literature became counterproductive forces encouraging each other and heading for the some goal. The first generation untouchables became either ideologies activists of the Dalit Movement. They in turn, made efforts to educate the masses and saw education as the most effective path to break the strongly-embedded caste dissemination and hegemony. In their writings, through journals, pamphlets, political addresses, novels and poetry, they ridiculed the efforts made by the caste-Hindu reformers and exhorted the Dalits to realise the utility of education.

Effective changes in the condition of "untouchable" was a direct result of constitutional and legislative efforts. But no concrete and collective social movement at a national level was taken up by the caste-Hindu enlightened sections. Even to the communists of this time the problem of untouchable was too `mundane' cause. Thus the Dalits could not muster much support from the non-Dalit sections.

Education became meaningful to the untouchables only in those institutions which were founded by the missionaries and Dalit reform organizations.

However, the available sources reveals that education did not do any thing concrete to alleviate their economic status. Evn the census reports does not indicate any professional mobility in any field. However, it produced the intelligentsia, social reformers, politicians, writers who in turn fought for Dalit rights and such rights were subject to legislation only in the post colonial society.

The non-dalit women were recognised as an entity to be reformed and educated in the late nineteenth and early 20th centuries. As a result many caste Hindu women achieved high status in political, educational and professional fields but, Dalits Women remained uneducated and excluded from schooling system.

Growth of Education (Caste-wise break-up in Andhra : 1891 - 1931 Percentage)

Caste	*1891*		*1901*		*1911*		*1921*		*1931*	
	Male	*Female*	*Male*	*Female*	*Male*	*Female*	*Male*	*Female*	*Male*	*Female*
Brahmin	72.21	3.73	67.30	4.55	68.19	9.91	59.66	14.98	68.2	9.9
Balija	20.12	1.44	11.70	0.73	20.90	2.03	22.46	03.25	20.9	2.0
Komati	60.46	0.88	49.47	0.86	52.11	2.50	52.13	05.37	52.1	2.5
Rapu/Redd	09.45	0.22	03.82	0.06	08.98	0.29	10.21	00.77	09.0	0.4
Kamma	03.41	0.24	04.79	0.15	12.21	0.69	13.56	00.48	12.2	0.7
Mangala	06.61	0.11	03.53	0.12	06.86	0.27	08.61	00.54	06.9	0.3
Mala	01.13	0.15	00.56	0.03	01.37	0.07	01.63	00.14	01.4	0.1
Madiga	00.46	0.02	00.23	Nil	00.82	0.06	00.89	00.11	00.8	0.1
Kamsali	28.53	0.56	16.45	0.47	25.05	1.35	27.61	02.55	25.1	1.4
Golla	02.66	0.06	01.02	0.07	02.76	0.14	02.90	00.25	02.7	1.1

Source: Census of India, 1891, Madras, vol. XII, p. 179; Census of India, 1901. Madras, vol. XV A part II, pp. 106-1-7; Census of India, 1911, Madras vol. XII, part II, pp. 80-81; Census of India, 1921, Madras, vol. XIII, part II, pp. 76-78; Census of India, 1931. Madras, Subsidiary Tables, pp. 315-316.

2

School Education

As per a general perception, the schooling system offers the Dalit children an opportunity, on equal terms with others, to gain knowledge and enable them to rise in socioeconomic status. It allows them to learn and develop along with other caste children, to see and imbibe values of higher communities, the experience of and exposure to which was possible not available to their parents and grand-parents. In short, therefore, education can be defined as a great human experiment in community interaction, a process of constant learnings. Therefore dropping out under scores an end of a potentially fruitful adventure, School drop-out indicates a withdrawal from a system which could eventually render a most valuable support to one's development. Then why do Dalit children drop-out from the school if the latter has the potency to deliver them goods? An attempt has been made in this chapter to answer this question in this chapter. It is observed that generally the explanations offered in reply to this question are too simplistic or evasive in nature with an implicit assumption that the actual situation does not admit of any complexities.

We can look into the reasons underlying the school drop-out of Dalit children. For this a direct question was asked to the parents. "Why did your child stop going to school?" Investigators who were entrusted with the responsibility to record detailed answer, probed excellently and came out with manifold dimensions of the problem. Table provides us with thirteen broad categories of responses in which the answers from Dalit parents are classified. One can observe that the question drop-out reasons elicited over two responses of discrete categories per case (623 responses from 300 respondents) and in this there was no conspicuous gap between Rasra and Ranipur Blocks (293 and 330 responses respectively).

Parents' Position

The most significant variable relating to drop-out is the incapacity of parents to meet the educational needs of the child (86 out of 300 cases). Such as expenses for books, exercise note books, slates, pencils, etc. On enquiry it was reported that the Dalit Welfare Office in the region or the offices of Basic education were supplying, at irregular intervals, such items as text books, copies (exercise books) etc. But these extremely inadequate supplies were limited to a few schools. Therefore, Dalits parents were vindicated in claiming that no assistance or help was rendered to their children in this respect (all the 300 parents replied that they received no help whatsoever from educational authorities). Besides this their poor financial conditions, the parents found it impossible to spend money towards these items. They helped the child as per their capacity. Indefinite scarcity of books and other material was stated to be the cause of child's declining involvement in school studies. Some school teachers, as part of their duty, requested the child to bring this material. Some reminded him of such basic equipment. The child was, in most cases, helpless, and so were his parents. This resulted in school drop-out of some Dalit children.

Financial Responsibility

Another variable (see again item ix of Table causing school drop-out was the direct monetary liability on the part of Dalit parents. Above 80 per cent of Dalit parents were required to pay between Rs. 2 and Rs. 15 per annum towards fees. Though game fees charged to the students were reportedly nominal, i.e., 10 N.P. per month. For each student, there were in some quarters other channels through which the school teachers reportedly used to collect money from students, both Dalits and Non-Dalits. These practices were generally known as 'Pass Karahi'; 'Centre Kharcha' and 'TC Expenses'. It was reported by some parents that the school children had to pay 'pass Karahi' meaning thereby payments for promoting the child to higher class. This payment, from varying Rs. 2 to Rs. 10 collected as a matter of right by some teachers. Some parents even alleged that when this payment was not made their children were detained in the same class by declaring them as failed students. The second practice relates to the contribution realized from children of Class V appearing for the Zilla Parishad Examination. This examination was usually conducted at the Junior High School premises. It was reported that payments ranging between Re. 1 and Rs. 3 were collected from children to defray hospitality expenses on the examiners. There were the times when even tea and other hospitality arrangements during the inspection of a school were made reportedly at the cost of the school children. The last practice known as "TC Expenses" relates to the payment demanded from the parents by the teaching staff to issue Transfer Certificate (TC) to the outgoing child. As the inter-school mobility was not very prevalent in the villages, this demand affected mainly those students who desired to join the Senior Basic School after getting through the class V examination.

Drop-out Causes Indicated by Dalit/Parents

Reasons	*Rasra Block (N=150)*	*Ranipur Block (N=150)*	*Total (N=300)%*
(i) Domestic work including the care of infants	25	45	70 (11.1)
(ii) For placing the child in gainful employment	26	21	47 (7.5)
(iii) Sickness/death in the family	25	36	61 (9.8)
(iv) Prolonged illness of the child	8	8	16 (2.6)
(v) Distance, location and other incongenial aspects of the school	11	18	29 (4.7)
(vi) Ill-treatment/Unhelpful attitude of school teachers	40	31	71 (11.4)

(vii) Ill-treatment/dominance by schoolmates	12	12	24 (3.9)
(viii) Unproductive school experiences, bad habits and traits in the child	14	22	36 (5.8)
(ix) Lack of monetary support books, copies and other educational aids	48	38	86 (13.8)
(x) Lack of interest in studies	37	40	77 (12.4)
(xi) Inability to meet physical needs of the child	30	30	60 (9.6)
(xii) Cultural factors beliefs and values	14	27	41 (6.6)
(xiii) Any others	3	2	5 (0.8)
Total No. of responses	293	330	623(100.0)

When asked to comment on the above mentioned practices many a school teachers not only refuted such allegations but tried hard to defend their schools and in the same breath pointed an accusing finger at other schools. A few teachers, however, admitted that their meagre salary did not permit them for spending lavishly on those conducting school inspection or examination. Whatever, the facts the poor parents being coerced to make gratifications is in itself a most disturbing phenomenon. Inspite of their Pathetic economic condition, Dalit parents continued to pay to the school teachers and thus becomes scapegoats. But as they found helpless financially they could no longer afford sending the children onto schools. Nearly one out of every three Dalit children was out of school due to lack of financial support and educational material (86 responses against Item-ix).

Another major reason cited for drop-out is the lack of child's interest in studies (77 out of 300 cases). This particular drawback among children was highlighted by some Dalit parents in a state of emotional disturbance. The child became less and less punctual in his school attendance and home assignments, grew careless about examination and felt more secure at home than in school. Combined with this attitude of indifference towards school, he displayed signs of mental irritation whenever asked about school activities. Some parents bemoaned that their child reached aggressively and stubbornly refused to study at home. A few parents were at a loss to understand the reasons behind such a sweeping change in the child from a peaceful and well-adjusted to a disturbed and aggressive behaviour. In some cases, the teachers reported the undesirable developments in the child to the parents and advised them to pay closer attention. In a few cases, the parents approached the teachers to request them for helping out the child in studies. But efforts such as these provided infructuous.

That the indifferent attitude of the teachers and illtreatment meted out by them to the Dalit students that forced as many as 71 of them (23 per cent of the total sample) to leave the school was another disturbing factor. Articulate parents gave a brief account of how their children were ill-treated, harassed and discriminated against a few instances are given below as reported by them. A major complaint of the parents in this group referred to the incidence of beating. A Dalit child was beaten up by the teachers for various reasons. It was, however, alleged by the parents that the teacher ill-treated the child simply because of letter's inability to fulfil their demands of 'Fee; Pass Karai; Donations (Chanda) etc.

Teacher's Fear

In some cases, the Dalit child got scared of his teacher after witnessing the way the other children were handled in the class-room. Other dimensions of the teacher's unhelpful attitudes. There were also incidents that the Dalit child was asked to sit away from other students. More humiliating were the assignments given by like teachers carrying their personal luggage, doing their domestic work and even rendering free help in agricultural operations. At some places that Dalit children were reported to have not permitted to touch the blackboard, chalk or a book handled by the teacher. It is paradoxical that teachers whose hands are supposed to shape the personality of the child in a constructive manner, should practice such subtle forms of exploitation and harassment.

"But this happened and happens every day", said one Dalit parent agitatedly waving his hands in the air. He added: "When my child casually reported these happenings in the school. I hardly believed them to be true. I went to school and saw with my own eyes that Dalit children were accommodated in the rearmost part of the class, huddled together on a shabby may (which later I came to know was bought by one of the Dalit boys from home). All of these children (they were nine in total), were looking alike in dress and in everything. Why this separation? Why this isolation on caste lines? How my child and other children can learn better human values in this atmosphere? He will grow and die in this world in the same degraded manner as I would and as my parents and grand-parents did. Education is force and nothing less than a force in the hands of these fanatic teachers".

He was trembling with anger when he ended his arguments. Could we say that he was projecting his prejudice and bias? No probably he was moderate in his expressions. We witnessed ourselves what we felt is that and heard of many such instances. It would appropriate to point out here that practices, as outlined above, hurt many a sensitive child. The parents could not find any justification in coercing the child to remain in the school.

Combined with this discriminatory, debasing treatment meted out by the teachers was the highhanded, arrogant and aggressive attitudes of school mates mostly belonging to the upper castes. Although this was not much prevalent it should not be ignored as trival matter. Most of the Dalit parents spoke very mighty of the cooperative and helping attitudes of the caste-Hindu children. But the parents whose children had to subject the unseemly deeds of these uppercaste children were severely critical about them. How exactly were the Dalit children treated in such cases? An examination in this score brought out a revelation that in some schools, the most pampered and arrogant caste-Hindu children harassed the Dalit child, particularly the new entrants, by pinching, hitting or pulling his hair. They used to hide his slate, book and pencil. At the height of mischief, they used to break the slate or tear the book to pieces. In a few cases, they used to form a group (should we call it a gang) of their own and beat the Dalit child, bruise his arm or leg. Such incidents were less in number but enough to alarm the whole community against the schooling prospect of a child. Nearly one out of every 10 Dalit children was a victim of such boyish banditry. Could we, then, simply dismiss this as an insignificant features of school system or consider it seriously as a breeding ground for caste-hatred and rivalries among children?

Significant Role

This has already mentioned that Dalit children played an active role in the household activities. In fact pressure of domestic work should cause the drop-out of 70 children (23 per cent of the total) is a surprising fact. On their own showing, the Dalit children seemed to be handling very many aspects of household routine. The responsibility of looking after infants and younger siblings might have presented a barrier in his way of schooling. As both the parents went out for making livelihood and remained out for uncertain hours, it fell to the lot of the unfortunate schooling child to wind up his studies in order to take care of the younger ones. The case of the Dalit girls was more indefensible than that of the boys because they were the first to be asked to leave the school should there arise any need or eventuality at home. The fact should not leave unmentioned here that some parents, albeit a minority, were selfish and short-sighted. They make the child to do the domestic chores without showing any consideration for their age, interest and aptitudes. They were guided by the immediate, short terms benefits, cattle-grazing, sheep care, grass cutting and collection of firewood at the expense of their school education. Of course, this was not the case with the majority. Most of them were living from hand-to-mouth and yet striving hard to educate their children. Being agricultural labourers, it was virtually impossible for them to take the little child along with them. Nor could they leave him alone, unprotected. The children were assigned with the jobs like experience gave them a lesson to be cautions of their little possessions like a pair of bullocks, sheep or goat which needed shepherding. Finding no alternative arrangements they were constrained to rely on the services of the school-going child. This ultimately resulted in the drop-out. We met many such families during the course of this enquiry and they confided their helplessness to us.

A far more pitiable fate than this was of those 47 families who discontinued the education of their children in order to employ them in some gainful activity. In what occupations could such young, tender-aged, semi-literate children be absorbed? As a full-time agricultural labourer? No, he was too young and ill-equipped to do that. He got occupied in such minor job as assistance to farm labourers in sowing, weeding operations, selling firewood or basketware in the market, shepherding for others, domestic work for land-owing castes, casual work at brick kilns etc. Economic hardships gnawed at the vitals of their living and parents were compelled to employ gainfully their younger sons and even daughters. At least one out of every 10 Dalit children in our study was condemned to adulthood tasks before be reached his teenage (see item ii).

This is not an easy task to establish a direct relationship between living conditions and the status of health. However we can make a reasonable guess that the Dalit families were not better placed in the matter of health. The factors like poor working and living conditions, financial worries including heavy indebtedness, recurring drought situation entailing hunger and starvation contributed negatively to their physical well-being. These apart in some cases atleast, the practice of liquor consumption, narcotic addition etc. could be found . Illness in the family was, there, a recurring phenomenon. Unsound economic condition prevented many of them from availing proper medical help and they tried indigenous herbal medicines which often failed to bring early relief. Prolonged illness of the bread-winner put out of gear the entire household economy. It further aggravated their plight. Schooling of the boys as well as girls, came to a screeching that as soon as the head of the family was bedridden. They were required to attend to the ailing and, luck and age permitting compensate for the loss of earnings through engagements in gainful activity. Death of the householder was a devastating mishap which directly had bearing on the schooling of the child. Each two out of 10 Dalit children were forced to leave their studies on the grounds of illness or death in the family. In 16 cases, prolonged illness of the school-going children resulted in their drop-out.

Another major aspect cited for drop-out relates to the inability of Dalit parents to comply with the physical needs and requirements of the child. What could be the physical needs of the child attending a primary school? Daily breakfast or meals depending upon the school timings, a pair of clothes and possibly a pair of shoes. The last item, *i.e.* footwear was often dispensed with and the Dalit children were accustomed to attend school bare-footed. Dress was however a problem to most of the Dalit families. When at home, the children could carry on in rags. But in school, when other children came dressed in better clothes, it was indeed humiliating for the poor Dalit child to sit alongwith them. At some places, particularly in the Dalit special schools, even the rags could scrape through; but some families could not afford their children of even higher age remained half-naked usually the upper garment totally torn or missing. In addition this were the subtle reactions of some sensitivity. Some purists among the teachers scolded the child for inadequate clothing and sent them back home for proper dress. Besides, some poor families could not keep a certain level of cleanliness and hygiene in respect of their children.

Unhygienity and personal hygiene may be the result of many cultural factors including poverty, but this, coupled with the untidy appearance of the child in the school, was a source of great mental conflict within the child. Parents did understand these problems but were either too helpless or insensitive to resolve these . How can they meet these expenses when many of them were acutely concerned about providing some minimum food to the school-going child? This question may appear superfluous but was in reality a valid one. There was such a pathetic level of poverty in some cases that families compelled to live on borrowed food or cooked herbs and plants to survive.

Poor Conditions

Sending a child to school in the morning was nightmare's

thought because the child had nothing to eat at home. Because of hungry or half-starved, he was hardly able to concentrate on his studies in the class-room. A number of school teachers referred to this pitiable state as they observed it day in and day out. Sometimes, they did extend a helping hand but they could not afford feeding them regularly. Some Dalit parents, on the other hand, felt compelled to ignore the physical needs of their child on account of abject poverty. All these factors caused the discontinuation of the child's studies which could not claim a priority in a situation where hunger and starvation reigned supreme.

Cultural values and beliefs among the Dalit community sometimes came as hurdles for the proper growth of children. Noticeably enough there was a near-unanimity among them on one issue that higher education to girls of their community was totally undesirable. There was strong feeling that the girls should not be educated beyond junior basic level.

> "What she must know in the school is how to read and write. After all she is somebody else's property. She will be married and sent away from this house. If she knows by way of schooling enough to write a letter to us from her new home, that will be the sufficient achievement on her part."

One Dalit parent commented on his expectations out of his daughter's education. This was the perception among most of the parents. There was a certain amount of diffidence and anxiety among them too. For instance, they thought that higher education would lead their daughter astray. Upper-caste fads and fashions encourage them to mix freely with children of the opposite sex and would ultimately bring a bad name to their family and community. Some of these fears were poignantly articulated by the parents who stopped the education of their daughters with these convictions.

With a few families, superstitions and beliefs of the elders cause the stoppage of the boys' education. Recurring fever of the school-going child, any major accident inflicting physical injuries and such other events were interpreted as bad omens resulting from his schooling. They put it thus: "Education is harmfuf to him. It will not do him any good. Even his father had suffered a similar accident in his school days and had left his studies." Such credulous, superstitious ideas haunted many a Dalit father and when they were overwhelmingly supported by their other family members or community people, the natural consequence was to save the child from potential deleterious influences of school. How incredible! yet these beliefs and values disrupted the educational career of 41 cases in our sample. (see Item xii)

In the case of 12% our sample (36 cases), unproductive school experiences were attributed to their drop-out. The explanation given by Dalit parents was that the child was learning bad habits, acquiring undesirable behaviour patterns. The major noticed in them were telling balatant lies, absconding from school and playing truants, gambling and smoking. Infuriated as they were, they thought it wise to control his movement and hence stopped his schooling altogether. In some cases, ther were complaints from the school teachers about the Dalit child being violent in the class-room quarrelling with others and coming to blows with them.

Various Factors

Though relatively insignificant factors such as distance and location of school also caused drop-out incidence in a few cases. Physical distance between the school and residence of a Dalit child was sometimes as much as two to three kilometres. Besides the aspect distance, there were other obstacles like absence of walkable pathways, existence of or drain-pits or similar obstacles which made the schoolward movement of a very young child extremely difficult and sometimes insecure. In rainy season the approach road to school was invariably inundated and it was a feat to reach school. Apart from this was the appalling physical condition of school buildings, their roots leaking from all sides. Drenched and shivering, the children used to face all these odds. Some school building had developed deep cracks in the walls and the supporting pillars and were thoroughly unsafe. Torrential rains or storm could easily bring down the entire edifice within moments. We were shown these cracks school teachers and the artificial props they had raised: These created much in some parents about their children's schooling in such ramshackle buildings. In short, therefore, nearly one out of every 10 Dalit children dropped out of the school because of its distance and location which made its' accessibility less easy and also because of its dilapidated physical structure.

Peculiar Problem

The forgoing analysis makes it more than clear that the problem of school drop-out among Dalit children is a complex one, having multiple reasons behind it. We may, however, integrate the items which have some proximate relationship among themselves and attempt to draw a coherent picture. There are 13 items in Table, detailing drop-out reasons. If we avoke the last category of a miscellaneous nature, we get 618 responses against 12 items by 295 respondents, i.e., Dalit parents. These responses classified into five broad categories as shown in Table.

The fact that emanates from the above statement clearly reflects that poverty and associated handicaps are chiefly responsible for the drop-out incidence among the Dalit children. The next contributory element to reckon with is the existing inadequacies of the school system. Punitive, unhelpful and impersonal attitudes of the school teachers as well as the aggressive and unfriendly acts of the school inmates seem to have created a credibility vaccum between the Dalit students and the school system. The last three categories are independent in themselves and relate to family or personal issues like sickness and death, declining interest of the child in studies and superstitious beliefs and values against the continuity of school education. In general, the economic backwardness of the Dalit families and unreceptive and discourteous atmosphere in the school constitute two major barriers that lie at the root of the drop-out problem among Dalit children.

Major Categories of Drop-out Causes
(based on the responses of Dalit Parents)

Major Category	*Inclusive Sub-categories and Responses*	*Total No. of Responses*	*%*
I. Poverty and Economic Hardships	(a) Child's gainful employment (47) (b) Lack of basic educational equipments (86) (c) Non-provision of physical needs (60) (d) Engagement in domestic work (70)	263	42.6
II. School and School related Factors	(e) Distance, location etc. (29) (f) Behaviour of the school teachers (71) (g) Behaviour of school-mates (24) (h) Unproductive school impact (36)	160	25.9
III. Domestic Existencies	(i) Sickness/death in family (61) (j) Prolonged illness of the child (16)	77	12.5
IV. Individual Deficiency	(k) Lack of interest in studies (77)	77	12.5
V. Cultural Factors	(l) Beliefs, values, community reactions (41)	41	6.5
	Grand total of Responses	618	100.0

Information available in peer literature relates to the drop-out reasons as indicated by the children themselves. It seems that there is a great deal of similarity in the responses obtained from the children and their parents. Lack of educational equipments such as books, copies etc. is a most dominating reason. Interestingly enough, over one-fourth of the children (45 out of 198) have stated that they left studies owing to lack of interest. Among parents too, over 25% had attributed school drop-out to this factor (77 out of 300, see Table).

If we group these items (excluding Item x) into broad categories as attempted previously (see Table) we would find identical gradations in emphasis. For example the category of poverty and economic hardships (items i, ii, vii, ix) would get 125 out of 271 responses, and would score a first position in the list. A less than half of its total, *i.e.*, 54 responses are against the second category, namely school and school-related factors (Items v and vi). Domestic exigencies or crises constitute a third major category with a total of 47 responses (Items (iii) and (iv)). A category coming under individual deficiencies has 45 responses and stands last in the numerical order. It is desirable to make mention here that the children, unlike their parents, made no reference to cultural factors. On the whole, there is substantial between children, *i.e.*, drop-out cases and their parents, regarding the causes that underline the drop-out incidence.

From other quarters also a supportive evidence can be availed. A question asked to village leaders and school teachers regarding the factors responsible for drop-out among Dalit children elicited very interesting information. In the same way, Dalit parents who had earlier listed specific reasons for drop-out of their children were further asked to point out the factors contributing to school drop-out in the Dalit community. Views of the parents, leaders and teachers are summarised into broad categories as shown in Table. Analysis of response categories shows clearly that economic hardships seem to play a major role in furthering drop-out situation.

Next significant element is one which relates to the apathy and indifference of Dalit parents and child's disinterest in studies. Significantly enough, even the parents have started showing serious concerns against the prevailing negative attitudes of the Dalit family towards education of their children, though earlier they did not apportion any blame to themselves in respect of school drop-out of their own children. It should be noted that the school teachers maintained a discreet silence over the inadequacies and deficiencies of the school system (only 0.7 per cent response). This can well be understood because they probably felt it a risky exercise in self-evaluation. But village leaders and parents are not so critical of the inhibitive and discriminatory aspects of the school system.

With some vigor both these groups have condemned the unhealthy, crippling and regressive caste and community practices. This had reference to a practice of early marriage, liquor addiction, family feuds over petty issues, indebtedness on account of avoidable expenditure on rituals and ceremonies and blind faith in superstitions. It was their finding that all these forces ran counter to the educational interests of the Dalit child. Domestic exigencies, which resulted in the drop-out of at least one-fourth of our sample (77 cases), find the rear-most place in the general assessment of the paernts, teachers, and village leaders.

Drop-out Causes indicated by Children

	Reasons	*Rasra Block (N=108)*	*Ranipur Block (N=90)*	*Total* (N=198)%*
1.	Domestic work including infant care	10	18	28 (9.9)
2.	For placement in some gainful employment	9	6	15 (5.3)
3.	Sickness/death in the family	21	22	43 (15.3)
4.	Prolonged illness of the child	1	3	4 (1.4)
5.	Distance, location and other incongenial aspects of the school	6	4	10 (3.6)
6.	Ill-treatment/unhelpful attitude of school teachers or school males	26	18	44 (15.7)
7.	Lack of books, copies and uniform	49	22	71 (25.3)
8.	Lack of interest in studies	21	24	45 (16.0)
9.	Physical needs not met	7	4	11 (3.9)
10.	Any others	3	7	10 (3.6)
	Total No. of responses	153	128	281(100.0)

Note: *Out of 300 drop-out children, 102 children (42 from Rasra and 60 from Ranipur Block) were not available/suitable, for interviews. Responses shown in this table are from 198 cases only.

A Composite Data in Respect of Major Categories of Drop-out Causes Indicated by Dalit-Parents*, Village Leaders and School Teachers

*Major Categories***	*Response Percentage*		
	Parents (N=300)	*Village Leaders* (N=60)	*School Teachers* (N=40)
(i) Poverty and Economic hardships	47.8	51.6	53.6
(ii) School and School related factors	13.7	12.0	0.7
(iii) Domestic Exigencies	0.9	0.5	8.4
(iv) Individual Deficiencies	24.0	24.4	16.1
(v) Cultural Community Factors	13.6	11.5	11.2
Total No. of Responses	(766) 100%	(209) 100%	(143) 100%

* Responses recorded in this table refer to a different question relating to general causes contributing to drop-out problem in a Dalit Community.

** Categories listed here include, in addition to sub-categories (See Table) mentioned earlier, the following:

Item I : Lack of facilities at home.
Item IV : Parental apathy and indifference.
Item V : Unhealthy caste and community influences.

Important Factor

If we take into account of the various reasons and factors causing drop-out among the Dalit children covered in our study, we may reach a conclusion that economic backwardness of Dalits is a dominant factor underlying drop-out, incidence. Other factors of varying significance can be listed as incongenial school atmosphere, domestic exigencies, absence of involvement on the part of parents as well as children in the school activities, and unfavourable influences of caste and community. All these factors singly or in combination, seems to generate an atmosphere in which the schooling of the Dalit child becomes virtually impossible. These factors may be analytically distinguished but cannot be separated in reality because of their interlinkage. Apathy of parents or vagrancy of th child may be the result of poverty conditions. Keeping this in view it was considered necessary to perceive the situation in its totality. Drop out is a complex event encompassing various trends. Evidence that we have here amply proves the point.

Age Factor in Dalit Children Drop-out Rate School System

Drop-out Age	*Rasra Block*	*Ranipur Block*	*Total*	*(%)*
Below 7 years	15	9	24	(8.0)
7 years	27	12	39	(13.0)
8 years	21	33	54	(18.0)
9 years	22	29	51	(17.0)
10 years	18	31	49	(16.3)
11 years	15	19	34	(11.3)
12 years	14	9	23	(7.6)
13 years and above	18	8	26	(8.8)
Total	150	150	300	(100.0)

Information on the age at which the Dalit child drops-out from the school system is vital because it can enable us to formulate suitable preventive programmes for such cases. Information in this respect (Table) suggests that over 72 per cent drop-out cases (217 out of 300) were below 10 years of age. Of these 217 cases , 100 belonged to the age-group 9-10 years. In other words, one out of every three drop-outs (100 out of 300) belonged to the age group 9-10 years. The mean age for the total sample stood at 9.3 years (9.4 years for Rasra block and 9.2 years for Ranipur block). This provides that the moment the children from the Dalit community reach a critical age of 8-9, or 10 years they withdraw from the school system. This stage onwards the usefulness of children for domestic help and outside activities becomes intensive. The Dalit families begin to view their children as working assets.

Now our attention can be focussed on other crucial aspects of the drop-out situation. Who in the family generally takes the decision about dropping the child from the school? The answer that we obtain in our study (Table) is some what unexpected. Even if in nearly seven out of ten cases (69 per cent) the decision is reported to have been taken by the father, mother or other elderly person from the child's family, it is really strange that in 30 per cent of cases, the drop-out child himself was the sole arbiter. Similarly, three out of every 10 children who dropped out of the school, were doing so on their own initiative.

Who in Your Family Took the Decision of Not Sending Your Child to School? (Parent's Version)

Response	*Rasra Block*	*Ranipur Block*	*Total*	*(%)*
Father	60	69	129	(43.0)
Mother	35	32	67	(22.3)
Child himself	45	47	92	(30.7)
Other Relatives	10	2	12	(4.0)
Total	150	150	300	(100.0)

Two reasons can be attributed to this trend. Firstly, the parents who were asked this question, might have felt little unnerved and hence might have shifted the onus of drop-out decision to their child to conveniently shirk the moral responsibility. Perhaps they did not like to shoulder the responsibility of forcing their child to leave school education half-way. A second explanation could be that the answers are representative of a true position: parents were unwilling or indecided but the child was bent upon withdrawing from the school system. It seems likely that in view of the drop-out reasons mentioned earlier, the latter may be the case. The Dalit child did not enjoy school education a very rich experience due to ill-treatment of teachers, unsociability of schoolmates and some incongenial aspects of school itself. He was also running out of books, copies and other educational aids which could help him sustain his interst in school activities. In some cases, neglect of his physical needs was the most dominant disincentive in schooling efforts. Lack of interest in studies (affecting 77 cases) could be a consequence of the above mentioned deprivations. These clearly indicate child's disenchantment with school education. It may, therefore, be possible that the child himself opted against the continuity of school studies. Beneficially speaking, however, the child's parents have taken decision in dropping him out of the school.

Chief Concerns

Why did the Dalit parents decide to drop their child from school? What was the main consideration behind their decision? Answers to this question are recorded in Table. Earlier parents had cited various reasons contributed to the drop-out of the child from the school. Here we shall deal with those factors which are of primary singnificance in the decision-making process. Similarly the statements or reasons advanced by the parents can be construed as major causes leading to drop-out decision. Understandably only 208 respondents have replied to the question as they were directly responsible for taking a decision in the matter. The data is quite instructive and once again highlights the economic inapacity of Dalit families. If we combine the figures against Items (i), (ii) and (iv), we notice that in nearly 50% of cases (146 out of 300), the Dalit parents decided to keep the child at home on account of their unsound financial condition, pressure of domestic work (which frequently emanates from economic hardships) and urgency of some economic support through the employment of the child. This finding squarely supports our earlier contention. It is interesting to note that 62 out of 208 respondents (over 20%) in a total sample of 300 decided to stop schoool education of their child on account of their beliefs and attitudes (which favoured less education) and unpleasant school experiences of the child. The former reason refers to their culturally-conditioned, tradition-bound way of thinking while the latter throws light on the unhealthy, discriminatory practices prevalent in the school. Generally, the economic helplessness, traditional thinking and unproductive school experiences were the three main considerations which acted as a driving force in drop-out situations.

It would be interesting to look into whether the issue of school drop-out of a Dalit child was treated as an insignificant, trivial matter in his family or whether it created some flutter, some argumentative situation with heat exchange of views between father and mother or between parents and other elderly persons in the family. It was indeed heartening to find that drop-out became a serious subject to discussion in 135 families (45% of the total sample). Whether it was father, mother or the child who ultimately decided to keep out of school, the very decision was discussed and debated in these families with some members supporting and some opposing the decision on various considerations. It is indicative of awareness and involvement of family members in the child's educational prospects. It is, however, unfortunate that in 55% of cases, there was no such anxiety or curiousity and the matter was allowed to be settled unilaterally by the father, mother or a child. In these cases no concern was shown about the future of the child's education.

Main Consideration Behind the Drop-out Decision

Main Consideration	*No. of Respondents*	
(i) Relief from school expenses	80	(38.5)
(ii) Physical help from the child	39	(18.7)
(iii) Cultural factors, beliefs and attitudes	32	(15.4)
(iv) Unhealthy school experiences	30	(14.4)
(v) Economic help from the child	27	(13.0)
Total	*208	(100.0)

* This figure excludes 92 cases wherein the respondents have treated the child as a decision-maker in drop-out situation.

Depressed Lot

It apparently clearly the parents who had enrolled their child in the school, should fee unhappy and dejected in the event of their child's dropping out of the school; this has indeed been the case in our study (Table). To a question: "What did you/your wife feel when your child stopped going to school?" 196 fathers, and 204 mothers were reported to have felt unhappy. Surprisingly, a some what different position obtains in regard to a drop-out child:

According to the parents estimate, nearly 40% of children felt `happy', over 10% indifferent and around 50% 'unhappy' immediately after drop-out. As a fact of the matter quite a large number of drop-out cases had no sense of grief over the loss of school education is very disconcerting. Were they too young and immature to evaluate their prospects? Did they consider a drop-out an opportunity to escape from frustrating and humiliating experiences in school and at home? We find no answers to these questions. But it needs to conclude that a majority of parents and a fairly number of drop-outs themselves felt anguished and disheartened for the loss following the discontinuation of school studies.

Feelings of the Father, Mother and the Child (Drop-out Cause) Immediately After Drop-out: (Parent's Version)

What did they feel?	*Father (%)*		*Mother (%)*		*Drop-out Child (%)*	
Happy	51	(18.9)	66	(22.8)	116	(38.7)
Indifferent	22	(8.2	19	(6.6)	37	(12.3)
Unhappy	196	(72.9)	204	(70.6)	147	(49.0)
Total	269	(100.0)	289	(100.0)	300	(100.0)

If feelings of happiness, indifference and unhappiness as equivalent to positive, neutral and negative reactions to drop-out incidence are taken into account, we obtain the following position (Table). All in all 266 families in whose cases the reactions of all the three persons were available, are distributed within two polar limits of extremely positive and extremely negative reactions towards drop-out situation. The result is clear enough to suggest that 62 families had a positive or favourable reaction; only 9 families seemed to be neutral while a large majority of 195 families (nearly two-third of the total sample) were negatively disposed towards drop-out. This further reveals that a large number of families have acted under compulsions of social and economic reality, giving scant regard to their personal preferences and volitions.

Family Reactions to Drop-out Incidence*

Reaction Range	No. of Families	(%)
Extremely positive	34	(12.8)
Moderately	28	(10.5)
Average / Neutral	9	(3.4)
Moderately Negative	104	(39.1)
Extremely Negative	91	(34.2)
Total	266	(100.0)

**Note:* It is a composite table based on the addition of scores assigned to each scale. Family includes father, mother and a drop-out case and the reaction evaluation is made by the respondent. For father and mother, a three point scale was given assigning scores as follows:

Happy-1; Indifferent 2; Unhappy-3.

For the child, a five-point scale was designed with the following values:

Very Happy-1: Happy-2; Indifferent-3; Unhappy-4; Very Unhappy-5. The computation was done in two stages. First, the child's score was recorded by assigning values as under:

1 to 1 or 2; 2 to 3; and 3 to 4 or 5.

Secondly, individual scores of father, mother and child were combined with a result that the total score range varied between 3 and 9.

The Rehabilitation

Even if we have ample evidence that a large number of children did not feel unhappiness or grief over loss of education, parents themselves have given us an inkling of the child's mind when a question in another direction was posed to them. When it was asked whether the child (drop-out case) had ever expressed his or her desire to rejoin the studies, 115 have answered the question in the affirmative. In other words, as per parents report, at least one out of every three drop-out children, had openly expressed their willingness to restart their chequered career. Of these cases, 62 belonged to Rasra while 53 came from Ranipur Block. When a somewhat similar question was asked to children themselves, 72 out of 198 cases (36%) replied in affirmative stating that they strongly felt like carrying on their studies. These are indeed significant results indicating the child's positive frame of mind in respect of school education. A more convincing evidence in this respect can be had from the school teachers. When asked, "Do you think that the Dalit children who dropped out were unwilling to discontinue their studies?", 23 out of 40 school teachers replied 'most of them', four 'some of them' and 13 'a few of them'. The major portion of the school teachers was of the opinion that most of the drop-out cases were in fact favourably disposed towards school education and had shown willingness for its continuation. It was perceived that withdrawal of a child from the school on a permanent basis might create at least in some cases, some behavioural changes among them. This assumption proved to be correct in 86 cases (nearly 29 per cent). These children displayed specific changes in their behaviour and dealings with their parents and other family members, friends and neighbours. Their behaviour immediately after drop-out alternated between over aggressiveness and passive, negative withdrawal. As one sensitive mother put it thus: "The day after his schooling was discontinued; he started cold-shouldering every one in the family, including his youngest sister. He roamed about in the neighbourhood listlessly and ignored even our slightest demand. He used to come home twice in the day, to take afternoon meals and spent the night. If I tried to penetrate into his thoughts, he would burst out saying, all were keen to tie him to the job on land and waste his life toiling. This temperament of his lasted for over six months".

More instances were quoted by a number of others parents as well. Weeping and crying; shirking work; spoiling food and breaking dishes; abusing parents; avoiding friends and relatives; these and many other behavioural postures were adopted by those children who felt seriously jolted by their drop out from school.

Dropping out of a child is not an isolated instance and it may have repercussions on a wider front. For instance, the drop-out of an elder brother might the students of the younger one. It might be an unhealthy precedent in the neighbourhood. In case, drop-out child happens to be sociable and has leadership qualities, other neighbouring children who felt secure and happy under his stewardship might soon follow suit. Therefore, it is necessary to consider the drop out problem as consequential, often times capable of introducing many undesirable trends in the family or locality. This argument receives some support from our data (Table). In 15% of cases, the parents have reported that the other school-going children in the family were affected by the drop-out of a single case. Either they stepped into his shoes or started comparing their own performance with that of a drop-out case. This resulted in quarrels and unpleasant feelings within the family. Another 17% cases were those where the impact had bearing in what locality. Children in the neighbourhood started to be negligent of their studies, a few even stopped going to school. Out of every 10 drop out cases, three were reported to be positively responsible for adverse effects on school going children in the family or locality. These facts got to prove that impact of drop-outs registers itself not only in the family but it also extends to the neighbourhood.

Question: Did the School Drop-out of Your Child Adversely Affect the Education of Other Child/Children of Your Family in the Locality?

Reply	*No. of Respondents (%)*	
Yes, family children affected	45	(15.0)
Yes, locality children affected	51	(17.0)
No none was affected	204	(68.0)
Total	300	(100.0)

The drop-out child himself suffered a badly in terms of learning owing too the dearth of opportunity to practise things at home. While at school, he could read and write, try his hand in drawing and painting, participate in cultural activities and above all play and make friends. Dropping out meant losing out chances to develop his faculties in any of these spheres. The data in this regard provides us with a clear indications of how the drop-out affected the Dalit children (Table). It was observed that out of 300 drop-out cases, over 57 per cent (172 cases) of them totally abandoned the practice of any of the school subjects or activities. Similarly, only four out of ten drop-out children practised at home what they earlier learnt at school. The data clearly explain that in each of these areas of learning, there was a steep fall in the number of children showing engagement in activities after drop-out. Surprisingly, even under the category of games and sports there were only 16 children reported to be actively associated with it. In the pre-drop-out situation, the corresponding figure was as high as 159. A comparatively higher number of children seemed to be retaining their knowledge of reading and writing. By and large the children who dropped out appeared to show little concern or involvement in the subjects or activities they learnt at school and which stimulated them most during the school career. In plain terms, this can be considered as a substantial loss both to drop-out cases as well as to the school administration which invested so much resources for imparting education.

Showing Drop-out Impact on Learning Areas/Subjects

Subjects/Areas	*No. of children practising subjects at home after drop-out*		*Percentage of children practising the subjects after drop-out (%)*
Reading and writing	77	(199)	38.7
Games and Sports	16	(159)	10.1
Arithmetic/Minor calculations	28	(110)	25.5
Singing /dancing etc.	12	(49)	24.5
Drawing / Painting	4	(45)	8.9
Clay modelling/Craft/Needle work	12	(42)	28.6

(Figures in bracket refer to No. of children reported to have learnt the subjects/activities during the course of schooling).

Everyday Practice

What was the daily routine of a drop-out child? In which

activities, did the drop-out child engage himself/herself? Data in this matter is recorded in Table. For the sake of comparison we have also recorded the routine activities in which Dalit child indulged during his school career. Results that we obtain from the table are quite starling. In the first place, it demonstrates (see the foot-note to the table) that the number of children who extended their help in household and other activities has increased from 256 to 289 after their drop-out. Secondly, the number of children in some activities has remained more or less stationary and these activities are: cattle or sheep grazing, household work, looking after younger children etc. One the drop-out happened more children have taken to farm labour, grass cutting, help in the studies of younger children and independent jobs for earning a livelihood and income supplementation.

Type of Work in which the Dalit Child was Engaged Before and After Drop-out

Type of work activity	*After drop-out (1) (N=289)*	*Before drop-out (2) (N=256)*	*Proportionate difference of (1) over (2) (%)*
Farm labour	55	34	+ 61.8
Grass Cutting	137	108	+ 26.9
Household work	141	144	- 2.1
Cattle/sheep grazing	124	126	- 1.6
Looking after younger children	65	67	- 3.0
Help in the studies of younger children	22	16	+ 37.5
Independent employment	83	16	+ 418.8
Any others	29	14	+ 107.7

(Out of 300 children, eight in Rasra and three in Ranipur block did not offer any help in domestic or other duties after drop-out. Corresponding figure in pre-drop-out situation was 44).

Indeed there has been a five-fold increase in the number of children doing independent jobs after drop-out. Parents of drop-out children opined that these jobs covered domestic work in the families of higher castes, work at construction sites, casual jobs like house repairing or processing at brick kilns, pulling of cycle-rickshaw etc. Taking into account that physical strength and age were the limiting factors, it is still amazing that over one third of the drop-out cases were engaged in independent employment. This finding vindicates the earlier evidence that the economic backwardness of Dalit families came in the way of the advancement of their younger generation.

If we remember at this juncture the parent's statement on drop-out reasons (Table) we would notice that only in 47 cases, did gainful employment constitute one of the factors in drop-out incidence: Later, we were told that only in 27 cases, the employment of the child remained a primary consideration (Table). Practically this number rose to 83 and this signifies the shaky status of the Dalit's household economy. The reason behind a large number of children have lost touch with what they had acquired in the school is vividly. Once loosened from the school context, the children tended to drift away. Domestic work which took only a small portion explained in this data of their time during school career, could now absorb most of their time. Irrespective of their willingness or not the Dalit child had to support the household in its daily chores, inside or outside. It was, as it were their inescapable destiny.

Differences in time devoted to household and related activities by the child while he was in school and after he dropped out are distinctly representative of dissimilarities in the rhythm of life, before and after drop-out. When in school, the Dalit child treated his school as a major interest and played at best a supportive role in the household affairs. But after drop-out, he had to devote the major part of his time and energy in attending to domestic assignments as well as to unsteady and strenuous outside employment which had poor remunerative prospects (Table).

Time Devoted by Children to Household Work and Other Activities Every Day

Daily work labours	*After Drop-out* (1)	%	*Before Drop-out* (2)	%
1-2 hours	9	(3.1)	154	(60.1)
3-4 hours	27	(9.3)	66	(25.8)
5-6 hours	83	(28.7)	34	(13.3)
7-8 hours	94	(32.5)	1	(0.4)
8 hours or more	76	(26.4)	1	(0.4)
	289	(100.0)	256	(100.0)

Considering this dramatic shift in their role and responsibilities, it is no surprise that most of them have passively acquiesced in the present economic status. Irrespective of aspirations they might have had in their school days, the present situation was one of hard, toiling labour outside home or engagement in domestic work inside. Once they sniffed there ties with the school, their potentialities remain undeveloped, talents, unexplored and their energy diffused over the wide assortment of uncreative jobs. In such circumstances the achievement motive of the individual is bound to be stultified. How else can we explain the data in Table, showing the level of aspirations of 198 drop-out cases.

Out of every 10 drop-out children, one child seemed to oblivious of any aspiration at all, about three preferred to remain as housewives (all girls' cases) or farm labourers. One wanted factory work or some skilled job, three wanted to join any unskilled job category and the remaining two wanted to start their business or take up white-collar occupations such as teaching, clerical assistance etc. It is clear that owing to an extremely low level of education, most of the drop-out cases have lowered their sights and desired to become what their own limited capacities of background would justify. These reflect unwholesome consequences brought about by their drop-out.

Positions aspired to by the drop-out cases: No. of children

Aspirational Level	*Rasra Block*	*Ranipur Block*	*Total*	*(%)*
No aspiration at all	18	5	23	(11.0)
Housewife	19	8	27	(13.6)
Farm Labourer	2	27	29	(14.6)
Factory Worker	6	3	9	(4.6)
Businessman Trader	12	11	23	(11.6)
Unskilled Worker	39	27	66	(33.3)
Skilled Worker	4	7	11	(5.6)
White-collar occupation	8	2	10	(5.1)
Total	108	90	198	(100.0)

Negative Side

It was a convincing and noticeable feature of the study that out of 198 children who were available for interviews, 65 have expressed their desire to rejoin their studies. In other words three out of every 10 drop-out children were aware even at this stage (with a comfortable gap of two to eight years) that they should educate themselves to improve their socio-economic position. A question is: How many of them can successfully translate their desire into action? Whether their families would be in position to relieve them from their present engagements? Answer appear to swing more in favour of the negative than the positive side. Economic compulsions would not allow most of them to devote sufficient time for educational activities, although they succeeded in re-admitting themselves.

It would be interesting to find out their present activities (till the time of this study). It is learned from parents that out of 300 children, 133 are unemployed but assisting them in household work and other activities while 167 are working independently in some gainful activities. In other words, nearly 56per cent of the drop-out cases are providing much needed economic support to their families. If we recall the earlier discussion (Table), we found that 83 children had entered into independent employment immediately after drop-out.This number of working children has become twice in a short span of 4-5 years (from 83 to 167). If we observe the present age of the drop-out cases, it can be seen that out of 300 children 62 per cent of them (186 cases) come under the age group of 14 years while remaining 38 per cent are above that age, only seven cases are above 21 years. As the employed children constitute 56 per cent of our total sample, it is very clear that quite a large number of children below 14 years of age are in independent employment, a fact that underscores the economic contributions of child labour in the Dalit families. Dalit households are limited to use child-power for livelihood.

The clearcut explanation on this situation in this chapter throws sufficient light, on the causes underlying drop-out and the consequences emanating from it. We are still unaware of the role of child's family in his educational efforts, the extent of contribution of school system and the nature of community influences. Every aspect of these has some part to play.

3

Government's Role

For emancipation, education is a very powerful instrument for emancipation. Further, it may be defined as the inculcation of knowledge, values, skills, and attitudes by means of institutions that have been built-up towards this end. It is an inevitable tool for the improvement of socio-economic conditions of people. Education helps to bridge wide disparity in social status, political assertation and income distribution. This also plays a significant role in transforming the existing social order and in defining the aims and objectives of human beings. One of the major objectives of education in the post-independence era, specifically in 1950 was to cater to the educational needs and development of Scheduled Castes and Scheduled Tribes children who have remained quite isolated from the ambit of education for over ages. It is only after independence, government started making systematic efforts to raise educational standard of dalits though the result has not been satisfactory in terms of its implimentation and outcome. Notwithstanding the education was an attempt at integration of dalits with the rest of the society, they continue to remain out of mainstream of life. This group of children are brought up in the society along with others but are away from the mainstream of life. It is only during the last three decades that there has been a social reorientation and acceptance.

In India, a good deal of emphasis has been laid, since independence, on the spread of education. The Constitution adopted in 1950, emphasized on central importance of education in national development and includes a Directive Principle to provide, by 1960, free and compulsory education for all children upto the age group of 14 years. Educational development among socially and economically weaker sections, such as SCs has been considered an important obligation under the Constitution. Article 46 states that "the state shall promote with special care the educational and economic interests of the weaker sections of the population and, in particular of SC, and shall protect them from social injustice and all forms of exploitation. But the dilemma of the ruling class/elite is manifold; they wish to honour the values of modernity, democracy and equality without effectively rejecting the values of old social order. That is why, though at the local and lower levels SC live in a society dominated by the values of varna and caste, effectively determining the fortune of millions, at the higher levels, the illusion of living in a modern state system is carried out. The state would attain modernity only when it destroys the entire values system of varna and caste.

The purpose of this chapter is to perceive at in a more in depth and larger perspective the education of the two groups, with specific reference to the state of Uttar Pradesh. Hence it is centred around certain themes :

1. Population of the Community and Literacy figures.
2. To Study the enrolment of SC students between primary level to the Higher Education including professional education.
3. To study the state responsibility in terms of policy implementation to bring SC students at par with general category.
4. To identify the reasons behind dropout among SC students and suggest possible remedial measures.
5. An attempt has been made to make an analysis of the constraints that has been responsible for the relatively slow rate of progress and the best alternative solution for accelerating the educational development of the SC children.

India claims to be a largest democracy in the World. The major factor makes democracy a success is the quality of its men and women. Democracy becomes meaningless to the people if they are to remain uneducated and the number of illiterates remain high. Even today the modern Indian state, despite its commitment towards addressing the problems of caste, has completely failed to address the questions of increasing Dalit access to modern education. The extent of development can be judged by an official estimate (1993) which shows that 80 per cent of Dalits are living below the poverty line. Out of the total bonded labourers dalits account for 66 per cent whereas nearly 55.27 per cent Dalits are agricultural labourers and 23.62 per cent cultivators (most of whose holdings are of marginal or small size). Besides 3.42 per cent were occupied in household industry. Whereas around 17.59 per cent of Dalits engaged under the category "Other Workers"; which includes employment in governmental organizations, factory sector, mining, construction, service sector and (transport, trade and commerce etc.). Approximately about 20% Dalit are `liberated' from age old imposed occupations and it is this proportion of the Dalit community which has been become capable of cashing in on any form of educational opportunity.

According to 1991 Census, the population of India had reached to 84.63 crores which was about 16 per cent of the World population (536 crores). The Census data also reveals that in 1991 the member of Scheduled Castes or groups notified was 1091 and that of Scheduled Tribes 573. The majority of the population belonging to the Scheduled Castes and Scheduled Tribes are illiterate even today. Dalit Shiksha Andolan (DSA), a voluntary educational action group working for the welfare of SC/STs prepared a report namely 'Dalit Data Bank'. It reveals that inspite of Welfare Schemes, provisions of reservations in jobs and educational institutions, the country has not been able to achieve the constitutional directives of universal primary education. The literacy rate has grown at less than one per cent per year while population has been growing at the rate of over two per cent per annum. Although it is claimed that Indian education is getting massive qualitative expansion at all levels but it still needs a kind of transformation to make up the staggering backlog. In India, 48% of the total population is illiterate even after 53 years of country's independence. The SC/STs are the worst victims of present educational system where 63 per cent SCs and 71 per cent STs are illiterate. The female illiteracy rate among them has been alarmingly high as 76 and 82 per cent respectively.

The report published in March 1998 by the Ministry of Welfare, Government of India, indicates the recent literacy figures of general communities as well as Scheduled Castes. According to Table , the general castes (male) literacy rate is 64.13 per cent whereas it is only 49.91 per cent in case of Scheduled Castes (male). While the literacy rate of women belonging to general communities was 39.29 per cent that of SC female was 23.76 per cent. If we include male and female, the literacy rate reaches 52.21 per cent among general castes whereas it is 37.41 per cent among SCs.

India	*Literacy Rate*	*Scheduled Caste*
Male	64.13%	49.91%
Female	39.29%	23.76%
Total	52.21%	37.41%

Source: Ministry of Welfare, Government of India, New Delhi, Report Published in March 1998.

Literacy Rate (Scheduled Castes)

Years	*Percentage*
1991	37.41
1961	10.27
1951	1.9

Source: Ministry of Welfare Report March 1998.

Only 1.9 per cent population belonging to Scheduled Castes were literate in 1931 which increased to 10.27 per cent in 1961. In other words, the literacy rate among the SCs increased by 8.37 per cent in first 30 years. . In 60 years only 37.41 per cent SC population were literate in 1991. The literacy rate among them increased by 27.24 per cent in next 30 years in independent India. It is very disappointing to see that the measures adopted to develop education among Scheduled Castes failed at every level. The literacy rate among them did not increase even at the rate of one per cent in a year. In other words, the literacy rate among SCs, came down in independent India as it was in pre-independence India.

Number of Illiterates and Literacy Rates

Year	*All Social Groups*		*Scheduled Castes*		*Scheduled Tribes*	
	Illiterates (in million)	*Literacy rate*	*Illiterates (in million)*	*Literacy rate*	*Illiterates (in million)*	*Literacy rate*
1961	334	31.00%	57.8	12.80%	27.9	10.62%
1971	388	38.20%	68.9	18.28%	33.7	14.07%
1981	424	43.67%	81.4	26.48%	43.2	20.31%
1991	482	52.21%	96.7	37.41%	51.7	29.60%

Source: Census Report 1991.

According to 1991 Census, India became more illiterate than it was in 1961. India had produced 54 million illiterates between 1961 to 1971; 34 million between 1971 to 1981 and 58 million between 1981 and 1991 and in 2000, the population increases upto 100 crores. In three decades 148 million additional illiterates added to our total population. Whereas the literacy rate increased by 21.11 per cent in 30 years which is very low in proportion to the growth of population.

Besides, 38.9 million illiterate Scheduled Castes added in actual illiterate population in three decades. However, the growth in literacy rate in the same period was only 24.61 per cent. In case of Scheduled Tribe, population growth was 23.8 million whereas literacy rate increased only 19.03 per cent in 30 years. The rapid growth of population has pushed up the country further with illiteracy. The literacy rates have been going up from 31 per cent in 1961 to 52.21 per cent in 1991.

The famous Poona Pact was signed between Gandhiji and Dr. B.R. Ambedkar in 1932, giving several concessions to the Dalits. Amongst those, State-sponsored free education to the Dalits was one of them. Consequently, the State offered universal freeship for all stages of education to Dalit students from all over the country. The Universal freeship policy was replaced by awarding scholarships, subject to the income ceiling of parents not being high. The scheme was further divided into two parts; the Central Government announced a scheme to cover students from the post-matric stage to that of higher education, and the state Government scheme to take care of students during the primary to pre-matric stage. The irony of the scheme is such that from the primary to pre-matric stage assistance is not offered universally, thereby meaning that few students selected from each school are offered scholarships. In consequences of income ceiling a majority of Dalit students failed to get pre-matric scholarship. If the income of parents is more than Rs. 25,000 annually, their sons/daughters are not entitled to avail fellowship. Failing to get financial assistance from the state and due to poor economic conditions of their parents, 49.62 per cent SC and 64.53 per cent ST of the total registered at primary schools dropped their education at primary level itself. As a result, the scheme has been insignificant all over the country. Similarly the PMS which begins for post-matriculation, does not cover assistance for M.Phil/Ph.D. programmes and therefore, effective impediment for higher education to Dalits.

The PMS was started in the academic year 1944-45 and till 1994-95, that is, in a period of 50 years, a total sum of Rs. 2002.46 crores was spent for Dalit education in the form of freeship and scholarship. This includes the total expenditure incurred by the state government.

Union Government decides the rates and other related provisions and the Govt. has time and again defied values of planning and ethics. For instance, per student the average spending per year was Rs. 548.08 in 1951. It went up to Rs. 1290.79 in the year 1992. But the Union Government had not taken into account the increase in Wholesale Price Index (WPI). If the increase in prices were to be taken into consideration this amount should have gone upto Rs. 6744.71 in order to at least maintain the real value of per awardee spending at the prevailing rates of 1951. Correspondingly, the total spending amount should have gone upto Rs. 1009.723 crores instead of the prevailing figure of Rs. 193.24 crores in 1992. In other words, in real terms there has been a decline in the per awardee spending. As it is clear from column 4 of the table, taking 1981/82 as the base year, per awardee spending in real terms has come down from Rs. 3245.77 in 1951 to Rs.621.17 in 1981 - a decline of about 80 per cent. Since Govt. did not take into account the rise in the prices, the PMS has been reduced to a mockery, as it no way makes education of SC/STs 'FREE'.

The ruling elite is often devoid of ethics and honesty in their life. The values of justice and the values of modernity are yet alien to them.

The recent hike in PMS rates is too low to come to any help to SC/ST students. The successive Govts. at the centre often resort to the pretext of the resources crunch. If it is true, then how can the Union Government find over Rs. 8500 crores for the financial year 1996-97 in the name of fertilizer subsidy whose beneficiaries are basically the land-owning classes? 98 per cent of the land owners comprise the upper caste communities. Government further spent hundred of crores of Rupees for paying remunerative prices to the foodgrain producers, to subsidized electricity, petroleum products etc. for the welfare of their vested interests. But they find it difficult to spare minimal amount of Rs. 1010 crores which can effectively mould the life of nearly one- fourth of total population of India, namely the Dalits.

Development of Education

Education is the soul of human civilization and development which is lacking among the Scheduled Castes. To compete with general communities, it is necessary to equip them educationally. The total population of Uttar Pradesh is 13.91 crores. Out of which the Scheduled Castes population is 2.92 crores whereas

STs are in a very small number, i.e. 2.87 lakhs. The literacy rate among the general population is 52 per cent whereas it is only 26.85 per cent and 35.70 per cent among the SC and ST respectively. As far as drop out rate is concern, 72.91 per cent SC and 80.68 per cent ST students dropped their education before they could reach high school. Unemployment rate is also very high as 453967 SC and 9849 ST educated youth are unemployed in Uttar Pradesh (Govt. of U.P. Report 1993). The data available from government of U.P. gives a detail of SC students studying at various levels.

SC Students Registered Between Primary and Ph.D Level

S. No.	*Class*	*Number of Students*
1.	Primary (1-5)	2411563
2.	Junior High School (6-8)	0734330
3.	High School (9-10)	0314686
4.	Above High School and upto Ph.D. Level	0234776
	Total	37,35355

Source: Government of U.P. Report, 1992-93.

The table reveals a very Pathetic picture of Scheduled Caste students registered at various levels. At primary level, around 24 lakhs SC boys and girls were registered. Out of this number only 729 SC students reached upto Post-graduation in science. In other words, in a state like U.P. where the SC population is around 3 crores, but not even 1000 students in this community are doing M.Sc. Besides 3 lakhs boys/girls students were studying in high school out of which only 11,000 boys/girls reached to the level of post-graduation. In most of the cases, it has been observed that the economic backwardness of Scheduled Caste family is the only barrier in gaining access to education.

SC/ST Students Registered at Graduation and PostGraduation

Graduate (Degree Course) Subject	*Class*	*Number* *SCs*	*STs*
Art and Literature	B.A.	37217	796
Science	B.Sc.	04966	175
Commerce	B.Com.	02737	076
Engineering	B.E. etc.	00091	065
Medical	M.B.B.S.	00182	042
B. Ed.	B. Ed.	1555	041
Total		46748	1245
Post-Graduation	Ph.D./D.Sc./D.Phil	0224	008
All Subjects			
Science	M.Sc.	0729	036
Commerce	M.Com.	0632	035
Art and Literature	M.A.	9526	492
Total		11248	571
Grand Total (Graduate + 47993 + 11784 Post Graduate = 59777)			

Source: Government of U.P. Report - 1992 - 93.

School Dropout

A conference of Heads of 9 states was held on 'Education for All' in Indian scenario, between 15-16 September 1993, in New Delhi. In which Ministry of Education, Government of India came out with a statement in the form of a booklet which dealt with the dropout rate among SC students at various levels.

The dropout rate given here is on an all India basis. There is specific mention/evidence about U.P. The dropout rate in U.P. is more or less equal to all India. Because, barring two or three states, the status of Scheduled Caste education is more or less the same. However, in many cases U.P. is in worst position in comparison to other states.

Table shows that among 100 boys/girls admitted in class 1st, 80 out of 100 dropped out before they could reach upto 10th and at the P.G. level numerically they were very less. For instance, in the year 1992-93, 24 lakhs SC students were registered at primary but only around 24,000 of them were able to reach upto P.G. level.

Percentage of Drop Out

Class	*Scheduled Caste*	*Scheduled Tribes*
Class 1 to 5	49.62	64.53
Class 1 to 8	67.78	78.08
Class 1 to 10	79.88	86.72

Source: 'Education for All' in Indian Scenario, Ministry of Human Resources Development, Government of India, New Delhi, 1993.

It enables one to raise several questions.

1. Several lakhs of SC boys/girls registered themselves in primary school but out of them only a few hundreds or thousands students could reach upto P.G. why? It is because these students are not interested in gaining education? If it is so, then why did they register themselves in primary schools.

2. Just imagine about those SC students who secured more than 70 per cent marks and had to drop their education. Because they spent their childhood in schools where modern education was not introduced and thus they failed to achieve further advanced education. Realising this dismal possibility of securing jobs, they opted out of their education.

3. Lakhs of Sc boys/girls failed to pass through 12th standard and these students certainly have crossed their 16 years of age.

4. Think about those SC students with the age ranging between 17 to 22 who have cleared their graduation and post-graduation either in third division or failed.

5. The representation of scheduled caste boys/girls in Science subject is too negligible. Are the scheduled caste students not interested in studying science, or they lacking proper guidance or even if they get admission in science subjects they lack resources to pursue their studies in science subjects.

It is said that 'the evidence reveal'. The government sources reveals that the Centre and State governments have not yet brought Scheduled Caste/Tribes education in their agenda. Educational level of SC/STs have been discussed on the following pages. The second largest number of illiterates from SC population are residing in U.P. Reason being, the inert and discouraging attitude of successive governments by not releasing funds allotted for SC/ST pre-matric fellowship. The absence of monitoring agencies at state level to review the policies and programmes taken up by the state for SC/ST education has encouraged the state to become more unaccountable towards dalit education. Besides, if we go by the general socio-economic profile of SC/ST they are not in a position to generate surplus to fund education of their children. As a result, state is producing more and more illiterates among SCs and STs in UP.

Need for Literacy

According to 1991 Census report, 73.5 Scheduled Castes population is illiterate which accounts for more than that of national average (62.60 per cent).

Basic Education

35.79 per cent of students failed to take admission in primary schools in Uttar Pradesh. Because of their parents were not in position to bear the cost of education of their children, most of their parents are agricultural labourers. But the land which is in their possession is either unproductive or very low productive. Therefore, it is impossible for parents to manage the expenditure of education from agriculture. Secondly, SC/ST children who do not get enrolled at primary level is mainly because of the scarcity of Schools and other facilities rather than unwillingness of their parents. The state and privilged class of UP never responded positively to the problem of SC/ST which has resulted in a high rate of illiteracy. Consequently, they missed the chance of education for ever.

Uttar Pradesh
SC School Going Age Group (6-11 Years)

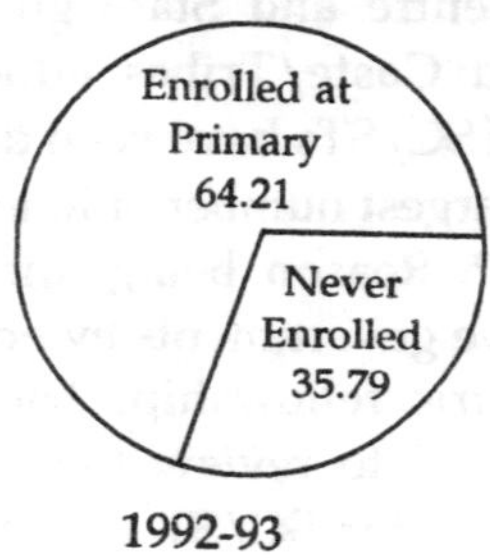

1992-93

Source: Dalit Shiksha Andolan.

Though the dropouts is a general phenomenon, it occurs more among the SCs than other population. Although the enrollment of the SCs at the primary stage is quite encouraging. Table shows a very high percentage of drop-outs among the Scheduled Caste is most of the states. In U.P. alone, 72.91 per cent of the total registered students in primary schools dropped their education before or upto to high school. According to report only seven states where dropout rate is lower than U.P.

Science and Technoiogy

Representation of Scheduled Castes students in science and other technical subjects is very less. According to the report of Ministry of Human Resources Development - Select Educational Statistics - 1993 in the total strength of SC students at Graduation stage, 84.11 per cent opted for humanities, and at Post-graduation stge, 88.31 per cent of the total strength went for humanities/ social sciences stream. Besides, only 6.69 per cent of SC students were pursuing their P.G. in science and other technical subjects. Since large majority of SC students acquired certificates and

Degrees in non-technical/non-professional streams of education they became virtually irrelevant in the job market of secondary and Tertiary Sectors of economy.

Uttar Pradesh SC Students in Under-graduate Stage

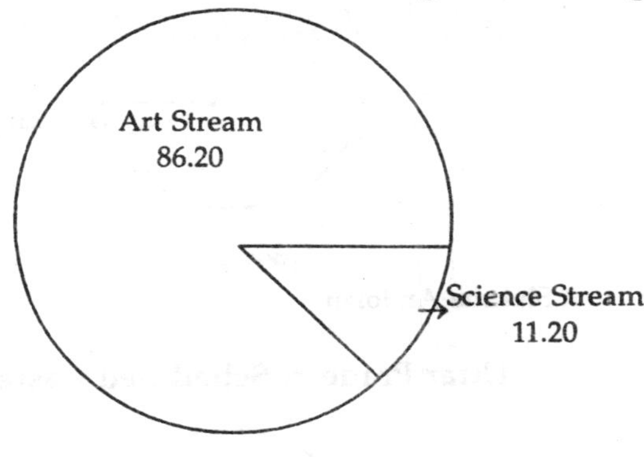

1992-93

Source: Dalit Shiksha Andolan.

The Economy

A study based on government documents (Dalit Aankara Bank - Granth Part I) reveals that 80.48% of the total population of Scheduled Castes in U.P. are economically very poor. Consequently they failed to provide resources to their boys/girls to gain education. According to study, 38.76 of the total labour force in Scheduled Caste are landless agricultural labourers whereas 42.63 per cent of them are landed agricultural labourers. The condition of small land holding agricultural labourers is also very bad because 95.66 per cent of the total cultivable land is distributed in marginal and small categories of tillers. 1.92 per cent of the chief labour force belonging to Scheduled Castes are involved in trade and commerce whereas 6.98 per cent are engaged in other services. Therefore, it is impossible to provide education to the SC without help on the end of Government. Without government's help the dream of education to SC will be unfulfilled.

Uttar Pradesh SC Students in Post-graduate Stage

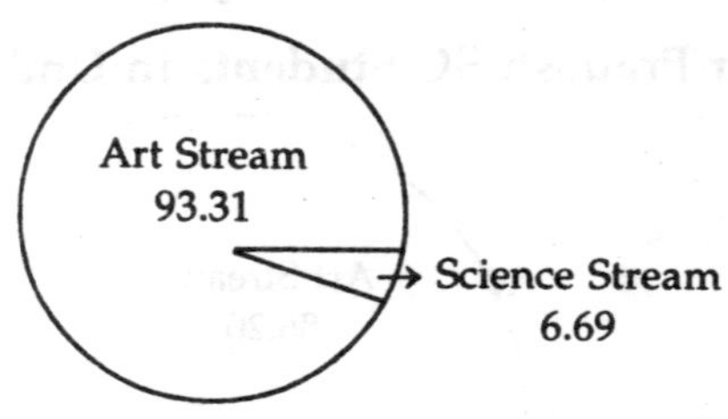

1992-93

Source: Dalit Shiksha Andolan.

Uttar Pradesh Scheduled Caste

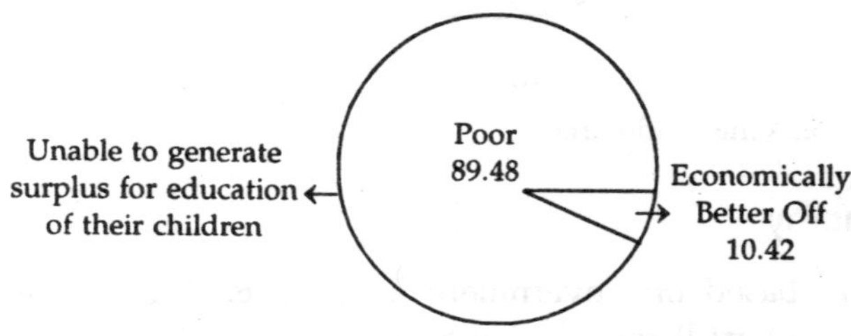

1992-93

Source: Dalit Shiksha Andolan.

Problem of Employment

According to the data available from Employment and Training Directorate, New Delhi (1993) the number of educated unemployed SC was 4,53,000. It is clear that now this number has gone double. The position of SC unemployed is much different from that of educated unemployed of general category. Because firstly SC youth complete their education in hardship and their parents are bound to sell off their belongings if they want that the education of their sons/daughters must be completed. In such circumstance, if there sons/daughters fail to get a job they have no other option except to face starvation. Secondly the economic condition of the parents of the SC/ST unemployed youth is very poor. Consequently, these unemployed SC/ST youth can not opt business also and the survival becomes the main problem.

Reservation will not work to improve/solve their unemployment problem. Therefore, government has to introduce an alternative to promote their economic conditions. Besides, a commission must be constituted at government level. The functioning of the commission is to be based on working out the search around 1 lakhs jobs for these unemployed SC youths. Because education is directly linked with employment. So if unemployment problems among SC cannot be solved, the SC may opt their traditional jobs for their survival. In such a circumstances it will be more difficult to educate them.

SC Population (All India)

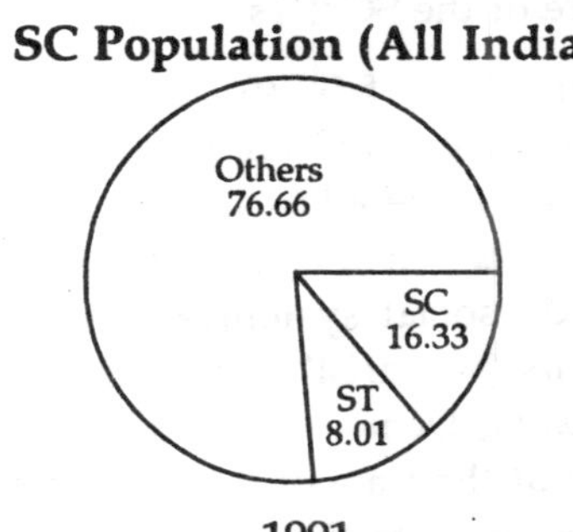

1991

Source: Dalit Shiksha Andolan.

SC/ST Population (Uttar Pradesh)

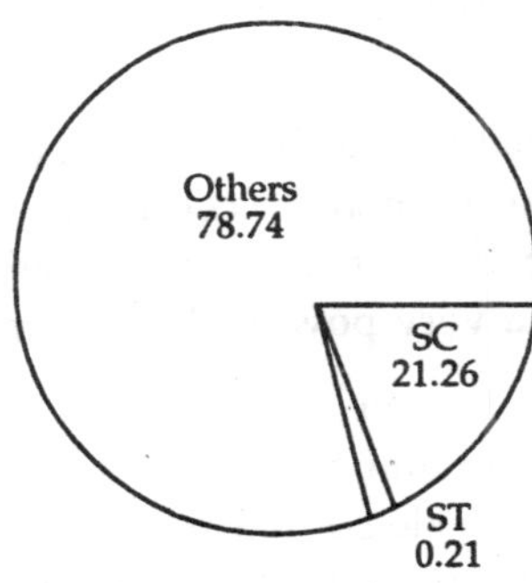

Source: Dalit Shiksha Andolan.

It is an established fact that SC/ST parents have a strong urge to give education to their children, but fail on this front owing to their abject poverty and lack of other infrastructural facilities. While a retrograde and essentially an oppressive institution, Indian State has transformed into a Republic albeit theoretically at the dawn of the second half of the last century. The society chose to continue with its obscurantist and retrograde world view and value system. Therefore, society is strongly biased against SC/STs, and wishes to retain the community away from the World of Learning. On the other hand, the institution of state has been at the disposal of political leadership of the country which refuses to confront society. This is clearly reflected in the policies and programmes evolved ever since Independence in regard to the welfare of the SC/STs.

The pathetic condition of SC/ST can trace its roots to the abject insensitivity on the part of Indian state. The Indian Republic which would like itself to be addressed as a 'Welfare State' has failed on both the fronts - neither did it bother to transform an essentially retrograde social system and nor did it sincerely attempt to acquire its 'welfarist' characteristics. Therefore, the noble values of equality, Democracy and justice which the State proclaimed to adopt at the time of its birth on January 26, 1950, continue to be dishonoured to the day.

In the light of the failure of the experiments of more than past five decades, the Dalits are not asking for something unjust but just for their rights to education. In concrete terms, following demands are proposed:

1. Immediate creation of a High Power National Commission for SC/ST Education at the centre as well as State level to deal with the problems of SC/ST education. When as educatioon is a very powerful tool of emancipation.
2. Withdrawal of Income Ceiling, the ceiling limit which is still Rs. 25000 annual should be revised at par with the revision of pay scale so that maximum students may get an opportunity to pursue their education.

3. The centrally - sponsored post-matric scheme to be extended to cover primary as well as higher secondary education.

4. Since most of the educational institutions and research organisations enjoy autonomy, they take escape-route of 'merit' and deny admission to SC/ST students. The 'autonomy' and 'merit question' should not be used to create social tension by ignoring adequate representation to SC.

5. Pre-matric and Post-matric scholarship rates are too low and have nothing to do with meeting educational expenses of SC student. Considering the fact pre and PMs must be revised at rate of current price Index.

It is hoped that dalit voice will be heard. Keeping one-fourth of the nation's population outside the world of education is a crime involving severe consequences for a nation and its people. Without providing equal opportunity of education to Dalits, any claim to democracy or modernity will be betrayal to the nation. The nation as well as states must make responsible to address the problems of Dalit education. Further denial of education to dalits ultimately will lead social tension and political disorder.

4

The Drop-outs

In a drop-out situation, the factors involved are predominantly related to the child's family background and school environment. Therefore, it is only proper that we should examine in more detail the role of both, the home and school in the child's educational life. It is equally important to examine the contributions, if any, of the child's community which includes his immediate neighbourhood, caste groups and also the village settlement as a whole. Community pressures for or against education is an important factor for determining the schooling prospects of younger generations. In a sociological perspective, all the three institutional units, i.e., family, school and the community have a strategic concern with the level of educational advancement of the children. School drop-out is a manifestation of failure or non-fulfilment of the basic objectives at the hands of one or more of these units. Do they perform their role satisfactorily? What are the shortcomings which they encounter in their task of meeting the basic obligations in the field of education? In the present chapter, we will deal with these apparently simple but basic questions.

Family Factor

By now, enough is known about the social and economic conditions of the Dalit households. We may recapture some major strands to keep a link in the discussion here. Dalit child, we have seen, has often inherited a social and economic legacy of which is not conducive to his future prospects. Economic hardships in some quarters, abysmal poverty in others, might have undermined the honest and determined efforts of many a schooling child. Added to these were the social and cultural factors, parental unconcern and carelessness and child's own repulsion towards school education. All these forces, acting singly or in unison, were responsible for the child's exit from the school. We must, however, bear in mind that it would be an error of judgment to consider Dalit families as universally irresponsible or careless in relation to the studies of their children. Such a sweeping generalisation would certainly do injustice to the Dalit homes, which have displayed affection, care, sympathy and some degree of involvement in the child's schooling.

We may recall, to provide a backdrop to further discussion, major aspects reflecting the involvement of the child's family in his educational activities. Despite the fact that most of Dalit parents were illiterate, it is they who had taken a major initiative in sending the child to school. Enrolment decision regarding the child's schooling was made by the parents in most cases. Apart from this, a large majority of them were careful in admitting their child in school at the right age, i.e., six years. Dalit parents were fairly well-informed about the child's progress in school, his likes and dislikes in respect of the outer world. It was, however, an enigmatic finding that out of 300 Dalit parents, only 53 per cent had visited the school, while the rest did not visit the school at all. When the school teachers were asked to give their definite opinion in this respect they too came out with identical responses in Table. A majority of them stated that the parents, visit to the school was limited to one or two occasions at best. Normally, these occasions related to the admission efforts, enquiries relating to the child's performance in annual examinations and the like.

Do Dalit Parents Visit Your School?
(School Teacher's version)

Answer	*No. of Respondents*
Rarely	9
Just once/twice a year	22
On quite a few occasions	6
On most occasions	3
Total	40

In comparative terms, parents from other caste groups were reported to be somewhat more particular in this respect. They used to visit the school oftentimes, enquiring from the teachers about the child's requirements, behaviour in the class and his performance in studies. School teachers, in turn, visited the homes of these children and, in the course of general discussion, kept the parents informed about the child's development in school. Some of the teachers belonging to upper castes were reported to be giving private tuitions to the children of caste-Hindus. Dalit children were not fortunate enough to enjoy such privileges. They had no means to engage the services of school teachers for private coaching. Some Dalit parents feel that attitude of school teachers who mostly belonged to socially dominant caste groups. Most of the school teachers enjoyed economically superior positions than that of even relatively well-off Dalit families. There was also a tendency in some of the school teachers to keep a conventionally legitimised social distance between themselves and the Dalit parents.

Some Dalit parents criticised the behaviour of teachers towards them. The latter would often keep them waiting outside the building, give evasive answers to their anxious queries and comment on the educational backwardness of their community. One Dalit parents described the situation thus:

> "When I went to my child's school once to find out why he was not doing any homework assignments, I was expecting a reasonably hospitable climate in the school. The school teacher who was Ahir by caste replied that Dalit child were better suited to jobs in agriculture than to schooling. They have no brain for ideas and no capacity for school work, the school teacher retorted. He further warned me that he would strike off the name of my child from the school roll if I ever again visited the school for seeking such clarifications. He misunderstood the purpose of my visit. He thought I was cross-examining him on his duties. I felt very much hurt by his derisive remarks. But what could I do in the circumstances? I left the school quietly consoling that it was better that I never went to school myself for education.

Social distance which the teachers try to keep from the Dalit parent was verbalised during such encounters. Such incidence as one just reported are capable of scaring away many a sensitive and self-respecting parent. In adequacy of contacts between the parents and teachers may partly be explained by such an unreceptive outlook of the teaching community. It is, however, erroneous to blame the school teachers alone for lack of parents' affinity with the school system. Some Dalit parents were equally responsible for this. They were totally unaware of their obligations towards their child's educational needs. Uneducated themselves they were apathetic and unconcerned. They thought that after an act of enrolling their child's name in the school, their commitment came to an end.

"Why should I go and visit the school? I have done my duty of putting my son in the school. It is my son who should go to school and learn something. I myself know nothing of basic alphabets. What can I tell the teacher who is the master of all knowledge. Now it is my son and that teacher who are concerned with each other. I am in no way connected with what goes on in the school. Don't you think I am right in my thinking?"

This is the response of one Dalit parent to this question. According to them, school education was a matter strictly between the school teachers and children, and parents had only a peripheral role in it. Why were these parents clinging on to a traditional and obsolete viewpoint? It is difficult to answer this question off-hand. However, our guess is that there are a number of factors responsible in making Dalit parents less responsive to the demands of the school system. And these can be enumerated as their illiteracy, culturally-conditioned inhibitions, lack of exposure to changing social responsibilities of the parents, unfriendly outlook of the teaching community, etc. Their inferior position in the status system of the village community further aggravate the social distance between the school and their family. This may explain why the Dalit parents were mostly unable to establish enduring links with the school system which, after family, was the next important for their child.

It was already explained that whatever knowledge or

information the parents had about the child's school, it could be gathered by them mostly through secondary sources. His own child, neighbouring children and others in the community shared their experience and opinions about the school education, facilities and the like. Sometimes Dalit teachers visited their locality and discussed the issues pertaining to the school. By far, the Dalit teachers formed the most important group that offered a link between the Dalit families and the school. Some of them were instrumental in motivating Dalit parents for enrolling their child in the school, in providing, guidance to Dalit children in studies and in meeting the basic educational needs of some poor children. In most of the cases, whatever inspiration or guidance that was available to the Dalit families, came from teachers of their own community. This also indicates how imperceptibly caste alignments take place in a village setting. By and large, however, the Dalit parents remained deprived of any direct information about his child's class-room behaviour, studies, regularity, etc. This is evident from the responsed in Table.

Question: Did the School Teacher Make any Specific Comments about the Child; His/Her Class-room Behaviour, Studies, Regularity etc.? (Parent's Version)

Response	*Rasra Block*		*Ranipur Block*		*Total*	
	No.	*%*	*No.*	*%*	*No.*	*%*
Received no comments	112	(74.7)	116	(77.4)	228	(76.0)
Made positive comments	17	(11.3)	14	(9.3)	31	(10.3)
Made negative comments	21	(14.0)	20	(14.0)	41	(13.7)
	150	(100.0)	150	(100.0)	300	(100.0)

Figures in Bracket indicate percentage.

Poverty and economic backwardness have many dimensions. It is reasonable to say that a Dalit home stands apart in its incapacity to provide adequate leverage to the youngsters to grow in a natural way, to embibe experiences compatible with their age and interests. Even school teachers have fully recognised this fact. When they were asked to explain the reasons for irregularity in school attendance of Dalit children, most of them have cited three factors, domestic duties including child care, minor agricultural jobs or tending the cattle or sheep, and starvation at home. They argued that compared to the above, reasons such as migration of the family, community or caste influences or lack of parental concern are not much significant in influencing school attendance. It was their opinion that children who are initiated into domestic tasks at a much lower age are more likely to develop tendencies of absenting from school. Some of the physical tasks done through the children in Dalit families were strenuous and unbearable for the child, eight or nine years old. It was economically compulsive for the Dalit families to engage the child in these unwelcome tasks, but its direct effect for the child was his declining interest in school activities. We are now beginning to experience how poverty conditions exercise their sway in different directions. Lack of food or other basic necessities, absence of adequate freedom to take part in school activities due to the pressures of domestic chores and physical strain linked with cumbersome manual tasks are responsible for driving a school-going child to a point of total withdrawal from the school system.

Influence of poverty can be seen in another context also. Out of 40 school teachers, 19 had stated that only a few Dalit students were able to pick up/learn easily the lessons in their classroom. When they were further asked to specify the reasons as to why some Dalit students have difficulties, they offered several responses in this respect Table. It is pointed out by the teachers that paucity of educational material, starvation and hunger and frequent absenteeism of the child are accountable for his poor classroom performance. It is entirely a new finding and perhaps a strategic one that domestic problems and anxieties accompanied by these are responsible for lack of the child's attention in the classroom. Observations recorded in the table go to prove that children with worst economic background have to encounter a series of obstacles to attain their goals. Poverty may reflect not only in his dress or school wallet but also in his mood, his behavioural patterns, his relationship with teachers and school mates. His whole personality may undergo a conditioning process. An attitude of listlessness or withdrawal in the class-room may be treated as only one expression of this conditioning.

The question is whether Dalit parents were aware of the educational backwardness of their children? Yes, some of them were. Out of 300 parents, 49 of them (nearly 17 per cent) stated that their children were much behind other students in class-room studies. They had this knowledge through school visits, observations of the child's goings-on at home and through the reports of school-going children in the neighbourhood. What efforts did they make to rectify the educational backwardness of the child? Nothing tangible as such. Some of them brought the matter to the school and implored the school teachers to 'improve' the child. Others warned their children of waywardness and supervised for sometime that their child does some lessons at home. But being uneducated or apathetic, the parents could hardly improve the situation. Still others watched helplessly and allowed the child to drift and waver in his own way.

Difficulties before the Dalit Child in Learning Easily the Class-room Lessons (Teacher's Version)

Difficulties	*No. of Responses (N=19)*
Lack of textbooks, exercise books, etc.	10
Irregularity in attendance	8
Mental preoccupation with household problems	7
Starvation and hunger	6
Lack of guidance/help at home	3
Any others—Poor innate capacity, lack of interest in studies, etc.	9
	43

From earlier observations, we are tempted to regard parental involvement in the educational activities of the child as sporadic and peripheral. It may also be noted that only 34 children (15.3 per cent) had received proper academic guidance from the family members in their educational efforts. Other children got only marginal attention in this respect or no attention at all. Would it then be correct to say that Dalit parents have no interest in the educational activities of their school-going child? Perhaps the questions has a misplaced emphasis on the term 'interest'. Most of the Dalit families were operating in a culture of illiteracy, with no long-standing tradition of learning or scholarship in their ancestry. Schooling of the child was thought to be an important issue and hence the enrolment of the child at the right age. Low social and economic status was the inhibiting factor which forced many a loving father to send his tender-aged son to the agricultural field rather than to the school. Their financial condition was hopeless for most of the year and yet they kept on bearing the expenses involved in educational activities. When asked whether the expenses relating to the school education of the child were within their capacity, only 95 parents (nearly 32 per cent) answered in the affirmative. In other words; two out of every three Dalit parents found the expenses out of their capacity to bear.

Provision of food, books and many other items required in the school, supply of kerosene and lamp for night study and relieving the child from much-needed domestic services are acts of parental concern and sense of obligation towards the schooling child. Apart from the few wxcepting most of the parents had the genuine desire of educating the child and had the willingness to make necessary sacrifices to attain that goal. They were hopeful that their child would rise above the conventional level and would make a mark. Academic guidance and support was available to only a few because they had literate and fairly educated family members around. Others were left unattended in this respect because their parents and other family members were not literate. It is, therefore, idle to conclude that Dalit parents were totally disinterested in the studies of their child. Even school teachers have supported this contention with a forceful logic. When asked to specify whether Dalit parents take interest in the education of their children, 33 out of 40 school teachers replied in the affirmative. In their opinion, parental concern and responsibility and are obvious through their anxious queries with teachers about their child's needs, requirements and class-room performance, meticulous care with which they ensure the regularity in school attendance of the child, some assistance in the child's homework preparations and the like Table.

By now, it is fairly well-established that Dalit parents, except a minority, were reasonally responsive to the educational needs of their children. Their financial insecurity as well as other constraints were largely responsible for lack of deeper involvement. From the description in the preceding pages, it can be safely concluded that the social and economic status of the Dalit family was not at all a facilitating factor in most of the cases. The home atmosphere was, in most of the cases, full of deficiencies and hardships. Physical help from the child was more a rule than a exception. It is already known to us that many a child had to leave his school owing to poverty and related contingencies. School and the teaching community were partly responsible for the drop-out of Dalit children and we will discuss their role at length later. For the present, it would suffice to say that most of the Dalit parents have played their role fairly satisfactorily, considering their limitations on different scores. A few of them might have erred seriously and none can pardon them for their inattention or neglect.

Parental Interest in the School Education of the Dalit Child (Teacher's Version)

Indicators	*Responses*		
	Basra Block	*Ranipur Block*	*Total*
Personal queries about children's needs, requirements and school performance	9	14	23 (39.7)
Help and assistance in child's home-work assignments	7	6	13 (22.4)
Ensuring regularity in school attendance/studies	6	3	9 (15.5)
Personal appeal to the school teachers to pay special attention on the child	1	6	7 (12.1)
Prompt supply of books, slates and other educational aids	3	3	6 (10.3)
	26	32	58 (100.0)

Figures in bracket indicate percentage.
(Report of the Education Commission, 1964-66, Ministry of Education, Government of India, 1966, p. 109).

Interestingly enough, a large majority of village leaders have spoken in favour of Dalit parents. They appreciated their role as responsible persons and sensitive to the needs of the schooling child. According to them, school drop-out among the Dalit children is largely a problem beyond the capacity of their parents to resolve satisfactorily. To a question, "Do you think that the Dalit parents are responsible for the drop-out of their children from the school?" 37 out of 60 village leaders emphatically stated "No, not at all", 15 of them held the parents responsible "to some extent", while the remaining 8 leaders felt that parents were responsible "to a great extent". Further, in support of their arguments, a group of 23 leaders (comparising last two categories) advanced reasons to justify that the onus of drop-out responsibility lies partially or totally on the Dalit parents (Table). They held that the parents failed to fulfil the educational needs of their children; detained them for domestic work, engaged them in gainful employment or placed them in a wedlock earlier than warranted owing to current economic compulsions. The last argument, none can deny, is a valid one and it stands to reason that the parents should not have hurried to get their son or daughter married at an early age. But the earlier three reasons, unless there are cases of brazen selfishness, avarice or cruelty on the part of Dalit parents are the result of economic backwardness of the family. This conclusion has been supported by the evidence obtained earlier.

Dalit Parents as Responsible for the School Drop-out of their Children (Village Leader's Version)

Indications	*Responses (N=23)*
Neglect of educational needs	20
Placement in gainful employment	12
Detention for domestic work	11
Early marriage of children	11
Any others Indebtedness, lack of contacts with school teachers, absence of guidance and encourgement etc.	05
	59

Now we shall turn our attention to other aspects of drop-out situation. It was interesting to observe that the school teachers came to know about the drop-out decision of the child at a much later stage in most of the cases. There were two distinct categories of drop-out cases. Firstly, the Dalit children who passed or failed in a particular class discontinued their schooling in a higher class or same class respectively. The fact that a particular child has preferred to stay away from the school came to the notice of school authorities one or two months after the school's reopening, some time around August or September. Secondly, there were cases who left the school during the academic year. Teachers often received delayed reports about drop-out of certain Dalit children. Out of 40 school teachers, only 8 stated that the Dalit children communicated their drop-out decision while 32 teachers complained that the children never let them know their drop-out decision. How did the parents act in this respect? Not quite responsibly, it appears. A majority of 22 teachers commented that none of the Dalit parents approached them to communicate the school withdrawal of the child. Teachers were left guessing most of the times.

From the viewpoint of preventive action, it is necessary that the school authorities should know about children who are about to withdraw from the school career. It was evident from our discussion with school teachers that in some cases they found it easy to identify the cases who would stop their education in the middle of the year. Increasingly tendencies of absenteeism, lack of attention in studies and similar traits of disinterestedness on the part of some children provided a basis for the teachers' judgment. But this was a very elementary way of making a judgment. Most of the teachers did not go beyond this exercise to effectively retard the very process of dropping out. It is necessary to point out that communication gap did exist between the teachers and the Dalit parents and in some cases, between the teachers and the Dalit children. We cannot, however, absolve the Dalit parents of their responsibility. This may be owing to lack of awareness, illiteracy or other cultural factors, they did not report to the school authorities about, discontinuation of their child's schooling. And this is a regrettable lapse on the part of Dalit parents. A situation such as this reminds us that a lot more effort needs to be made to bring

Dalit parents and school authorities together. Withdrawal of a child from the school at any point of time indicates, in some measure, the tendencies dominant in Dalit parents to view educational activities as outside their comprehension and scope. Whether their feelings are justified or not is entirely a different matter. It is indeed an unsound practice that drop-out decisions in most of the cases are not timely communicated by the parents or ascertained by the teachers.

Do the Dalit parents try to re-admit their children later? An affirmative response was given by 35 out of 40 school teachers. They said that the Dalit parents do try to send their children to school after a gap of one or two years. In cases where children have left school on their own accord, the parents make persistent efforts to send them back. They further stated that in cases where temporary domestic crisis had resulted into drop-out of a child, the parents put the child back into the school once normalcy was restored. How far were their readmission efforts successful? A rough estimate is provided by the teachers in this respect (Table). A majority view was that out of 10 only one or two drop-out cases are able to make successful re-entry in the school. In other words, nearly eighty per cent of the drop-out cases belong to the category of confirmed school leavers. This is indeed a serious phenomenon. It means that even parental efforts for re-admission remain, to a large extent, infructuous. It also shows the gravity of the situation because once the child is out of school, no matter for what reasons, it is difficult, it seems, to bring him back to the fold of education. It looks as if drop-out decisions, once taken, assume a form of finality.

Question: "Out of Every Ten Drop-out Cases among the Dalit Children, How many Rejoin their Studies? (Teacher's version)

Response	*Respondents*
Six to eight	04
Three to five	10
One to two	25
None	01
Total	40

Let us now see the actual position. Our sample consisted of 300 confirmed drop-out cases. When the Dalit parents were asked whether they made any readmission efforts in respect of their children, only 32 (10.7 per cent) replied in the affirmative. This shows that nearly 9 out of 10 parents did not make effort to readmit the child. In the above cases, drop-out decision was final. This is a somewhat conflicting evidence because the school teachers had stated, as we have seen a little earlier, that Dalit parents try for readmission. It is difficult to resolve this controversy in absence of relevant details. It follows from the above that a small number of Dalit parents genuinely make attempts for the readmission of their child. Still smaller is the number of those Dalit children who restart their educational career with fresh determination and sense of stability. For the majority of drop-outs, it is a total and complete scopestation from the school system.

This brings us to the final summary of contributions of the Dalit family to the educational life of the Dalit child. It may not be out of place to highlight the drawbacks inherent in the Dalit families. Almost all of them live below poverty-line, families living in some comfort can be counted on ones finger-tips. Most of them were fulfil the basic educational requirements of the child on a continuing basis. Quite a significant number among them was unable to provide food to their children. In this backdrop of poverty and deprivation, it is not surprising to witness an exodus of Dalit children from schools. Another dimension of the family life of the Dalit child is a social one, and refers to low literacy level in the family and lack of experience in dealing with the school system. Some of the beliefs and values prevalent in the Dalit community were doubtlessly counter-productive. These were responsible for shortening the educational career of the child. The social life of the Dalit community was restricted to a small, cloistered groove with caste boundaries. Personal contacts and interactions acquired intimacy and a touch of informality only within the context of caste. Conditions like these put severe limitations on the availability of information, exchange of ideas and experiences within a broader community framework. It is in view of these factors that the Dalit child appears to have received less than adequate attention and support from his parents. There were innumerable difficulties at home that could eventually distract the attention of the schooling child and compel him to relinquish his contacts with school. Observations of teachers in this respect are quite penetrating (Table).

Difficulties and Problems Facing Dalit Child at his home that come in the way of his Educational Pursuits (Teacher's Version)

	Responses Categories	*No. of Responses (N=40)*	
1.	Lack of physical and other facilities such as space, kerosene, lamp, etc.	28	(24.7%)
2.	Pressure of domestic work and other onerous responsibilities outside	22	(19.3%)
3.	Lack of guidance/encouragement from parents or other family members	16	(14.0%)
4.	Unhealthy community influences; bad habits in children, etc.	16	(14.0%)
5.	Lack of food; starvation and hunger	16	(14.0%)
6.	Lack of clothes, books, etc.	16	(14.0%)
	Total	114	(100.0%)

School teachers have provided a perceptive outline. On the difficulties of the Dalit child at home Table. Absence of basic physical necessities at home and pressures of household duties were reported to be two major barriers (50 out of 114 responses). Other inhibiting factors are lack of parental guidance, undesirable community influences and absence of food and clothing (64 out of 114 responses). Observations of the teachers aptly illustrate the handicaps of the schooling Dalit child. All these difficulties may not show up in each and every Dalit household, but a combination of two or three of the above mentioned difficulties is enough to discourage and dissuade a Dalit child from schooling. Difficulties just enumerated may precipitate the drop-out action among Dalit children and this has happened in most of cases. Evidence such as this shows that the education of the Dalit child should not be viewed as an isolated phenomenon. It is closely linked up with the family set-up, its social and economic status. So far we have seen the performance of Dalit families and their limitations as well. Now we shall have a closer look at the school administration in order to analyse its role in relation to the education of the Dalit child.

School Factor

By and large the village schools were under the personal supervision of the Head Master who usually had a long teaching experience in various schools in the region. Under him there were three to four teachers on junior grade. Special schools for Dalit which received grants from the Department of Social Welfare, had the advantages of Dalit teachers being on their staff roll, while the girls schools were under the complete charge of the Head Mistress and the female teachers. By and large, the school teachers came from the higher castes and from families of agriculturists. These SC teachers mostly belonged to the families of low income group. Most of them were reported to be landless or marginal holders. Monthly income from teaching varied from Rs.175 to Rs. 250 depending on their length of service and designation in a hierarchy. Most of the school teachers lived within a reasonable distance from the school, say 4 to 5 kilometres. This helped them to travel easily to and from school daily.

The school buildings, in most cases, were in poor shape An old rickety structure with broken pillars and cracked walls was the common mark of a village school. In some schools, during the monsoons children of all classes were herded together in one safe room, as there was no dry space around. Shortage of space was a perennial problem before the school teachers and during the summer days, they conducted the classes in the open. Children and the teachers settled themselves under the shade of trees to overcome the problem of overcrowding and suffocation in the class rooms. Senior basic schools had comparatively better buildings. On the whole, the physical conditions of the schools were of deplorably low standards.

There was no separate room for the office of the Head Master or Head Mistress of the school, no common room for the students either. Some schools were provided with basic furniture like tables, chairs, cupboards, etc. But these were age old and the school authorities had not bothered to repair or replace them. As such, most of the furniture and other material remained out and hence mostly was of no use. Mats made of coarse jute were provided to schools but were insufficient in number. Lacking replacement, the torn mats were used by the students for sitting purposes. Some students brought mats from their homes. Other paraphernalia like blackboard, bucket, tumbler, chalks, textbooks, maps, etc. were well short of the actual requirements. Teachers often complained about the lack of these essential materials. Some of them reportedly brought the matter before the authorities during the time of school inspection, others wrote to the higher authorities at the district level. But nothing much happened and most of the schools we visited, remained neglected as always.

In spite of these odds and inconveniences, some teachers ran the school activities with skill and resourcefulness. Some of them were residents of the very village in which the school was located. They could fruitfully mobilize the village community resources for specific tasks. The teachers who came from distant places could not exercise as much influence. It was reported that some teachers were making sincere efforts in enrolling the village children in the schools including those in Dalit communities. Teachers themselves explained to us the ways in which they increased the enrolment of Dalit children in their schools. By far the most important and effective strategy they adopted was visiting the *Dalit bustees* and individual households. They tried to motivate the parents in personal meetings. Even during casual contacts they tried to explain them the advantages of school education. It was also revealed during these discussions that the SC teachers were more successful because of their caste affinities and exalted status in their community. In most of the schools, the task of visiting the SC localities and contacting the parents was assigned to the Dalit teachers. Another method for enhancing enrolment was requesting the school children at the end of the term to bring with them their friends after summer vacation.

Despite the use of many techniques for increasing the enrolment position among the Dalit children, there was no encouraging response from some Dalit parents. Out of 40 teachers, only 14 stated that they faced no hardships in their enrolment efforts. The remaining 26 teachers described their experience as tough and sometimes unrewarding. What were the reasons behind the unreceptive response from Dalit families? The teachers replied that in some cases, the parents were apathetic and indifferent, in others, conditions of acute poverty and helplessness came in the way, in still others, the families wanted to use the services of the child at home. Anti-literacy environment in the family, unhelpful community influences and lack of proper incentive structure at schools were also the factors at work which kept the enrolment figure in the Dalit communities at a low level. The teachers, however, emphasised that there is slow but perceptible change in Dalit community and parents are becoming conscious of the significance of enrolling the child in the school.

But once the Dalit child enters the school, the school teachers do not seem to make deliberate attempts to involve his parents in the educational activities of the child. Out of 300 Dalit parents, only 121 (40.3 per cent) were specifically invited by the school teachers and this suggests that the initiative to introduce the parents to the school system was not taken by the school teachers in majority of the cases. It is further noticed that parental visits to school were mostly related to problematic issues or formal occasions. No stable relationship could possibly be invoked through such sporadic and problem-oriented contacts Table. This reinforces our earlier stand that Dalit parents were placed at a distance by the school system. It was, therefore, plausible that the Dalit families did not consider the school as their own institution which had intimate connection with their values and orientations. In a majority of cases, the Dalit parents displayed inertia and teachers overlooked the need to combat it by establishing fruitful rapport with them on a durable basis. This lacunae remained unattended to in most of the village schools.

There is a substantial gap between what the Dalit parents and school teachers say on the same issue. As many as 60 per cent of Dalit parents alleged that they were not called by the school teachers at all. Teachers on the other hand assert that it is their usual practice to invite parents on a number of occasions, formal as well as informal (37 out of 40 teachers made this claim). It is not easy to judge who is right in this matter. But it appears that not all the school teachers maintain close contacts with the Dalit parents. Out of 40 teachers, only 25 maintained that they know closely most of the Dalit parents. In the remaining group of 15 teachers, seven said that they have close contacts with some of the parents while eight stated that they have contacts with a few or none of them. A result like this suggests that there certainly exists a distance between the teachers and Dalit parents. In a rural setting where schools are located at close distances, it should not have been difficult for the teaching community to maintain closer ties with all Dalit parents.

Nature of Occasions for Parental Visits to the School (Teacher's Version)

Purpose of visits	*No. of Responses*
(i) To enquire into irregularities/absenteeism of the child	20
(ii) Failure in examination/deficiencies in studies	14
(iii) Special programmes/festivals	14
(iv) Admission/examination formalities	11
(v) Behaviour problems/bad habits of the child	08
(vi) Lack of personal hygiene and cleanliness or absence of educational material.	06
	73

Some teachers, however, had an inner desire to develop and maintain contacts with the parents of lower social strata. Calling them to school or at their own residence, visiting them at their *bustee* and providing help and guidance in their domestic probems were some of the ways through which the school teachers had built up a good image for themselves. Unfortunately, their number was not large enough. Some teachers complained that their efforts to go near the Dalit people were not appreciated by the caste Hindus. In some villages, the caste feelings were so intense that the teacher who should sympathy with Dalit was instantly rebuked for his behaviour. Some of them were told not to pamper the members of the Dalit community. In such atmosphere, it was well-nigh impossible for the teachers to deviate from the traditional image of his calling and brave the criticism of the village elders. Hence, the teachers adopted the safest course of maintaining a customary distance from people of Dalit community. The hope for building bridges between the school and the Dalit community, therefore, lay in the Dalit teachers. They had caste moorings and a common cultural environment. Their own residence was in a *Dalit bustee* and they were part of the Dalit community. They could, therefore, easily motivate the parents. The teaching community admitted that the Dalit teachers made efforts to bring children of their community into the educational system. They played their role with sufficient tact and resourcefulness. Their special efforts for enrolment, accompanying the Dalit children while going to schools, close attention on their studies and extra curricular activities and occasional financial and material help to poor children, unmistakably indicate the Dalit teachers' concern and feelings of identification with their community.

What was the image of the school teacher in the Dalit community? We had asked the Dalit parents to comment on the school teacher who taught their children. Their comments covered a wide range of attributes like character, approach towards studies and Dalit children, regularity and discipline in the class, familiarity with parents, etc. These comments were further classified into favourable and unfavourable attitudes depending upon their positive and negative emphasis. After going through this exercise we observed that out of 300 Dalit parents, 203 (67 per cent) were favourably disposed towards the school teachers while the rest, i.e., 97 (33 per cent) were totally critical about them. In other words, two out of every three Dalit parents had a favourable opinion about the school teachers. It is a somewhat painful observation that over one-third Dalit parents should have a negative estimation of the school teachers. As a matter of fact, all or at least a very large majority of school teachers should have received a word of praise from the parents.

The leaders' opinion also points towards a similar trend. When asked to mention the attitudes of the teachers towards Dalit children 40 out of 60 leaders stated that the teachers were mostly helpful and sympathetic to SC children. Another nine leaders characterised the teachers' attitudes as indifferent while the remaining 11 leaders commented that teachers were unhelpful and prejudiced. This minority opinion of the leaders indicate that there are some teachers who are found wanting in sincerity of purpose and evenhandedness. This is, indeed, an undesirable situation and needs immediate attention. There are many ways through which the image of the teachers gets eroded. His behaviour, attitudes and actual dealings with the Dalit child and his parents give indications of his role and underlying motivations. As many as 107 Dalit parents (36 per cent of the total sample) stated that their children reported at home the incidence of beating, scolding, harassment, or excessive punishment meted out to them in the school. On occasions, the incidence of beating or harassment involved the Dalit child and the children of the caste-Hindus as well. The teacher's behaviour received critical comments in some places. His tendency to exploit student labour, giving punishment to the Dalit child through upper caste children, isolating him in a class-room, were some of the themes that were brought before us in general discussion. One Dalit teacher reported that menial jobs like cleaning the mats, arranging school furniture, etc. were done through Dalit children by upper caste teachers. Dalit children were reportedly not allowed to draw water from the hand-pumps or wells. One teacher also stated that in some schools in another region, the Dalit children were generally not allowed to participate in dramas, musical concerts, etc. which were to be staged as public performances.

School teachers, on the other hand, seem to hold a somewhat different opinion. They are of the opinion that by and large Dalit children are favourably disposed towards them. When asked to specify the attitudes of Dalit students towards them, 23 out of 40 teachers described these as 'very favourable', 14 as 'favourable' while only three mentioned these attitudes as 'just alright'. It follows that, according to teachers, the Dalit children have no grouse or complaint against them. Rather, the children felt happy and secure in the company of school teachers. In explaining the feelings of the child, the teachers gave examples of how the child sought their help and assistance in studies, games and other activities, how the child followed them when other children picked up a quarrel with him. Really speaking, very few teachers could correctly analyse the feelings of the Dalit child towards them. In most of the cases, they interpreted the qualities of meek obedience, servility, fear complex and the like as indices of their affection and love towards their teacher. But an examination of our interviews with the teachers showed that most of the teachers were unable to feel the pulse of the Dalit children in true sense. It appears that, excepting a few teachers, a majority of the teachers could not successfully identify themselves with the Dalit children. This inference going further strength by the testimony of drop-out cases. Out of 198 children whom we interviewed only 88 stated that their teacher was helpful and cooperative. As many as 110 children firmly stated that teachers were not helpful or cooperative to them during their school life.

Dalit parents were articulate enough to describe the feelings of their child towards his school, teachers and classmates. We have already detailed the aspects which the Dalit children liked most in their educational pursuits. Now we shall examine the other side of the coin. To a question: 'What were the things which your child did not like in his/her school?' the Dalit parents gave multiple answers (see Table).

It is indeed an interesting exercise to compare the figures under 'likes' and 'dislikes' of the Dalit children as conveyed by their parents. With the exception of liking for two items, i.e., curricular and extra-curricular activities, in all other respects, the greater number of Dalit children had developed a dislike and a sense of grievance. In as many as 95 cases, there was positive disapproval of the behaviour of the schoolmates. Similar criticism against teachers was levelled in 75 cases. The largest single group of responses (111 in all) relates to the physical aspects of the school and this denotes the distance, inaccessibility during rainy season, poor sitting arrangements; lack of drinking water facility and other similar factors. Even the drop-out cases themselves came out strongly against some of these deficiently. By and large the evidence that we have is sufficient to reach a conclusion that the school system did not much succeed in forging durable and satisfying relationship with most of the Dalit children. Its staying or holding power was very weak.

Some of these shortcomings are poignantly shown by the village leaders in our sample (Table). They were highly critical of the role of the teaching staff in the village schools. Adjectives such as 'unco-operative' 'vindictive', 'inept' and 'inefficient' were used in describing the performance of the teachers. Some of the leaders went to the extent of branding them as 'caste supremacist' and prejudicial to the interest of Dalit children. Distance, poor approachability, lack of equipments and basic facilities like water, were other factors which the village leaders felt as responsible for creating a negative image of the school. They also feel that these factors are positively linked to the drop-out incidence among the Dalit children. It is thus imperative that these limitations are countered to improve the holding powers of the school.

Question: What were the Things which your child did not like in His/Her School? (Parent's Version)

(Figures in bracket indicate the number of responses from Table showing positive disposition towards the aspect).

	Responses	*Disliked (No. 227)**	*Liked*
Curricular programme	34	(12.2%)	(133)
Extra-curricular programme	11	(3.9%)	(168)
Behaviour of schoolmates	95	(34.3%)	(33)
Behaviour of school teacher	75	(27.1%)	(22)
Physical aspects and others facilities in the school	111	(40.1%)	(5)

*Out of 300 parents, 23 did not give any response to this question.

How do the school teachers react to the drop-out situation? What steps do they take to minimise the number of drop-out cases from the Dalit community? School teachers made it clear that, to the extent possible, they tried to make the school life of Dalits children bearable and satisfying. Some said that they maintained excellent relationship with these children, offered them help by words or deeds, supplied them books, copies, etc. and at times gave them food to eat. Some gave them clothes too. But such humanitarian souls were not many. A large majority of the teachers answered that they personally approached the parents, conducted group meetings in their locality and made efforts to convince the parents to readmit their child in the school. They, however, expressed their helplessness in dealing with the drop-out problem. They said that acute poverty among the Dalit families was mainly responsible for drop-out of the child. A large number of these families, they submitted, were compelled to use child labour for economic support. Some of them also agreed that low education level among the Dalit parents made their task difficult in convincing them on advantages of higher education. In short, the school teachers were mostly unsure of themselves and felt that they would not succeed in curbing the drop-out problem of Dalit children. Part of this defeatist attitude among the school teachers can be safely ascribed to the nature of issues involved. Economic hardships and resultant domestic instability were clearly outside the manoeuvrability of the school teachers.

Shortcomings of the School which Directly or Indirectly are Responsible for the Drop-out among Dalit Children (Village Leader's Version)

Shortcomings	*No. of Responses*
No limitations at all	4
Uncooperative, inefficient teaching staff	42
Distant location, poor approachability	37
Lack of educational equipments, aids, etc.	32
Lack of incentives, facilities to Dalit students	18
Poor physical structure	17
Lack of drinking water facilities	12
No proper incentive to teaching community	8

This apart, there was no organised community support available to the teachers in effectively dealing with this problem. Most of the teachers blamed the lack of cooperation from any individual or village organisation in motivating Dalit parents to continue their child's education. "It is nobody's concern whether Dalit children go to school or slog in the agricultural field. There is complete inertia and apathy among the villagers, including the community leaders" - opined one teacher frankly. When asked whether they contacted the parents of drop-out cases to convince them to send their children back to school, three teachers replied no, never; 15 stated that in a few cases they made attempt: 12 stated that in some cases they made attempts and only 10 teachers 'in all cases' tried to contact the Dalit households to get back the cases. Out of 37 teachers who made some efforts in this direction, 21 stated that the Dalit parents patiently listened to their arguments and some of them even promised to consider the readmission issue. The remaining 16 teachers explained that the Dalit parents reacted unfavourably and paid no heed to their persuasive efforts. There is some truth in what the school teachers, have claimed to be doing in certain cases. Most of the village leaders (32 out of 60) have testified that the school teachers did approach the parents in Dalit localities to encourage them to send their children back to school. These trends suggests involvement of some teachers in the educational activities of the Dalit child. Their efforts might not lead to any spectacular change in the attitude of the Dalit child or their parents yet we cannot overlook the advantages inherent in the personal approach of the school teachers. This might help in dispelling any doubts or apprehension the Dalit parents carry with regard to weaknesses of the school system and also dispel strains in interpersonal relations of ill-treatment meted out to the Dalit child.

It is indeed a matter of satisfaction that almost all teachers whom we interviewed perceived school drop-out among Dalit children as a problematic situation. Out of 40 teachers, 27 considered it as a serious matter that required immediate attention. It is, however, unfortunate that the drop-out problem did not receive much attention from the higher administrative machinery. In actual practice, no major steps seemed to have been taken to counter the menace of the dropping out of the Dalit children. Out of 40 teachers, only 14 reported that they discussed the drop-out issue with the higher authorities. It was during school inspection, examination or other cultural programmes that the teachers conveyed their anxiety about drop-out of Dalit children. Did the higher authorities make any serious efforts to examine the problem? The answer that we get is quite frustrating. Out of 40 teachers, 32 categorically emphasized that the higher authorities, did not at all refer to the drop-out problem in personal meetings, inspection visits or through correspondence. These responses fairly demonstrate that in the higher echelons the drop-out problem did not arouse much interest and hence it was given very low priority in the scheme of things undertaken at the higher level. The picture that ultimately emerges is more dismal then encouraging. At the higher levels of the administrative hierarchy, there is insufficient awareness about the problem. At grassroot level, i.e., school, feeble efforts are made by some crusading school teacher. There are, as we have noted earlier, many substantial shortcomings under which the village schools are functioning. Improvements are required on many fronts in order to effectively bring down the rate of drop-out incidence among Dalit children.

Community Factor

The village community can play an important role in promoting educational standards. For any village school to grow and prosper, the support of the rural community is considered an essentiality. However, these articles of faith have often remained in the domain of ideals and in practice we rarely see demonstration of positive community pressures working for the growth of education in a rural setting. Our experiences in this regard were not at all encouraging because in most of the villages there was a lack of any serious community action or involvement in the educational sphere. No doubt in two or three places there was a contrasting picture but it was mainly owing to personal interest and devotion of village leaders who themselves made to bring up the school. But it was also true that they had failed to rally other people round in their missionary enterprise. In this atmosphere of general apathy, it is rather too much to look out for any specific contributions of the village community towards the school system. All the same, it is necessary to analyse correctly the attitudes of the village community and reasons for their lack of continued participation in the school activities.

It may be mentioned that caste system, played a dominant role in every aspect of village life. Caste-Hindus believed in the concept of pollution and as a result, they did not often tolerate the violation of the commensal rules and prescriptions. Caste-Hindus did not accept even water from the Dalits, leave alone sharing food with them. Dalits were not normally allowed to draw water from the wells located in the settlements of caste Hindus. Dalits were usually not permitted to enter the house of a caste-Hindu and they had to wait in the outer courtyard if they wished to visit someone from the caste-Hindu family. Separate utensils or earthen wares were kept in some high-caste households to serve water or food items to the members of Dalit families who worked as labourers in their farms. These were common disabilities which the Dalit had to put up with. In the economic sphere, the Dalit occupied the lowest rung of the ladder. Most of them were landless or land poor, meaning marginal or sub-marginal land owners. Many Dalit families were traditionally attached to certain caste-Hindu households for undertaking all kinds of manual labour. They could not break away from this traditional bondage because they had secured monetary and material help from the caste-Hindu families. Sevility and bonded about had its effects on many a Dalit household.

The *Gram Sabha*, a village organisation, that came into being for the fulfilment of *Panchayati Raj* objectives has unwittingly become an instrument of perpetuating the existing caste hierarchy and fissions. In most cases, the leadership position of the Gram Sabha was in the hands of caste-Hindu. The role of Dalit community in the *Gram Sabha* deliberations and activities had been at best a symbolic one, with no effective influence to determine its policies and programmes. Their social and economic handicaps have further weakened their position in the *Gram Sabha*. Leaders of Dalit community complained of neglect and inattention shown to their basic grievances by the Gram Sabha representatives. It was their opinion that the Gram Sabha was not an effective agency to promote the interests of the weaker sections in rural areas. Rather, it was used by the caste-Hindu as a source of strengthening their social and economic hegemony at the cost of the poorer sections of the rural community.

In a socio-economic matrix discussed above, it is difficult to imagine that the village school could preserve its separate identity and ably perform its duties without fear or favour. The caste of school teacher was a matter of great significance to the village community. A teacher belonging to a higher caste was respected and given recognition by the Caste-Hindus; If he came from a far away place, he was given accommodation and other basic facilities in the village where the school was located. For Dalit teachers, there were many difficulties. It was essential for him to observe correctly the conventions and cultural prescriptions of the caste hierarchy. His caste and not his professional status often determined his relationship pattern with the village community. Even his colleagues at school maintained a definite distance from him. At one place, it was reported, that the Head Master of a school who was a Brahmin by caste had asked his Dalit colleague to bring a bucket and tumbler from home in spite of the fact that these were already provided by the school administration. This Brahmin teacher did not want that the Dalit teacher should defile' the bucket and hurt his values on ritual purity. The Dalit teacher who gave us this piece of information begged of us not to reveal his identity as this might cost him his job in the village. Example of similar nature are abound and it was common knowledge that discrimination on caste lines was practised, though in a muted form, in other village schools also.

As stated earlier, there was not much enthusiasm in the village community to take part collectively in the school activities. Literate members of caste-Hindu families as well as other influential persons like the lekhpal, land-lords, etc. were reported to be maintaining a somewhat closer relationship with the school teachers in order to guarding the interests of their school-going children. It was also evident that in the families of upper castes, encouragement and material support was available to the schooling children. In some households regular private tuitions were reportedly arranged to assist the children to improve their learning capacity. For this work, the school teachers were paid in cash or kind or both. Besides, some teachers were keeping intimate relationships with the emerging power structure which predominantly favoured upper castes. Partly out of fear or insecurity and partly owing to their own caste biases and predilections, some caste-Hindus teachers had no desire to act independently or to safeguard the interests of the Dalit children. Tendency to maintain physical distance from the children in the school, failure to provide them even drinking water from a well—owned by a caste Hindu; insistence on getting all kinds of manual work done through them; negligence in establishing rapport with the Dalit community and endearing them to the cause of education, the practice of punishing their own colleagues because of caste appellation; all these are clear indications of how some members of the teaching community failed to use a school system as an agency of social equality. Instead of the school bringing in new ideas and social experiences in a village community, it was itself moulded and conditioned to respond to the existing caste-based conventions, values and practices. A silver lining to as otherwise dark picture was provided by the encouraging efforts of some Dalit teachers, and a few others belonging to upper castes but imbued with the real desire to help the poor and vulnerable families.

It is necessary to stress on the contributions of Dalit teachers in the field of education of the backward classes. Possibly due to their own past experiences of living in poverty they were reported to be helping the other Dalit children in more than one way. Books, copies, slates and pencils, uniform and even food articles were provided by the Dalit teachers to those coming from poverty-stricken families. Apart from free tuitions and guidance, some of them even gave monetary help to deserving Dalit students to take up higher education at district place. A word of assurance and help was certainly an incentive for parents to take more interest in the education of their child. Leaders in the Dalit community also took positive interest and helped the Dalit teachers in their mission. Though most of them were uneducated they realised the value of education to the Dalit children and to their community. Most of them felt that an educated Dalit was far more effective to serve the cause of the downtrodden community. Dalit leaders were mostly from poor families and hence could not lend any financial help to others. Yet their indirect contributions in the form of encouraging and stimulating individual cases to continue schooling; arranging meetings between school teachers and Dalit parents, motivating parents, to send their children to school regularly; Dalit teachers at school to enquire about the general progress of the Dalit children and pleading the case of more material and financial help to poor and deserving students, cannot be denied.

Village leaders most of whom to upper socio-economic strata were somewhat reticent and less active in this direction. Teachers maintained that village leaders' contributions was limited at best to issues like maintenance and repair of the school buildings, organisation of cultural programmes or sports meet, financial help in purchasing prizes or other minor items of educational importance, etc. It was reported that as per the directive of the Basic Education office, a local Advisory Committee was required to established in every school to help the teachers to develop communication between the school administration and community. Another aim behind the formation of this Committee was to develop the school as a socially viable institution, responsive to the needs and demands of all sections of the village community. But we were informed by the school teachers that the committee experiment had not yet taken the roots. In some villages the Committee did not conduct even its first meeting even after lapse of 10 to 12 months. In others, the committee had not conducted serious deliberations worth mentioning. It was argued that experiment such as this needs long-term planning and organisational resources which at present are missing. Whatever may be the strength of this argument, it was our experience that the village elders did not display requisite spirit and involvement in educational matters. Enrolment or drop-out issues were regarded by most of them as outside their initiative and leadership functions.

In respect of rural education, even *Gram Sabha's* role has been minimal and largely related to material and not human aspects. To exemplify, the Gram Sabha helped the school to carry out repairs and provided free manpower and material towards that end. In some places, expansion of school buildings by constructing additional rooms was done with the financial help of the *Gram Sabha*. In some villages, money was provided to the school authorities by the *Gram Sabha* for purchasing educational material, prizes or refreshment items. In two villages the Gram Sabha constructed pucca roads and provided water facilities. By and large, however, most of the *Gram Sabha* units revealed limited involvement in the affairs of the village school. According to school teachers, it required continuous prodding to stir the Gram Sabha members for bringing about some betterment in the schools. Dalit school at Rasra functioned within the jurisdiction of the notified area and yet it did not receive substantial help or assistance from the councillors. Out of 40 school teachers belonging to different village schools, 28 stated that their school got no help from the *Gram Sabha*.

It is necessary to mention that although village leaders did not actively participated the promotion of educational standards in the Dalit community, they were aware of the importance of education to the community. Village leaders categorically stated that education constitutes a very valuable experience to weaker sections. Responses received from 60 village leaders signifies that importance of school education to Dalit children in terms of rise in social and economic status (41 responses); personal growth, good habits and manners (40 responses); better job opportunities (36 responses); relief from inferiority complex and low status (27 responses); accumulation of fixed assets like housing, land, tube-well, etc. (13 responses), and smooth and early social assimilation (11 responses). There are, according to leaders, direct and indirect advantages to the Dalit family which educates the child up to a certain level. These were listed as; rise in the economic level (47 responses); change in the social status of the family (38 responses); a better future outlook towards education (27 responses); increase in family resources (26 responses); freedom from unhealthy family tradition and wasteful community practices (11 responses); and relief from indebtedness (6 responses). If we analyse these perceptive answers we feel that the village leaders fully recognised the utility and beneficial impact of school education for Dalit children.

It is somewhat perplexing that even though there is clear awareness, the village leaders had failed to exert their influence in the education field and to help Dalit children to take benefits from the school system. We may identify two main reasons for the lack of involvement of village leadership in promoting the cause of education among the Dalit community. Firstly, those leaders (and they are the majority in any village) who have landed property feel that the schooling of more and more Dalit children would ultimately result in reduction of manpower for agricultural work. It goes against their economic interest that the low caste children should receive education and choose occupations of different kinds. This would also constitute a break from traditional bonded relationship that existed in villages. Many leaders expressed these doubts and fears. Secondly, the present leadership which is predominantly in the hands of higher caste is likely to face competition if the younger generations of the Dalit community secure higher education and thereby strengthen its economic position. Such a direct threat has been felt by the leaders in some villages. A respectable government position, regular income and expansion of agricultural holding have been possible in some cases because the Dalit youth had acquired sufficient education. Such successful Dalit though they are few are now in the forefront of their community leadership. Village leaders may conscious that it is difficult to rule the literate and educated Dalits.

Against this background of very limited involvement of village leadership in the educational sphere, it is not surprising that out of 300 drop-out cases, only 36 (12 per cent) received some kind of attention from the neighbourhood. Dalits parents of these cases showed that neighbours, friends, relative and school teachers had approached them for readmission, discussed with them their problems and difficulties coming in their way of readmitting children in schools. In the remaining 88 per cent of the cases there was not the slightest evidence of concern shown by the village community towards a drop-out child. This finding further reinforces our opinion that by and large, other village institutions, organisations or influential persons had not taken up a positive role with regard to the educational activities of the Dalit children.

It is also important to note that there are very few formal, organised groups within the Dalit community and these exist in large villages only. Apart from their functions are largely related to the cultural, religious or political aspects and they hardly address to the educational needs of the Dalit community. Whatever involvement or participation in the educational activities of the Dalit children that we saw in the villages, came from a few individuals like influential persons from the Dalit community and some village leaders. Similarly, some Dalit and caste-Hindu teachers were seen struggling to bring more and more Dalit children into the schools and helping them keep up their studies. But these efforts betray lack of consistent and determined involvement to promote educational goals among the lowest social group, i.e., Dalit.

The whole question of the school drop-out needs to be seen in a wider context of social and economic framework that exists in the villages. Caste variable assumes significance due to its social as well as economic current and under-currents. Hence the prevention of drop-out or other remedial measure should take into account the broader dimensions of the problem. In this respect, the Dalit family, the school system and the village community can help reduce the magnitude of the problem through their specific contributions. It is necessary to study the approaches in relation to drop-out prevention as felt by the Dalit parents, school teachers and the village leaders.

5

College Education

It is through socialisation that, an individual acquires his/her self-concept or self image through the socialisation. From a psychologist's it as an individual who moulds his self-image on the basis of early experiences with family and society and encounter with life situations. Social background has also on major in both achievement and motivation. As a matter of fact it means social background determines the future of an individual to a large extent. High ritual status and historical advantage have been attributed to higher achievement by the upper caste Indian in education than a dalit born and nourished with historical disadvantages.

The another important feature that requires to be examined is the communitarian dimension of dalit life. In the rural areas of India, in the slums of the country and even at times in urban settlements for fear of being polluted, dalits are made to live apart from other caste people. While, on the one hand caste people are to live close to dalit settlements for fear of being polluted, dalits themselves prefer to live separately as a community with their fellow kinsmen and women. It is the community living together in settlements that provides a sense of security and protection to the dalits specially during violence andatrocities on them.

In their own groups several other Dalits close to values are found which a part of dalit lives. Competition perceived to be something alien to dalit culture. An individual belonged to any Scheduled Castes share whatever they have and cooperate with one another. Their identity is more a group identity than an individual identity. An individual belonged to any upper caste is nurtured and brought up with values of competition and a sense of achievement the various vicissitudes of life and the need to be secure from caste groups primarily, a dalit identifies himself as a member of a community. It is a fact when an individual dalit defies a caste law, even today in rural areas the whole group is punished very cruelly. Only the individual gets punished in the case of caste people. The image of inferiority that one is born with, gives the dalit a feeling of diffidence, impurity, low self-esteem, fear, anxiety and various other negative emotions that obstruct learning. As a result of their social background their inferiority complex comes as an obstacle for dalit success and achievement.

Traditions and Values

Before delving deep into the poor success rate of Dalits in higher education, it would be significant to examine the value system of higher education. By its very nature, higher education is elite. Only 6 per cent of the relevant age group enrolls in higher education. Most of these are children of politicians, bureaucrats, land-lords, businessmen and the professionals hailing from upper castes and classes with a clear value system of their own. A few years ago a survey was done on the beneficiaries of higher education indicated that 80 per cent of the students who attend universities came from the top 20 per cent.

Why it is so? Apart from the social economic aspect these youngesters have an academic history. The culture of the universities played significantly in moulding their culture. An "individual" self-image is inculcated in children of the higher castes from birth. The values of competition are ingrained right from cradle. Memory work is encouraged in the study of slokas and sacred tests even prior to enrollment in schools. The parental values are unconsciously imbued by children. The whole culture of education is the culture of the upper castes and classes. Can a child be brought up in poverty and communitarian values with low or negative self-esteem, with feelings of inferiority and diffidence ever find it easy to get into the culture of individualism, competition, memory work and a totally alien culture of higher education? One may not fully grasp the lack of success of dalit students in higher education unless and until the whole question of dalits in higher education is viewed from the perspective of dalit culture.

Owing to their internalised caste values in the universities and colleges dalit students feel inferior. The students from upper caste communities feel superior and treat dalit students in line with the internalised caste values. What are the centres of higher education do is merely perpetuate the notion of purity and impurity, superiority and inferiority, high and low - the very same caste sentiments existing in society. This is the reason behind many drop outs among Scheduled Caste students for they find the environment not congenial. Those who survive either pass out with a feeling of inferiority or get coopeted by the higher castes and classes. By moving them out of their social milieu, the higher education system gives body blows to the culture of the dalits.

Who determine the culture of the universities? The caste culture which is prevalent in higher education is the creation of caste teachers and administrators who teach and administer the centres of learning. Generally caste teachers are not expected to behave very differently in colleges and universities than the way they behave in society. Consciously or unconsciously the teachers and administrators do perpetuate through their own interactions with dalit students their internalized caste values, thus posing a threat to the achievement of dalit students. Thus a dalit student besides getting rid of his own internalized self-image of inferiority, pollution, self-rejection, impurity and fear has to encounter teachers and students who too have a hostile attitude toward him. Does one expect them to excel in studies with caste centred attitudes against them? In realtiy such attitudes sometimes even destroy the little self-image they have had. Educational system does not function in a vacuum. It is built on our social system of caste. And it is the very same caste people who oppress and unleash atrocities on them, manage and administer our colleges and universities. Ambedkar had rightly said "no real progress can be made in education, if education was entrusted to the teachers from the brahmin community whose minds conceived an abhorrence for the lower classes and showed callous disregard for the intellectual uplift of any other classes". (Muralidharan 1996). In his book "Educational Priorities and Dalit Society" the author quotes a parent of a dalit boy:

"I went to school and saw with my own eyes that Dalit children are accommodated in the rearmost part of the class, huddled together on a shabby mats (which later I came to know was brought by one of the Dalit boys from home). All of these children (they were nine in total) were looking alike in dress and everything. Why this separation? Why this isolation on caste lines? How my child and other children can learn better human values in this atmosphere? We will grow and die in this world in the same degraded manner as I would and as my parents grand-parents did. Education is force and nothing less than a force in the hands of these fanatic teachers" (Muralidharan 1997). Can anybody expect these children to enter the portals of higher education?

The Difficulties

In India there is a dual system of higher education. The posh English medium schools have always been under the domination of the upper castes, the rich and the powerful. These institutions are reserved for the children of politicians, businessmen, professionals and bureaucrats - all hailing from the upper strata of society. The institutions with high standards in our country like the Jawahar Lal Nehru University, Birla Institute of Technology, Pilani, Indian Institute of Technologies, Indian Institute of Managements and others demand a very high standard of English. Those who have not had their education in English medium schools one cannot be expected to compete for these Institutions. Given their poor economic condition as a community, Dalits cannot afford sending their children to these schools. Most of these schools too are located in the cities and urban centres. Eighty per cent of the dalits live in villages making it practically impossible for them to benefit from these institutions.

Besides, illiterate and uneducated dalit parents are unable to introduce their children to the culture of the elite which the elite educational system represents. They are forced to send their children to village schools where teaching staff and the infrastructure are in poor shape. That is why even those who aspire for higher education compelled to join liberal B.A., B.Sc. and B. Com. programmes. In the year 1995-96, according to the data supplied by the Ministry of Human Resource Development. Government of India 2,73,568 Scheduled Caste students in the B.A. programme, was mere 11 per cent. In the B.Sc. they were 70,285 (7.19 per cent) and in the B.Com 60.084 (5.35 per cent). At the post-graduate level once again the Scheduled Caste enrollment in M.A. was 13.47 per cent. In the M.Sc. they were 7.13 per cent and M.Com 7.57 per cent. Only 3.66 per cent Scheduled Caste are pursuing their research degrees.

No. of Scheduled Caste Students Studying in Higher Education 1995-96

Stage	*Boys*	*Girls*	*Total*	*Percentage*
B.A.	199704 (14.08%)	73864 (7.25%)	273568	11.23
B.Sc.	47794 (7.54%)	22491 (6.48%)	70285	7.19
B. Com.	44833 (5.65%)	15251 (4.62%)	60084	5.35
B.E.	17492 (6.43%)	3592 (7.95%)	21084	6.64
MBBS	6391 (8.83%)	3570 (9.36%)	9961	9.01
B.Ed.	8902	3633 (12.39%)	12535 (7.22%)	10.26
M.A.	28695 (17.40%)	17607 (9.73%)	36302	13.47
M.Sc.	5212 (8.24%)	1854 (5.18%)	7066	7.13
M.Com	4760 (7.85%)	1227 (6.67%)	5987	7.57
Ph.D	1158 (3.87%)	356 (3.10%)	1514	3.66

Source: Ministry of Human Resource Development, Government of India, 1977.

How is that they have not even been able to fill up their quota in all disciplines in spite of reservation? Answer to this lines with the political management of the country. In the state directed expansion of education the benefits primarily go to the upper caste elites, the managers of the state. In recent years the caste politicians have coopted even certain leaders from the Scheduled Castes. As a result of an inegalitarian educational system, these Scheduled Caste politicians have succeeded in garnering dalit vote banks in the name of power. Once in power, instead of lobbying and working for their community, they have stopped to the level agents of caste leaders leaving their community in deprivation, allowing the state to continue their age old biases and prejudices against dalits and their education.

After establishing with educational institution for higher education by middle castes or dominant caste groups further weakened the Scheduled Castes. The Reddys and Kammars in Andhra, the Lingayats and Vokkaligas in Karnataka, the Nairs and the upper caste Christians popularly known as Syrians in Kerala, the Nadars and Vallalas in Tamil Nadu and other dominant groups in other states have gone on a big way for establishing institutions of higher education - Engineering Colleges, Medical Colleges and Colleges of liberal education. These are known to be caste colleges that do display caste prejudices and discrimination in the supposedly secular and modern environment of learning. Dominant OBC groups having internalised caste beliefs prefer avoid, ignore, pass sarcastic comments and exclude dalit students from curricular and co-curricular activities. Scarcity of resources owing to their poverty to start their own institutions and the caste prejudices exhibited by these dominant caste have acted as a factor in obstructing educational mobility of Scheduled Castes.

In consequence most of the Scheduled Castes confine in government colleges and universities. We are all aware how these institutions run. Apart from the dearth of teaching staff those who are on the regular roll don't regularly teach. Classes are hardly held. These social institutions are characterised with student unrest. Political interference by politicians to further their own cause and interests is frequent. It is only to tell the Scheduled

Castes that the state is interested in their education that such institutions are run. If the state can run first class institution like I.I.Ts and IIMs so efficiently and effectively for the elite, why are then these colleges frequented by the poor run so badly? Seemingly there is a definite design to keep the Scheduled Castes in their backwardness while at the same time mouthing slogans of social justice.

Effort for Change

If concrete changes are to be taken place in dalit higher education, one may have to have a recourse to dalit culture. If caste culture has prohibited them to climb the ladder of success in higher education, can dalit culture bring about a change in their self-perceptioon and lead them to empowerment? Is it possible for dalits to change their self-image denouncing the caste image they have acquired by announcing a new image that is historically theirs?

One may ask whether dalits have a culture of their own. Historically dalits, claim that they had a rich culture. Here is a statement by B.R. Ambedkar:

> "The Hindus wanted the Vedas and they sent for Vyasa who was not a caste Hindu. The Hindus wanted an epic and they sent for Valmiki who was an untouchable. The Hindus wanted a Constitution and they sent for me" (Dr. B.R. Ambedkar Marati 1978).

The crux of this statement is that it makes a bold claim to a great spiritual and academic tradition and culture. Their culture is centred on three ideas:

Makers of Culture. The folklore that normally expresses the struggles of the masses, the epic that symbolize the mystical union of God with humankind, the village art and music that expresses fellowship among human beings are all expressions of creative life among the dalits. Present at the length and breadth of the nation dalits express themselves through street theatre art, dramas and paintings, their rich cultural heritage. The Indus Valley civilisation is believed to be an example of their history and culture.

Earlier Inhabitants of the Country. Dravidians, despite considered to be outcastes are said to be the earlier inhabitants of the Indus Valley. All over the country today is a large section of awakened stake the claim that they were the original people of the country. Their claim for separate electorates, demand for a pre-Aryan status by a section and recognition as non-hindus derives from this claim. There is a belief in current that untouchable had been Buddhists pushed to the outskirts of the village when Brahmanism won over Buddhism well over a millennium ago. Their original culture connects them to a rich heritage of egalitarianism, rationality and humanism.

Militant People. They were believed to be a militant people who used their strength in a self-sacrificed way for their people. There is common belief among that they had been the bravest warriors in defense of the subjugated peasant community. Hinduism is nothing but violence and tricky ideology. Peasants are exploited by Brahmins by the means of religions trickery and violence. So dalit society should not be based upon the false nationalism of a Brahmanic elite but on the energy of the Shudra-Atishudra masses. That is why the urgent need is to replace the hindu superstitious social order by a universalistic, equalitarian and rationalistic religion—religion of humanity.

Social reformers of the community had laid the firm foundation for non-conformist movements in India. This major figures of them are Buddha, Bhakti saints, Tukaram, Guru Nanak, Ambedkar, Phule and Guru Ravidas. One may wonder what has all this to do with dalits and higher education. It is my view point that unless and until the question of culture is rightly handled, dalits are unlikely to succeed in higher education. They are required to internalize new beliefs as they reject the old ones and evolve a counter culture. Ambedkar writing in the Harijan in 1933 noted "The outcaste is a by product of the caste system. There are outcastes as long as there are castes. Nothing can emancipate the outcaste except the destruction of the caste system. Nothing can help to save hindus and ensure their survival in the coming struggle except the purging of this odious and vicious dogma: (Harijan 1933). In reconstructing their culturl heritage it is quite important for Dalits to express themselves through a common identity. Today they want to be known as "outcastes" outsiders to the caste structure. The idea behind is that dalits want to remain as representataives of the original casteless human community. This is the most important factor for gaining their original human status."

If Dalits have to succeed in education it is essential that they must bring about a counter-culture. Concretely it would mean the entire dalit population should be made.

- awareness of the dalit status into which they were forced
- raise consciousness in them of being a part of a casteless community and their rich cultural heritage.
- awareness that their assigned inferior status was imposed on them by a humanly created system .
- help them to reject the mythical Brahmanical order which has perpetuated captivity.

Founding a "counter culture" is as important as discarding the existing one. It may be even necessary at the phase of transition to have exclusive centres of higher learing for dalits where they could learn in a spirit of fellowship, exchange knowoledge through cooperative learning, exhibit their folk culture and value it, thus establishing communities of solidarity for social change. SCs have not been benifitted with reservation policies, especially in internalizing the egalitarian values of their culture. Exclusive schools of their own can provide a tremendous impetus for dalits students to evolve an educational system of their own at least at the phase of transition. Let me conclude with the words of Ambedkar the value of higher education for Dalits.

"Coming as I do from the lowest order of the Hindu society, I know that what is the value of education. The problem of raising the lower order is deemed to be economic. This is a great mistake, the problem of raising the lower order in India is not to feed them, to cloth them and make them serve the higher order as is the ancient ideal of this country. The problem of the lower order is to remove from them that inferiority complex which has stunted their growth and make them slaves to others, to create in them consciousness of the significance of their lives for themselves and for the country, of which they have been cruelly robbed by the existing social order. Nothing can achieve this except the spread of higher education. This in my opinion is the panacea of our social troubles".

Social Factors

The poor achievement of higher education among Dalits can be attributed to many reasons like failing in examinations, higher role of drop outs and stagnation caused by their poor socio-economic background and educational training, lack of proper guidance, etc. Even the majority of those who stay in colleges and universities usually do not perform well in their studies and secure relatively poor grades or percentage of marks in examinations. Recently some quantitative but not much qualitative changes have occurred in their educational achievement. Even though these observations are correct these cannot be widely generalised. As a rule, there are variations in social adjustment and educational performance of students of these communities depending upon variations in their socio-economic background, nature of institutions they join, and type of courses they opt for. Hence the elements generally related to social background of these students and social and academic environments prevailing in educational institutions joined by them affect, in meaningful manner, their representation and performance in higher education. But in fact, these are not uniform; rather, these vary from institution to institution and from an individual student to the other.

Therefore, it is suggested in this chapter to look into variations in socio-economic background of the Scheduled Caste/Scheduled Tribe students and their social and academic adjustment in institutions of higher education. Attempt is also made have to examine correlations of their varying socio-economic background and educational performance in particular programmes of study which they pursue. Lastly, efforts also taken to identify a number of factors which affect their social and academic life, in an averse manner, in educational institutions.

Analytical Approach

A number of general impressions about the Scheduled Caste students enrolled in various institutions of higher education are also given. Some of these are that they hail from poor socio-economic backgrfound and from families with no tradition of formal education. Above all, they always do bad performance in their educational pursuit. However, in both the cases contributions made by the policy of protective discriminations during the last five decades are either undermined or exaggerated and individual variations with regard to socio-economic background and educational performance of the Scheduled Caste students are kept aside. Perhaps the reason of this is due to two contradictory reasons. Firstly it is construed that the government is providing a lot of facilities to foster educational achievement of the Scheduled Castes and is despite their poor performance in their studies. But we have mentioned elsewhere (Ram 1981: 20-24) that these facilities are inadequate and are not available particularly at the time when these are really most needed. This apart, most of these students unlike students of other castes and communities have to shoulder certain family responsible and contribute to their family's subsistence even during their study period. This badly affects their performance in a particular programme of study. Secondly, protective discriminations in the case of education and other spheres also have helped only a small section of the Scheduled Castes and their majority are still illiterate and quite away from benefits of the reservation policy. Those benefitted from the facilities vary in terms of their socio-economic achievement and educational performance. However the above mentioned impressions are with subjective bias and they muddle different variations in the case of socio-economic background and educational performance of the Scheduled Caste students.

The perspective in which data relating to the Scheduled Caste students of a particular institution of higher education has been analysed in this chapter is comparative in its adherence. It takes into consideration variations in socio-economic background and educational performance of the Scheduled Caste students admitted in institutions of higher education. Contrary general impression mentioned earlier, it analyses a specific situation and looks into a number of variations in the case of Scheduled Caste students. The perspective legitimately proceeds grounded in the facts that as the protective discrimination measures have affected positively though in limited manner, the socio-economic background of quite a few Scheduled Castes varies. This also gets cleared from social background and educational performance of students from these castes and tribes. However, the Scheduled Caste students admitted in various institutions of higher education find it difficult in their adjustment and performance as stated in the previous chapter. But it does not mean that there is always a definite correlation between their social background and educational performance; nor these students perform always worst than students of other castes and communities admitted on 'merit'.

In the given perspective the data analysed in this chapter pertaining to socio-economic background and educational performance of the Scheduled Caste students admitted during 1978-82 in an institution of academic excellence, namely Jawaharlal Nehru University (JNU), New Delhi. However, data used here are secondary in nature and have been taken from records available with the office of the Dean of School of Social Sciences. To be precise information have been extracted from personal files of the Scheduled Caste students enrolled in graduation and post-graduation programmes of study in various Centres (departments) of the School.

The given analysis in this chapter would have perhaps given clear and sounder results had some of the Scheduled Caste and non-Scheduled Caste students been interviewed in person. But the author's familiarity with the state of affairs in the university in general and with the School in particular and his frequent interaction with and observation of the Scheduled Caste students have provided a good deal of insights and understanding of their background and problems of their adjustment and educational performance. Hence, analyses made and conclusions drawn here may not be regarded as impressionistic but they bear a testimony of the author's constant and continuous observation of the situation.

Educational Angle

It is evident that a very few Scheduled Caste students get enrolled for higher education. Their representation in institutions of academic excellence including professional and technical ones is very negligible despite a specific quota of seats reserved for them. Apart from many other reasons these institutions emphasise on 'merit' in their intakes of students and are afraid of declining their 'academic standard' if they administer fully the quota system. Thus, they indirectly view the quota system as an encroachment on the rights of the 'meritorious' students drawn from other castes and communities. This generates a social atmosphere not favourable to the Scheduled Caste students in these institutions and they often get discouraged when admitted therein. However, there is variability in social and academic atmosphere prevalent in various institutions of higher education though these may not be regarded as ones laying their unconditional favour to the Scheduled Caste students.

Just contrary to the situation described above, there are some institutions of higher education which have also displayed a good deal of interest in education of students from minorities and other socially and economically deprived sections of society. J.N.U. is one such institution. As a research-cum-teaching university, it has maintained somewhat different social and academic structures. In reality, it was established in 1969-70 with the broad objectives of promoting "the study of the principles for which Jawaharlal Nehru worked during his life time, national integration, social justice, secularism, democratic way of life, international understanding and scientific approach to the problems of society". More precisely, the University has stood for pursuing academic excellence through research and teaching, national integration, and cultivating and safeguarding educational interest of the socially, educationally and economically deprived sections of the society. For this end, it evolved as early as in 1974 a system of admitting students for its different programmes of study which was novel to the history of higher education in the country. Taking into account of the varieties of disparity among different sections of society the admission system laid a considerable weightage to socio-economic background of candidates (though there emerged within the University a strong opposition to the earlier existing policy which succeeded in 1983 in replacing it by incorporating `merit' of the candidate in the admission test) seeking admission along with their merit in the admission test. To a great extent this had promoted higher education among the socially, educationally and economically deprived sections of the society.

However, since the academic session of 1983-84 the University has laid heavy emphasis on the 'merit' obtained by a candidate in all India test administered for the purpose of admission. Thus, in its pursuance the University had in a way taken a digression from its earlier principles and joined the category of purely 'meritocratic' institutions in the country. As a result, number of the SC students admitted for different programmes of studies since 1983-84 had gone considerably down and in the academic session of 1989-90 it was hardly 8 per cent which was much below the prescribed percentage of quota of 22.5 meant for these communities. In general some is the situation in other academic institutions like I.I.Ts., medical colleges, Indian Institutes of Management, etc. In view of this the University Grants Commission (U.G.C.), New Delhi had asked all the universities and institutes in the country to admit the Scheduled Caste students to the tune of quota of seats reserved for them without administering the test criterion of admission on them so long their quota of reservation was not filled in. However, universities and other institutes have widely ignored the UGC instructions and have not admitted students from these castes and communities as per the percentage set by UGC.

The faculty in J.N.U. (henceforth university) are regarded well qualified, secular in their outlook and have a scientific approach in analysing social problems in general and dealing with problems of students in particular. Unlike many universities, classes are being conducted here through the medium of English which is a language of elites in India. It follows the semester system and an internal assessment of performance of students providing full academic autonomy to the teachers. As for the social and cultural life of students on the campus, the university believes broadly in principle of individual freedom, self-aggrandisement and self-help in personality formation. This is with the perception that as the students are mature in age and have already acquired certain level of academic standard, they are matured enough to judge things with right perspection. Then, the teachers' roles are only to guide them for a more intensive and systematic understanding of the subjects besides making them equipped with conceptual clarity. More so, teachers are also supposed to generate in them a scientific and rational outlook, democratic values and a profane culture.

In principle, both academic and personal lives of students in the university are considered separate from each other, though the students have to meet certain desired academic requirement. This examplifies an *inter alia* emphasis on their academic life but in reality their social and personal lives are not neglected as is clear from the existence of a number of institutional arrangements like that of Dean of Students' Welfare, Wardens, Students' Counselling, Programme Adviser, etc. (and all of them happen to be teachers). In reality, the programme advisers and hostel wardens are, in principle, supposed to be overall custodians of academic and socio-personal life of students in the university.

About 45 per cent of the total students pursue their studies leading to the pre-Ph.D and Ph.D. degrees. In some way about 60 per cent students at both the graduation and post-graduation levels get scholarships/fellowships. The students from amongst the Scheduled Castes are also include. But with the new scheme of the National Elighibility Test conducted by the U.G.C. for award of the Junior Research Fellowships, the number of such fellowship holders has come down. Nevertheless the overall social and academic environment in the university is quite favourable students including the Scheduled Caste students as mentioned earlier.

Eight Schools (including the School of Creative Arts and Aesthetics which is currently inoperative are there in the university and each School has a number of Centres (departments) which pursue varieties of teaching at Master, pre-Ph.D and Ph.D. level courses and research in specialised fields of study. These include School of Social Sciences (SSS), School of International Studies (SIS), School of Languages—both Indian and foreign (S.L.), School of Life Sciences (SLS), School of Environmental Sciences (SES), School of Computer and Systems Sciences (SC&SS), and School of Physical Sciences (SPS). The Schools of Social Sciences and International Studies are popular for both their master and pre-Ph.D. and Ph.D. level courses in the country and outside. The School of Languages provided courses of three levels. These are – Master level courses of five years in foreign languages and of two years in Indian Languages – Hindi and Urdu; three years diploma courses and one year certificate courses in foreign languages. Inspite of the fact that there are pre-Ph.D and Ph.D level courses both in Indian and foreign languages but the School attracts more students for its undergraduate programme. The School/Course-wise break-up of students admitted/enrolled during 1978-82 in the university can be seen in Table.

It is clear that courses in the School of Social Sciences and International Studies, besides the School of Languages, are much popular and there is always much competition among candidates for seeking admission to the various programmes of studies in these two Schools. The major reason cited for this is that knowledge vis-a-vis degrees adhered to in these Schools cover a wide range of study and provide better job-opportunities in the market. Other Schools are also well known for their academic pursuits. But every School and Centre differ in their methods of pursuiting knowledge and academic standards.

School/Course-wise break-up of students admitted in J.N.U.

	*Schools/Courses**	*1978-79*	*1979-80*	*1980-81*	*1981-82*	*1982-83*
1.	S.I.S.	254	454	178	153	225
2.	S.S.S.	533	929	388	431	228
3.	S.L.	1,690	1,701	1,225	1,157	1.147
4.	S.L.S.	52	123	40	32	32
5.	S.C. & S.S.	16	39	15	16	18
6.	S.E.S.	34	90	18	18	17
	Total	2,579	3,336	1,864	1,807	1,727

* The School of Physical Sciences was set up much later. Hence, not include here.

Source: *Annual Reports* of the University and *J.N.U. News Bulletins*, 1978-82.

Presence of SCs

Earlier it has been mentioned that representing of the Scheduled Caste students in higher education is meagre owing to obvious reasons. But J.N.U. enjoys the credit of having honoured the national commitment of providing reservation to the Scheduled Caste candidates in their admission right from the inception of its teaching and research programmes. The students from such background are admitted against 22.5 per cent seats reserved for them in all programmes of study, though satistics indicate that only about 15 per cent of the reserved seats have been filled in so far. As stated earlier this percentage has declined further in the recent years. However, these students are given facility like hostel accommodation and some of them get financial assistance in the form of merit-cum-means (MCM) scholarships. In many ways thus the facilities provided to the Scheduled Caste students are, better here than in any other institutions of higher education in the country.

Apparently, the State take seems to take care of the overall cost of study of the Scheduled Caste/Scheduled Tribe students. However, considering the net high cost of living and a kind of apathetic attitude (which sometimes becomes prejudicial also) of many teachers and others on the campus the Scheduled Caste students are usually faced some financial and academic constraints which, in a way, affect badly their performance in a particular course of study pursued by them. On this count, their poor socio-economic background and inadequate previous educational training also-contribute a lot. But this again cannot be accepted uniformally in the case of all the Scheduled Caste students admitted in J.N.U. We shall come to this after a while.

Here, we had better to have a brief look at the pattern(s) of admission of the Scheduled Caste students in the university over a period of time. As for the many programmes of study, their less representation is caused by an in-built social and structural constraints. These operate both at the levels of their family background including social and economic positions, their previous educational training, and above all a highly stimulating but challenging academic atmosphere which is prevalent in the university which also demands hard labour to cope with. Thus, keeping on the view of the course/School-wise strength of students in a particularly year of admission the representation of the Scheduled Caste students is not fully in accordance with the quota reserved for them which may otherwise be filled in to the extent as the university claims. This is likely clearer when we look at their representation in the total number of students admitted during the period under reference.

Our observation regarding to be less representation of the Scheduled Caste students in the various programmes of study in this university is true as is evident from Table . Then, there question arises as why and how this happens. A related question is equally important to mention here. That is, what are the Courses/Schools/ Centres which have adequate representation of these students. Such questions are of much relevance as these are often raised with regard to proving academic incompetence of the SC students and their preferences for subjects and educational institutions low in the hierarchy of academic prestige. We shall try to answer below these and other related questions.

Many of the developing countries in general and India in particular have adopted formal education system, by and large, on the pattern exist in western countries. In its long stretched experience the realisation has down on India the need of evolving specialisation in many branches of study, especially at the level of higher education. In consequence of this, two forms of education namely higher education with greater specialisation and general education with elementary knowledge of as many subjects as possible have been emphasised on. The higher education with greater specialisation needs high aptitude, high I.Q. and hard labour along with more investment of money whereas general education is to require average aptitude, I.Q. and less labour. It has a direct link with employment not requiring much specialisation. There is tremendous emphasis on the latter type of education in the Draft of the New Education Policy of 1986, in accordance with which a large number of students (majority of that will obviously be Scheduled Caste) need to be checked at the level of higher secondary education and be asked to go for vocational education. In short they may be deprived of opportunity for the higher education.

Generally feeling that majority of the Scheduled Caste students have aptitude for general education. It has also been proved by a number of empirical studies. (see for example, Chitnis 1981) that a large majority of the Scheduled Caste students go for such subjects of study even at the higher level of education which require less hard work and provide less lucrative jobs in the market. This is partly true from their enrolment for the courses/Schools over a period in J.N.U. (see Table). We can not help agreeing one fact that such students are usually discouraged in one form or the other, both at the time of seeking admission and pursuing their studies in a more specialised course. This is done on the ground of their supposedly having 'low' level of aptitude, less 'merit' (Singhi 1979: 279-82), and encroachment on 'merit' and thereby lucrative jobs in market (Ram 1981: 20-24; Desai 1981). It is also done in the name of a heavy rate of drop outs and stagnation among these students and thus wastage of public money. But we have found contrary to the general impression about low aptitude among the SC/ST students (Sharma, Ram et al 1974; Pandey and Ram 1978: 297-98).

Various Schools and Centres in J.N.U. do not maintain uniformity in their intakes of students. Accordingly, the representations of the Scheduled Caste students differ in these Schools and Centres. Then, an observation that the majority of the Scheduled Caste students get admitted in courses/subjects which do not foster high academic stimulation and, in turn, fail to provide lucrative jobs in market is not true at least in the case of such students in this university. In Universities like J.N.U. a candidate is to opt for three subjects/centres for seeking admission and question of his/her choice for a specific subject arises only when he/she gets admitted to more than one subjects/Centres. The representation of the Scheduled Caste students in various subjects/ Centres is determined by a number of socio-structural constraints varying in nature. This fact is evident from the following discussion on their admission in the School of Social Sciences of the University.

The Discrimination

Eight Centres are there (departments) in the School of Social Sciences. These are: Centre for the Study of Social Systems (CSSS), Centre for the Study of Regional Development (CSRD), Centre for Political Studies (CPS), Centre for Historical Studies (CHS), Centre for Economic Studies and Planning (CESP), Zakir Hussain Centre for Educational Studies (ZHCES), Centre for Studies in Science Policy (CSSP) which is currently inoperative, and Centre for Social Medicine and Community Health (CSMCH). Out of these the last three Centres have only M. Phil/Ph.D. level programme and thereby their intake capacity is much lesser than that of the first five Centres.

It has been stated earlier that the socio-economic background of the Scheduled Caste students pursuing higher education varies in the individual cases contrary to a general impression that such education, being more expensive, draws students only from the families of upper class and higher income. However, the Scheduled Caste students hailing even from poor socio-economic background can afford higher education owing to the strategy of educational development adopted by the government. The representation of the Scheduled Caste/Scheduled Tribe students in J.N.U. has been facilitated by the admission policy of the university as stated earlier. Here, in the case of their socio-economic background we shall put our focus on their rural urban background, occupation and income of fathers and their previous educational background.

Total number of the Scheduled Caste students admitted at the graduation level in the School during 1978-82 were 104 and 100 respectively. Out of this 82 SC students hailed from rural and 22 Scheduled Caste from urban areas. In the same way majority of the Scheduled Caste students admitted to the M.Phil/Ph.D. programmes in the School came from rural areas. Thus, such representation of the Scheduled Caste students may be in the linear direction with regad to concentration of majority of the Scheduled Caste population in rural areas. This may not be seen clearly in other situations as in an institution of higher education students generally hail from the urban middle and upper-middle classes background. But in the case of most of the students studying in this university their parents are located in urban areas though these students might be giving their background as rural. Further, after their studies the students themselves prefer to stay back in towns and cities owing to their job-placement. Therefore, in strict sense the strategy of educational development in the country in general and in the case of the Scheduled Caste in particular is not favourable of those staying in rural areas. Rather, it facilitates a process of imbalanced educational development in the country.

The reservation strategy with regard to educational development of the Scheduled Caste is also imbalanced at least keeping in mind the proportional representation of these two minority communities in total population in the country. For example representation of the Scheduled Caste students in different Centres of the School of Social Sciences was not in accordance with seats reserved for them (See Table and Table) nor with percentage of the population of their caste in the country. On the other hand, educational devlopment of the Scheduled Tribe was much ahead as their representation in the Social Science School was more than the seats reserved for them or their proportional population in the country. It is also clear from the given Tables that such an imbalanced educational development among the Scheduled Caste was clearly on upto 1979-80 when the number of the ST students was more than that of the Scheduled Caste. Even though it was brought in order during 1980-81 and 1981-82 but again in 1982-83 it was restored to its earlier pattern. Two reasons were cited for this. Firstly, the strategy of educational development in the form of reservation of seats in admission has not strictly been adhered to the demarcation made for the Scheduled Caste students and has been guided by the provision of interchangeability. That means, if there is the scarcity of suitable candidates amongst the Scheduled Castes, the benefits can be given to the Scheduled Tribes and *vice versa*. Secondly, the merit of the Scheduled Caste candidates in the test for admission in various programmes of study in the university has for long been measured *inter se* which has favoured more to the Scheduled Tribe than to the Scheduled Caste students owing to their previous educational training.

Nevertheless, the Scheduled Tribe students admitted in the

university generally came from better socio-economic background in comparison to that of the Scheduled Caste students. It is evident from the fact that the majority of the Scheduled Tribe students admitted at graduation (82 per cent) and post-graduation (63 per cent) levels in the School hailed from families where their fathers were occupied either in agriculture, or employed in government jobs, or in business. Unlike this 67 per cent Scheduled Caste students admitted at graduation and 47.7 per cent at post-graduation levels in the School came from a moderate background and none of the Scheduled Caste students belonged to the business family. Similarly, 26 Scheduled Caste as against 6 Scheduled Tribe students belonged to labour class families.

As for the income position, more than 70 per cent Scheduled Tribe students admitted at graduation level hailed from families with monthly income of less than Rs. 500 in contrast to 60 per cent Scheduled Caste students coming from such income category. Contrary to this, more than 50 per cent Scheduled Caste/Scheduled Tribe students admitted at post-graduate level in the School belonged to income over Rs. 500 per month. As the admission policy of the university had provided in the past some benefits to the students coming from poor economic background as stated earlier, it may be possible that the Scheduled Caste/Scheduled Tribe students also, like students from other castes and communities, perhaps not informed about the actual income of their father. Inspite of this on the basis of information supplied by them in their application forms for seeking admission it is clear that they varied not only with regard to income but also occupational positions of their father.

Thus, it is evident that there can't be found uniform socio-economic background of the Scheduled Caste/Scheduled Tribe students admitted in institutions for higher education in general and in J.N.U. in particular. As a rule, variation ranges from absolutely poor economic position to a 'rich' position as in quite a few cases their fathers/guardians have drawn their monthly emoluments over Rs. 2000 or so. In the way variation also exists in terms of their rural-urban background as stated earlier and education of other members in their family. Their such background could not be viewed in relation to that of non-Scheduled Caste/ Scheduled Tribe students due to lack of information relating to the latter. However, it has been recorded that in majority of the cases both the Scheduled Caste/Scheduled Tribe students hail from the families where other members, especially younger ones, are educated upto certain level. Even structure of their family varies as in many cases number of dependents on parents or guardians is not more than five. In the cases of both Scheduled Caste and Scheduled Tribe students hailing from illiterate families other members do realise the relevance of formal education imparted specially in an institution like J.N.U. which provides fairly good deal of material and other facilities to the students though it may not counsel the wards in the desired way.

All these points social and structural variants in social background of both inter- and intra-groups of the Scheduled Caste/ Scheduled Tribe students pursuing higher education. Such variants exert influence on representation and educational performance of the Scheduled Caste/Scheduled Tribe students. As the university is having its academic programmes at master level and beyond as mentioned earlier, the students are required better equipped with some education background prior to their getting admitted here. This is applicable, though in oblique manner, even in the case of the Scheduled Caste/Scheduled Tribe students. However, their previous educational training, like that of several other students, may not be sound and uniform combined with this variations in their socio-economic background affects their social and educational adjustment in an institution of higher education like J.N.U. We shall discuss this in detail in the following section.

There is no uniformity in higher education with regard to the contents, syllabi, medium of instruction, and in a word, the standard of administration of knowledge and its evaluation all over the country. This get more conspicuous in the form of medium of instruction opted by students before they join J.N.U. Less than one-third Scheduled Caste/Scheduled Tribe students (the number of Scheduled Tribe students was more) had opted English and rest had either Hindi or a regional language or a mix of these languages as the medium of instruction prior to their coming here. Since the university has adopted English as medium of instruction as stated earlier, a major portion of the Scheduled Caste/Scheduled Tribe students as many students from other castes and communities face the problem of communication and thereby understanding and comprehending the imparted knowledge at least at the initial state. Had the medium of instruction been any regional languages they would have easily understood and comprehened the ideas imparted to them. But this is not our major concern in this chapter.

Social and Cultural Elements

Patterns of evaluation of performance of their students differ in different institutions of higher education. Consequently, levels of performance of students also vary accordingly though mesures have been evolved in the term of percentage of marks or grades to establish equivalence or variance in their merit. As it has been mentioned at the outset about a general impression that the Scheduled Caste/Scheduled Tribe students admitted for higher education do not perform well in their performance. Hence, we shall see here briefly their performance in the qualifying examinations and in the admission test before going deeply into their performance in the various programmes of study which they join in J.N.U.

If we have a look at performance of those Scheduled Caste/ Scheduled Tribe students in the qualifying examinations who were admitted at both the graduation and post-graduation levels during 1978-82, it can be observed that about 40 per cent of them (N=300) had obtained more than 50 per cent marks. A few of them had also obtained more than 60 per cent marks. But surprisingly, in the case of quite a few students (97) the results of the qualifying examinations were not known at the time of their getting admitted in this university. So the number of the Scheduled Caste students who had obtained above 50 per cent marks in qualifying examinations and got admitted both at graduation and post-graduation levels in the School was more (73) than that of the Scheduled Tribe students (57).

The variants discussed above affect representation and later educational performance of the Scheduled Caste/Scheduled Tribe students in varying degree in the university. To be more precisely how and to what extent these affect them can be seen in terms of whether they got admitted on the prescribed merit, completed the programme of studies which they had joined and if yes, with what levels of performance. Apparantly the various Schools and Centres within Schools in the university had prescribed varying minimum merit (percentage of marks) for admitting students in the past. Such differences also varied from year to year. As of now under the new admission policy a students is required to secure at least 50 percentage marks in the qualifying examination to be eligible to apply for admission in the university. But in the case of the Scheduled Caste/Scheduled Tribe students only the pass percentage in the qualifying examination is require to make them eligible to apply. In the same way students from general category are supposed to score at least 40 per cent marks against 35 per cent marks for the Scheduled Caste/Scheduled Tribe students in the admission test to make their berth secure in the admission to the M.Phil/Ph.D. programmes in various Schools and Centres. Such requirements of marks for getting admitted to the master programmes are 25 per cent for general and 18 per cent for the Scheduled Caste/Scheduled Tribe students though the minimum percentage with which the students especially from the general category get admitted in the university is more than the prescribed percentage. But a point must be mentioned here that the minimum merit for admission in the university had been determined, under the earlier admission procedure on the basis of giving some weightage to previous academic qualification of candidates, their performance in written test and viva-voce held for the purpose, and also weightage on their socio-economic background as stated earlier.

However, keeping in view of such differences among the Schools and Centres over different periods a good deal of effort has been made here to find out whether the Scheduled Caste/ Scheduled Tribe students were admitted with the minimum prescribed merit or below that during 1978-82. Data pertain again to different Centres in the School of Social Sciences. It is then clear from Table 5 that 44 per cent Scheduled Caste/Scheduled Tribe students were admitted both at the graduation and post-graduation levels with minimum merit (cut-off points) and about the same percentage (43.3 per cent) below that prescribed for the purpose. In about 12 per cent cases it could not be known. Although sufficient data is not at our disposal about the candidates from other castes and communities for making cross comparison, yet between the Scheduled Caste/Scheduled Tribe students the latter had a little edge over the former on such count. This perhaps is due to their better articulation through English or their previous educational training. However, in both the cases of the Scheduled Caste/ Scheduled Tribe students admitted during 1978-82 (and also 1983-89) their performance in the admission test—written and oral *vis-a-vis* their number to be admitted for various programmes of study had some reflection of the prejudices of a few teachers in different Schools and Centres in the university.

An alternative way of measuring educational performance of students in whether they complete the programme successfully. Thus, unlike the general perception about heavy rates of drop out and stagnation among the Scheduled Caste/Scheduled Tribe students, a portion of these students in the university had successfully completed in time the programmes of their study (see Table 5). In a few cases they had taken a little extra time in completing the programmes of their study but some were cases from amongst general students also. In reality, the university extents opportunity to the students to improve their performance (grades) in subsequent attempts available in the stretch of two extra-semesters. The reasons for could not be ascertained but this obviously would have been caused by both the academic and non-academic factors. Although the financial constraints also would have caused drop outs in some cases, yet it might have not been the only reason for this as mentioned earlier.

Finally, we have measured the levels of educational performance of the Scheduled Caste/Scheduled Tribe students on the basis of cumulative grade points average (CGPA) obtained by them towards the end of completing their programme of study. As students take a little more time to get adjusted in the new socio-educational set up and this certainly causes a adverse impact on their educational performance at least in the beginning of the programme, we first thought to record their semester-wise performance to find out gradual improvement in that. Rise and decline in their performance in various semesters could also be witnessed. We had therefore, looked at the CGPA of graduate students (but the same was not available about the post-graduate students) and found that it ranged from B to B+ (50-59 per cent) and placed them in high second class in the merit. There were quite a few students who had obtained B- (40-49 per cent) and some even A- and A (Above 60 per cent). This was, generally in accordance with their performance before they got admitted in the university though this did not rule out the possibility that some students who had not performed well earlier would have further improved their performance and those who had done well earlier would have not improved at all in their programme of study. But one thing is to be remembered here that the academic standard and thereby performance of students at other institutions of higher education in the country cannot be equated with that in J.N.U. as stated earlier.

However, this does not mean that there existed inter-or intra-group uniformities in educational performance of the Scheduled Caste/Scheduled Tribe students in this university and elsewhere. As a matter of fact, after getting admitted to the university the ST students had improved their performance though the Scheduled Caste students had also done fairly well (see Tables 4 and 5). Though putting students from these two groups together they would have not done as fair as that of the students from other castes and communities, but whatever educational achievements the Scheduled Caste/Scheduled Tribe students had obtained cannot be undermined in view of the socio-structural constraints they faced with. Yet, their educational performance could not be compared at the exact and precise level with that of the general students because of the unavailability of data pertaining to students of the latter category.

As it has been mentioned earlier that the Scheduled Caste/ Scheduled Tribe students by and large, do not perform well in higher education owing socio-structural constraints they face with both at the levels of their family and the educational institution they join. This is caused by their less orientation to the study (due to structural problems) and apathetic and sometimes prejudicial attitudes of the teachers (Singhi 1979) as stated earlier. This has been observed in the case of the Scheduled Caste/Scheduled Tribe students in this university also. A growing impression of this sort is there among both the teachers and students in general in the universities. But in the specifically in the case of the Scheduled Caste students their impression runs that they are awarded grades less than they deserve by the non-Scheduled Caste/Scheduled Tribe teachers who are allegedly guided by caste and communal prejudices. This has been publicly displayed also in some cases of the Scheduled Caste students in the recent times. Teachers, on their part, confer of non-orientation and low aptitude of the Scheduled Caste/Scheduled Tribe students towards higher education. Hence, a non-faith atmosphere prevails in institutions of higher education.

Question, then, arises as to why this happens and how to resolve it. The answer to this question is relevant because this may help the Scheduled Caste/Scheduled Tribe students to improve their performance in higher education and to build a healthy educational system in the country. For this, the students are required to work hard in their study despite the various socio-structural constraints encountered by them. Only such commitment to higher education will help them in overcoming their different shortcomings. As for the teachers, they only find the Scheduled Caste/Scheduled Tribe students academically inferior but fail to appreciate their poor socio-economic status and their prior training deficiency. Therefore, instead of rejecting their problems completely the teachers need to emphathise with them and removing their educational deficiency. This, of course, is a time consuming process and requires more patience on part of both the teachers and the Scheduled Caste/Scheduled Tribe students.

The above question can be answered obliquely in a different way also. The Scheduled Caste/Scheduled Tribe students may be given higher education by teachers with the same caste/community background in the institutions established for the purpose. Some advancement can also be seen in this direction, though the State generally discourages this. Such a move is legitimised from the Scheduled Caste/Scheduled Tribe point of view on the ground of their being discriminated against in the common institutions of higher education. However, fact of the matter is that the institutions of higher education managed primarily by teachers of the same caste/community background may not help the Scheduled Caste/ Scheduled Tribe students in their educational pursuit unless they are motivated and they work hard. This is necessary because these students have to compete, though in limited way, with general students at the level of getting employment. Again, whereas teachers of the same social background may better understand and appreciate the socio-structural constrains of the Scheduled Caste/ Scheduled Tribe students, they have to be well qualified to deliver their academic worth. So absence of all this may further strengthen the congruence between social segregation and educational segregation of the Scheduled Caste/Scheduled Tribe students which may go against the prime objective of the State policy in India. This is also not desirable from the point of the Scheduled Castes/ Scheduled Tribes as it may promote the principles of 'equal but separate' instead of 'equal and common' and the ghettoisation of the Scheduled Caste/Scheduled Tribe students.

Contrary a general impression about the poor socio-economic and educational background of students from the deprived communities pursuing higher education, differentials in their such background need to be explored on a larger sample. Such enquiry is relevant owing to the fact that the various government schemes and self-initiatives of these castes and communities have definitely improved their socio-economic status and educational background in all these years though this may not be as good as of the people in general. But between the Scheduled Castes and Scheduled Tribes the latter in some regions enjoy edge over the former because of the reasons like adherence to benefits of the government's developmental and welfare measures, some specific policies protected in their interests, and their being away from the stigma of untouchability and social degradation. Though they lived with prolonged isolation from the general population, their access to the moratorium of the missionaries and later interaction with others have compensated, in a way, their loss of the yesteryears. All these have contributed to emergence of socio-political awareness among them and have raised their urge for achieving higher education.

It is apparent from the discussion made in this chapter that the Scheduled Caste students usually have better educational standard in terms of percentage of marks obtained by them in their qualifying examinations. But they lag behind in their performance due to their adoption of Hindi or other vernacular languages as the medium of earlier instruction. Further, they come across face more socio-structural constraints than the Scheduled Tribe students both within and outside the institutions of higher education. This may even be caused by extension of the historical legacy prevalent in the country which continues with two faces of apparently favouring higher education among the Scheduled Castes and Scheduled Tribes and also discouraging them, in subtle manner, at the level of materialising it.

The policy of reservation for educational development among the deprived communities like the Scheduled Castes and Scheduled Tribes has helped them to the extent that there exist variations in their socio-economic status and educational achievement. But at the same time, it has not fully met their expectations and aspirations in absence of its proper and systematic implementation. Subsequently, there has arisen a small section of the Scheduled Castes and Scheduled Tribes population who have benefitted from this policy though in the imbalanced form as analysed in this chapter. However, benefits of the policy have not yet reached to the masses of these castes and communities who have not witnessed any substantial change in their educational status.

6

The Concessions

In the Constitution, Articles 15(4) and 46 provide special safeguards for the educational uplift of Dalits and enable the State to make special arrangements for their educational advancement. The directives enshrined in the Constitution have been reflected in various Five Year Plans which have sought to raise the level of education among Dalits. In the First and Second Five-Year Plans, the educational schemes introduced for Dalits were the following:

1. Scholarships (pre-matric and post-matric);
2. Opening of Schools in Dalit localities;
3. Grants of books, hostel fees;
4. Opening of Residential Schools, Balwadis, Community Centres, etc.

Gradually the scope of programmes for educational development in the various five-year plan periods increased. A mid-term appraisal of the Fourth Plan revealed that nearly half of the Backward Classes Sector allocation (48 per cent) was mainly spent on educational programme alone. The pattern of educational programmes for the Scheduled Castes of the Government of India and of the State Governments is given below :

Centre's Role

A number of Centrally Sponsored programmes are being continued for Dalits. They are:

(i) Post-matric scholarships;

(ii) Pre-matric scholarships for children of those engaged in unclean occupations;

(iii) Boys' and Girls' Hostels;

(iv) Book Banks;

(v) Upgradation of merit of SC/ST students;

(vi) Coaching and allied schemes;

(vii) National Overseas Scholarship and passage grants for higher studies abroad; and

(viii) Grants-in-aid to voluntary organizations.

In addition to these, two schemes in the central sector have also been approved, viz.

(ix) Educational complex in low literacy pockets for development of women's literacy in Dalit areas, and

(x) Special educational development programmes for Scheduled Caste girls belonging to very low educational levels.

These programmes are in addition to the special thrust provided to the weaker sections in the general programmes for educational development like opening of schools, running of Non-Formal Education (NFE) Centres and Adult Education Centres, schemes of Operation Blackboard, upgradation of merit of the Dalit students, etc. Except the National Overseas Scholarship Scheme, all others are of the type of 50:50 sharing basis between the Centre and the States.

State's Role

1. Scholarships and stipends at various levels;
2. Supply of textbooks, stationery, equipment, uniform, sports material;
3. (a) Administration of Balwadis, Primary Schools, Middle Schools, Higher Secondary Schools;

(b) Attendance prize to students;

4. Residential schools;
5. Amenities to boarders in private hostels and financial assistance for sharing rental accommodation;
6. Hostels (and reservation of seats in general hostels);
7. Merit Scholarships;
8. Expenses of those studying in public schools;
9. Reimbursement of examination fees and tuition fees at different levels of education;
10. Excursions;
11. Mid-day meals;
12. Loans to students for carrying on education;
13. Vocational craft classes;
14. Introduction of modern trades and training centres for self-employment;
15. Coaching and study centres;
16. Awards to teachers;
17. Houses for teachers.

In addition, the Ministries of Education, Labour and Agriculture and the University Grants Commission have also been providing various other facilities to Dalit students, namely:

(i) Reservation of seats in educational institutions including Engineering and Medical colleges, Technical Institutions, Sainik schools and Navodaya Vidyalayas, Kendriya Vidyalayas;

(ii) Relaxation in age and marks for the purpose of admission;

(iii) Research scholarships and fellowships.

There is no separate programme for award of scholarships/ stipends to the Dalit students under the Ministry of Education. However, reservations have been made for the Dalit students at pre-matric level under the two following schemes of the Ministry (now Ministry of Human Resource Development).

The Stipends and Scholarships

Rural Talent Scholarships Scheme. The objective of this scheme is aimed at greater equalization of educational opportunities by providing a fillip to the development of potential talents from rural areas by provided to them in good schools. Under this scheme, scholarships are granted to talented students from rural areas from classes VIII to XII. The total number of scholarships available under this scheme at present is 43,000 per year. Out of this, 13,000 scholarships are reserved for the SC/ST students. The rates of scholarship range from Rs. 30 to Rs. 100 per month in accordance with the stage at which the student is enrolled and whether he or she is a hosteller or non-hosteller. The selection of students under this scheme is done at two parts. In first part, selection is made through an examination conducted at block level. The selected candidates have to appear in a test at district level in the second part. Final selection is made with Community Development Block as a unit and the top students in the order of merit are awarded scholarships blockwise.

Junior Research Fellowships. The University Grants Commission organises a national level test for recruitment to the post of Lecturers and for the award of Junior Research Fellowship (JRF) to ensure minimum standards of the entrants in the teaching profession and research. SC/ST candidates are given relaxation upto 10 per cent cut-off marks for the JRF test and all the SC/ST candidates qualifying for the JRF are awarded Fellowship. If no vacancy is available, UGC provides Supernunerary positions of JRF to the universities. The JRF is available for five years.

Fifty JRFs are awarded every year in Science and Humanities including Social Sciences to SC/ST candidates who take the National Eligibility Test (NET) and qualify the eligibility test for lecturership.

Research Associateships. The UGC awards Associateships to carry out research in the field of Science, Humanities, Social Sciences, Engineering and Technology and Gandhian Studies. The

Associateship is tenable initially for a period of three years and extendable further for another term not exceeding two years.

The total number of awards under this programme is 260 every year, out of which 40 positions are reserved for SC/ST candidates. The Associateships are awarded in various slabs ranging between Rs. 2800-Rs. 3300 to Rs. 4325-Rs. 5,000 per month. The award also covers a contingency grant of Rs. 7,500 p.a. and Rs.10000 p.a. for Humanities and Science subjects respectively.

Research Fellowship in Engineering and Technology. The UGC awards 60 research fellowships every year in Engineering and Technology including Agricultural Technology, to undertake advanced study and research leading to Ph.D. The age limit for this award is 40 years which is relaxable by five years for SC/ST candidates.

Teacher Fellowship. The UGC provides short-term teacher fellowship of one year duration to enable teachers in affiliated colleges to do M.Phil or Ph.D. Teachers are given a living expense allowance of Rs. 750 per month, and a travelling allowance to and from the research centre. A contingency grant of Rs. 5000 per annum for teachers in Humanities and Social Sciences, and Rs. 7500/- per annum for teachers in Science subjects is also provided under the Scheme. Fifty Teacher Fellowships (20 for Ph.D. and 30 for M. Phil) are awarded to teachers belonging to SC categories.

National Talent Search Scheme. The NCERT operates a scheme of National Talent Scholarships identifying and nuturing talent at the post-secondary stage. Under this scheme, 750 scholarships are awarded every year to talented students of which 70 scholarships have been reserved for the SC candidates. These are available from class XI onwards upto post-graduation level.

Scholarships in Regional Colleges of Education. Scholarships are awarded to the SC students admitted to the four regional colleges of education run under the NCERT. The rates of scholarships is different for various course.

All the Scheduled Caste students admitted to the course of educational and vocational guidance are awarded scholarships.

ITI Scholarships. A stipend is awarded to the SC trainees admitted to ITIs. To supplement the Government of India stipend, some State Governments like Andhra Pradesh, Himachal Pradesh, Madhya Pradesh, Maharashtra, Orissa, Tamil Nadu, Uttar Pradesh, Delhi and Pondicherry have introduced their own schemes for award of scholarships/stipends to the SC students undertaking studies in ITIs. The rates of stipends, however, differ from State to State.

Apprentice Training. All apprentices recruited under the Apprenticeship Act, 1961 are paid stipends at the rate mentioned under Rule 7 of the Apprenticeship Rules, 1962. These range from Rs. 400 to Rs. 700 per month. The Boards of Apprenticeship Training make serious efforts to provide training facilities to all the applicants belonging to the Scheduled Castes even in excess of the quota earmarked for them. The candidates under the Apprenticeship Training Scheme are chosen by the industrial organisations/establishments, and necessary guidelines are given to them to ensure selection of all the SC candidates who apply for training under the scheme.

(i) *For study in Agriculture and Veterinary Sciences.* No less than 240 scholarships @ Rs.300 per month with a contingent grant of Rs. 750 per annum are given exclusively to the SC students to study at graduate level in Agricultural and Veterinary Sciences.

(ii) *Fellowships awarded by ICAR.* Twenty per cent of scholarships are kept reserved for the SC students in Junior Fellowship, Senior Fellowship and Post-Doctoral Fellowship awarded by the Indian Council of Agricultural Research. These are for Masters, Ph.D. and Post-doctoral courses respectively.

Note. It is possible that the rates under the various schemes, mentioned in the foregoing paragraphs might have been revised by this time.

Official Programmes

Post-matric Scholarships Scheme. One of the most important Centrally Sponsored schemes under the Backward Classes Sector is the scheme to award post-matric scholarships to the SC/ST students undertaking their studies in recognized educational institutions in India. The Elyperumal Committee on Untouchability, Economic and Educational Development of the Scheduled Castes regarded the post-matric scholarships Scheme "as the most extensive in coverage and far-reaching in significance in the educational advancement of Scheduled Castes". The objective of this scheme is to provide financial aid to the SC students studying at post-matriculation/post-secondary level so as to enable them to acquire higher education in College/University as well as through Correspon-dence Courses including distance and continuing distance and continuing education. This is an open ended scheme under which the number of beneficiaries is not fixed by the plan outlay and all the eligible SC students are given scholarships. The level of expenditure reached at the end of each plan period becomes committed and is handed over to the States. Only the outlays, over and above that level, whether because of an increase in the number of scholarships or an increase in their rates, or both, are met by the Central Government. Started during 1944, the scheme was meant exclusively for the Scheduled Castes and its implementation limited to the then British Indian Provinces only. The scope of the scheme was extended in 1948-49 to benefit the Scheduled Tribes also. During the first year of its implementation 114 Scheduled Castes students got the scholarships and in 1948-49, the number of the Scheduled Castes beneficiaries was 647 and 84 respectively. Till 1958-59 the programme was implemented by the Ministry of Education, but with the rising number of scholarships and for quick disbursement of scholarships, the Post-matric Scholarships Scheme is now implemented through the State Governments/ Union Territory Administrations, in accordance with the regulations framed by the Government of India. The scheme was transferred from the Ministry of Education to the Department of Social Welfare in January 1968 and after that to the Ministry of Home Affairs and it is now being administered by the Ministry of Social Justice and Empowerment, which disburses funds to the States/UTs for the operation of the Scheme.

The Post-matric Scholarships Scheme includes maintenance allowance, reader charges for blind students, reimbursement of compulsory non-refundable fees, expenditure on approved study tours and preparation of thesis/dissertation papers, and book allowance for students undergoing correspondence courses, etc. As per the Government of India regulations governing the Post-Matric Scholarships Scheme, the Scheduled Castes (Hindus, Sikhs and neo-Buddhists) and the Scheduled Tribes are eligible for award of such scholarships irrespective of their place of study. Those undertaking their post-matric studies outside their home State/UT are also sanctioned scholarships by their respective State/UT to which they belong. The Scheduled Castes converted to Christianity are not entitled to Government of India post-matric scholarships. Those in full-time employment but continuing their post-matric studies are not provided maintenance allowance under the scheme. The means test meant for the Scheduled Caste students is also now applicable for the Scheduled Tribe students. Those students whose parents' annual income exceeds Rs. 44,500 are not entitled for award of this scholarship. The scheme also benefits only the first two children of the parents and the third and subsequent children are not provided benefits of such scholarships. This restriction has been relaxed in case of girls with effect from October 1, 1995.

Before 1974-75, the rate of post-matric scholarships was fixed at Rs. 27 per month for day scholars and Rs. 40 per month for boarders in undergraduate classes. The rate for students pursuing professional courses was fixed at Rs. 60 per month for day scholars and Rs. 75 for boarders. The rates were revised during 1974 which ranged from Rs. 50 to Rs. 100 per month in case of day scholars, and Rs. 75 to Rs. 125 for hostellers depending on the course of their study.

The scheme has been later modified w.e.f. 1.10.95, thereby revising the maintenance allowance rates, income ceilings for entitlement and study courses. It has been decided to revise income ceiling once every two years and to link it with the Consumer Price Index for Industrial Workers. The current rates of maintenance allowance under the scheme of Post-matric Scholarships for the SC students are as in Table.

Students pursuing correspondence courses including distance and continuing education are now entitled to get book allowance of Rs. 500 p.a. in addition to reimbursement of compulsory course fees.

The scheme also entitles the study tour charges up to Rs. 500 per annum thesis typing/printing charges up to Rs. 600, and a reader allowance for blind scholars of Rs.100, Rs. 75 and Rs. 50 per month for courses in Groups A, B, C, D and E respectively.

In addition to the Government of India scholarship amount, the Government of Andhra Pradesh has sanctioned full mess charges to the SC hostellers. Under this scheme, the entire boarding and lodging charges, which are higher than the rates prescribed by the Government of India, are sanctioned by the State Government, and the expenditure over and above the Government of India rates is met from the State funds. The SC students of postgraduate and professional courses residing in College/ University attached hostels, are also provided full mess charges and pocket allowance of Rs. 25 per month per boarder over and above the Government of India maintenance allowances. The additional amount paid by the State Government to the students of intermediate and postgraduate courses is Rs. 25 and Rs. 55 respectively, and is meant for hostellers. In addition to the above, the State Government also provides book grants and stipends for the students conducting their research.

The Government of Tamil Nadu is supplementing the Government of India post-matric scholarship amount. The amount of State post-matric scholarship being higher than the amount sanctioned by the Government of India, the difference in the amount is borne by the State Government. The rates of Post-matric scholarships prescribed by the Government of Uttar Pradesh for various courses of studies are also higher than the Government of India rates and the difference of the scholarship amount incurred over and above the rates fixed by the Government of India is provided from the State funds. The Government of Karnataka sanctions extra boarding and lodging charges up to a maximum of Rs.150 per month, if the Government of India post-matric scholarship holders reside in recognized hostels.

Maintenance allowance rates under the Post-Matric Scholarship Scheme Groups courses in Brief

		Rate of Scholarship	
		Day Scholar	*Hosteller*
A.	Degree and Post-Graduation level Courses in Medical (including B.A. M. & S. etc.) Engineering, Agriculture, Veterinary Science, Fisheries, etc.	Rs. 190	Rs. 425
B.	Diploma level courses in Medical, Engineering etc. Commercial Pilot License course, Degree and Post-graduation Courses in Business Administration, Nursing/Pharmacy, etc. Post-gra-duate courses in Science subjects. Other diploma courses in Professional and technical subjects.	Rs. 190	Rs. 290
C.	Certificate courses in Engineering/ Technology, etc. Diploma courses in Agriculture, Pharmacy, Veterinary Science, Fisheries, Dairy Develop-ment, Degree/Post-graduate and Diploma courses in Teacher's Training, Library Science, Physical Education etc. Post-graduate courses in Arts and Commerce subjects.	Rs. 190	Rs. 290
	General Courses up to graduate level (2nd year and onwards)	Rs. 120	Rs. 230
E.	Classes XI and XII in 10+2 system, Intermediate courses and first year of general courses up to graduate level.	Rs. 90	Rs. 150

In Kerala, students who are awarded Government of India post-matric scholarships are also entitled to enjoy the financial aid from the State Government scheme to the extent the Government of India scholarship falls short of the amount of State scholarship.

About 169.99 lakh SC/ST scholars including roughly 34 lakh belonging to the Scheduled Tribes have been benefited by this scheme during the period 1985-86 to 1996-97 as shown in Table.

Number of SC/ST Scholars Benefiting from the Post-Matric Scholarship Scheme

Year	*Number of Students Covered (in lakh)*	*Source*
1985-86	9.90*	
1986-87	10.89	a
1987-88	11.30*	
1988-89	11.70*	
1989-90	12.24	b
1990-91	14.18	c
1991-92	14.97	d
1992-93	15.31	d
1993-94	14.90	d
1994-95	15.34	d
1995-96	18.47	d
1996-97	20.79**	e

* estimated ** anticipated

Sources: (a) p. 304 of Twenty-eighth Report of the Commissioner for SC/ST.

(b) p. 15 of Annual Report of the Ministry of Welfare, 1992-93.

(c) p. 13 of Annual Report of the Ministry of Welfare, 1993-94.

(d) p. 16 of Annual Report of the Ministry of Welfare, 1995-96.

(e) p. 22 of Annual Report, Ministry of Welfare, 1996-97.

So nearly 2.50 crores of the SC/ST students had been covered by this scheme up to 1996-97. Out of this about 47 lakhs were STs and the remaining 2.03 crores were SCs. If it is presumed that on an average a student enjoyed this scholarship for a period of four years, then at least 51 lakh Dalit students had so far been covered by this scheme, the bulk of whom (46 lakhs) belonged to the post 1969-70 period.

Although the value of each scholarship is low and the gap constantly increasing with inflation and a similar gap in the matter of the 'Means Test' exists, the scheme is very useful owing to its open-ended nature, i.e. all eligible SC students are eligible for the scholarships at all levels of post-matric education. Considering the fact that during the last 25 years not less than 46 lakh students have been benefited by this scheme, impact of the scheme is an impressive achievement. One has, however, every right to question who are these 46 lakh recipients, to which caste and sub-caste they belong and what is their contribution to the uplift of their brethren.

A Centrally Sponsored Scheme of pre-matric scholarships to children of those engaged in unclean occupations like scavenging of dry latrines, tanning and flaying, irrespective of what religion they were introduced from the academic year 1977 in order to provide good school education to them. It was noticed that persons engaged in such occupations were doing great service to the society but the percentage of school drop-outs among their children was much higher and this resulted in their continued backwardness. Under the scheme, 1,000 scholarships were given to those children studying in Classes VI to X in institutions having hostel facilities. These facilities were made available to the children of those parents whose income did not exceed Rs. 500 per month. Not more than one child in the family was entitled for the award of this scholarship. The rate of scholarships was Rs. 100 per month to meet the expenses of tuition fees, cost of boarding and lodging, cost of books and other incidental charges. An additional allowance of Rs. 45 per month was also given to cover expenditure on uniforms, clothing, towels, toilets, etc. The scholars were not supposed to render any help to the parents during the course of their studies. This scheme is being financed jointly by the Centre and States on matching grant basis from the year 1979-80. Central assistance is provided to the State Governments on 50:50 basis over and above the committed liability, i.e. the total expenditure incurred on the scheme in the terminal year of the previous Five Year Plan. The State Governments/Union Territory Administrations are the implementation agencies for the scheme.

The main objective of this scheme is to provide good quality education to children of those involved in unclean occupations by keeping them away from the dirty and unhygienic surroundings under which their parents live. There were, however, certain inherent shortcomings in the scheme and hence the response of the State Governments towards it was not satisfactory. The scheme was suitably modified during 1986-87. The children from the families of sweepers who have traditional association with the job of scavenging have also been included in this scheme from the year 1986-87. The other modifications made in the scheme are the followings:

(i) Raising rates of scholarships from Rs. 145 to Rs. 200 p.m. for Classes VI to VIII and Rs. 50 p.m. for Classes IX to XI;

(ii) Raising the income ceiling limit from Rs. 500 p.m. to Rs. 1000 p.m.

(iii) Provision for renting hostel buildings where hostel facilities are not available;

(iv) Provision for appointment of a full-time hostel warden where the number of children is large, otherwise one of the school teachers may be appointed as hostel warden on some extra remuneration.

During 1985-86, the expenditure incurred on this scheme was only Rs. 0.25 crores against an allocation of Rs. 2.50 crore and the number of students to benefit was only 9,286. With the modification of the scheme during 1986-87, the coverage of children which had been very slow all along, was supposed to improve. But even during the year 1988-89, only 12,820 children could be covered under this scheme. Since this scheme covered only hostellers and not day-scholars, the Working Group on development and welfare of the Scheduled Castes during Eighth Five Year Plan (1990-95) suggests modification of the scheme suitably in order to include day-scholars also with scholarships of Rs. 40 p.m. for Classes I to V, Rs. 55 p.m. for Classes VI to VIII and Rs. 75 p.m. for Classes IX and X; increase the scope of children residing in hostels from Classes III to X and provide an amount of Rs.500 per scholar per annum to all hostellers and the income ceiling limit from Rs. 1,000 to Rs. 1,500 per month.

These recommendations revising of the Working Group were acted upon and from November 1, 1991 the scheme covered day-scholars from Classes I to X, for whom the scholarship rates were

Rs. 25 p.m. for Classes I to V, Rs. 40 p.m. for Classes VI to VIII and Rs. 50 p.m. for Classes IX and X. The scheme also covered hostellers from Classes III to X. The scholarship rates for hostellers in Classes III to VIII were Rs. 200 p.m. and Rs. 250 p.m. for those in Classes IX and X. The scholarship was given for 10 months in a year. An *ad hoc* grant of Rs.500 per annum to all hostellers and day-scholars was also given. The income ceiling limit was increased to Rs.1,500 per month. The scheme has been further modified with effect from 25th February 1994. Now there is no income ceiling and also there is no limit as to the number of children of the same parents who would be entitled to award of scholarship upto Class VIII, subject to the condition that if a third or subsequent child is born after 1.4.93 a total of only two children in the family would be eligible for such scholarships. In respect of Classes IX and X, only two children of the same parents would be eligible for the award of scholarships. Income ceiling has been done away with.

The modified scheme attracted a higher number of students. The coverage under the scheme was 90,912 students in 1991-92, 99,254 in 1992-93, 1,30,715 in 1993-94, 1,76,253 in 1994-95, 2,40,628 in 1995-96 of general courses up to graduate level. Rs. 90, Rs. 150 and 2,50,000 (provisional) in 1996-97. Though large number of students are being covered under this scheme, the children of those engaged in flaying and tanning have remained almost excluded from this scheme as systematic surveys have not been carried out to identify eligible children for this scheme. Without more focussed and systematic efforts at identification, the scope of the scheme will remain limited and its basic objective of providing formal education to all children of these groups, so as to open up other opportunities for them in the future, will remain unrealised.

Central assistance disbursed to various State Governments/ UTs were 4.00 crores in 1991-92, Rs. 6.39 crores in 1992-93, Rs. 5.61 crores in 1993-94, Rs. 6.25 crore in 1994-95, Rs. 8.92 crores in 1995-96 Rs. 5.55 crores in 1996-97 (upto 31.12.96).

Until recently, some of the scholarship rates provided under the scheme were more favourable than the rates prescribed for Post-matric Scholarships. However, these also now need immediate revision keeping in mind increases based on indexing with All

India Consumer Price Index (APCPI) for industrial workers so that its effectiveness is not lost.

Hostel Facilities

It has been observed that the SC/ST girls have lagged far behind the SC/ST boys in the matter of education. It was with a view to give impetus to girls education among these communities that the Centrally Sponsored Scheme of construction of girls' hostels was began during the Third Five Year Plan (1961-66). The scope of the scheme initially provided for the construction/extension of hostel buildings; it was later widened during the Fifth Five Year Plan (1974-79) to include provision for the construction of hostel buildings, award of stipends, maintenance of hostels and facilities for meeting special needs of the SC girls studying in middle and higher levels of education. The integrated scheme was aimed at enabling the hostels to develop into multipurpose institutions where the Scheduled Caste girls may be trained in arts, crafts, skills, games, house-keeping, etc. In one hostel 100 inmates can be accommodated, of which ten per cent of seats may be reserved for non-SC/ST students. The ceiling limit of grants-in-aid for construction of girls' hostel building was modified in May 1979 in 1985, and again in 1994-95 when the ceilings on the cost of construction of hostel buildings were removed. Now the cost of construction of a hostel is to be worked out based on State/UT PWD rates. However, if a State/UT is following CPWD rates the cost shall be worked out on the basis of the rates, whichever is lower. In the case of State/UT following only CPWD rates, the CPWD rate will be applicable.

During the Fifth Plan period (1974-79), Rs. 1.95 crores were spent under the scheme in all the States and during the Sixth Plan period, a provision of Rs. 13 crores was made under this scheme for hostels for both the Scheduled Caste and the Scheduled Tribe girls. During the Seventh Plan period an allocation of Rs. 31.95 crore was made. Outlay for the Eighth Plan for this scheme was Rs. 26.00 crore.

Since 1979-80, the expenditure on this scheme is shared by the Centre and the States on matching basis (50:50). Central assistance is also given through State Governments/UT Administrations to the Voluntary Organizations/Non-Government/Private Organizations only for the extension of hostels, provided the organization is ready to bear ten per cent of the total expenditure and remaining 90 per cent in such cases is shared between the Central and State Governments on 50:50 basis.

Up to the end of 1978-79, 916 girls' hostels were built in the States/UTs. Since then the number of girls' hostels has gone up and by the end of 1989-90, about 1900 hostels had been constructed under this scheme benefiting more than 90,000 girls. The yearwise release of Central aid, number of hostels sanctioned with capacity of students during the Eighth Plan period are as shown in Table.

Yearwise and Sanction of Release of Central Assistance Each Hostel with Capacity of Girl

(upto 31.12.96)

Year	*Amount Released*	*No. of Hostels*	*No. of Inmates*
1992-93	5.33 crore	177	9,547
1993-94	6.00 crore	213	19,452
1994-95	6.20 crore	73	7,208
1995-96	5.65 crore	90	7,546
1996-97	4.37 crore		

The impact of the scheme is, however, affected in a number of places due to inadequate planning and construction delays, in appropriate site selection, and poor management and provision facilities by the concerned State Governments. These deficiencies seriously harm the efforts at promoting the education of girls in particular, in view of the special requirements of location, watch and ward, etc. in the case of girls' hostels. In addition to construction costs, central assistance should consist of a realistic one-time grant for certain basic non-recurring items of expenditure which are necessary for improving the quality of life, such as a library, utensils, and cots, at very little extra cost.

The Working Group on development and welfare of the Scheduled Castes during Eighth Five-Year Plan recommended that all the educationally backward districts in the country, particularly in States like Uttar Pradesh and Bihar, should be covered by constructing hostels for the SC girls during the Eighth Five Year Plan for which an amount of Rs. 200 crore would be needed. It is disheartening to note that States like Bihar, Rajasthan and Uttar Pradesh, where literacy rate of the SC women is as low as less than 11 per cent as per the 1991 Census did not come forward with concrete proposals for raising the capacity of hostels for the SC girls.

One of the most important reasons for the slow pace of growth of the educational development of Dalit is the lack of adequate hostel facilities. The Working Group on the development of the Scheduled Castes during the Seventh Five Year Plan (1985-90), therefore, felt the necessity of including a centrally sponsored scheme for construction of boys' hostels during the Seventh Five-Year Plan on the pattern of the existing centrally sponsored scheme for girls hostels so that there could be a minimum of two hostels for boys in each district headquarters in the country. The scheme was introduced in the year 1989-90. It is implemented on the pattern of girls hostel. The Working Group on development and welfare of Dalits during the Eighth Five-Year Plan has made recommendation that this scheme should be extended to cover all the educationally backward districts in the country.

The outlay for the Eighth Plan under this scheme was Rs. 33.00 crores against which an amount of Rs. 41.20 crore has been disbursed upto 31.12.96. The yearwise release of Central assistance, number of hostels sanctioned with capacity of students during the Eighth Plan are as shown in Table.

Yearwise Release of Central Assistance and Sanction of Hostels with capacity of Boys

Year	*Amount Released (in crore)*	*No. of Hostels*	*No. of Inmates*
1992-93	5.00	200	10,270
1993-94	6.50	101	7,020
1994-95	10.00		
1995-96	6.20	134	11,297

It appears that Andhra Pradesh and Karnataka have evinced

keen interest in implementing the scheme followed by Gujarat, Bihar, Maharashtra, Tamil Nadu and Uttar Pradesh. It is not understood as to why States like Madhya Pradesh having sizeable SC population with low literacy rate among the SCs has not shown any interest in the scheme of construction of hostels for the SC boys.

Free Books

Dalit students who generally come from the economically weaker sections of the society, cannot afford to buy all the costly books of medical and engineering courses. In pursuance of the recommendations of the High Power Committee, the Union Ministry of Home Affairs, therefore began a centrally sponsored scheme for establishing Book Banks in several medical and engineering colleges in the country from 1978-79 for lending sets of textbooks on medical and engineering degree courses to the SC students.

This scheme having proved to be beneficial to the SC students in pursuing medical and engineering courses, the Working Group on the development of the Scheduled Castes, during the Seventh Five-Year Plan, suggested that the scope of this scheme might be extended to cover all the professional courses which would help a large number of the SC students in pursuing professional education. In order to make the scheme more effective and meaningful, the Working Group thought it desirable to give a set of textbooks to each SC students pursuing a professional course and who was entitled to post-matric scholarship. The Working Group on development and welfare of the Scheduled Castes during the Eighth Five-Year Plan also suggested the expansion of the scope of this scheme for covering other professional courses like Veterinary Science, B.Sc. (Agriculture), Law and Polytechnics, etc. during the Eighth Five-Year Plan and provision of one set of books to each students. The Ninth Plan Working Group felt the necessity extend the scheme to cover all post-matric scholarship recipients in categories "A" and "B" courses of that scheme.

At present, under the scheme, Books Banks are set up not only in Medical and Engineering Colleges, but also in Veterinary and Agriculture Colleges and Polytechnics. Indian systems of Medicine and Homeopathy are also covered under the scheme. Earlier one set of books was used by four students. Now each set of textbooks is to be shared by two students.

The scheme which is administered through the State Governments/UT Administration, is being funded jointly by the Centre and the States on a 50:50 basis from 1979-80, subject to the following ceiling on costs per set of textbooks for various courses.

Courses	*Ceiling Cost per set (in Rs.)*
Medical (including Indian systems of Medicine/Homeopathy)	7,500
Engineering	7,500
Veterinary	5,000
Agriculture	4,500
Polytechnic	2,400

The life period of one set of books has been fixed as three years; this means that every three years funds will be given for getting new sets of books. A provision of Rs. 3 crores was made for this scheme during the Sixth Plan but unfortunately the expenditure during the period was only Rs. 0.96 crore. For the Seventh Plan, an outlay of Rs. 2.25 crore was given for this scheme. During 1985-86 the number of SC beneficiaries was 16,822 rising to 21,000 in 1990. In 1991-92, Rs. 56.26 lakh were disbursed as central assistance to benefit 24,245 students. During the Eighth Plan period, an amount of Rs.11.24 crores has been released (up to December, 1996) benefiting 108,946 students. The yearwise break-up is given in Table.

Yearwise break-up of amount released for Book Banks during 1992-97

Year	*Amount released (Rs. in crore)*	*No. Benefited*
1992-93	0.67	11,582
1993-94	3.33	32,120
1994-95	3.50	37,877
1995-96	2.64	27,367
1996-97	1.10	

Merit Schemes

Under this scheme, central assistance is provided on 100 per cent basis to State Governments/UT Administrations for providing remedial and special coaching to the SC/ST students. The scheme was started in 1987-88 by the Ministry of Human Resource Development (Department of Education). It was later transferred to the Ministry of Welfare in the middle of 1993-94. This is intended to help the SC students studying in Classes IX to XII by providing them extra coaching both remedial and special in an effort to remove their social and educational deficiencies and facilitating their admission to professional courses such as Medical and Engineering, etc. where entry is based on competitive examinations. The outlay for the Eighth Plan under the scheme was Rs. 2.60 crore. The total grant released during 1993-94 was Rs.0.15 crore to benefit 334 SC students in only five States. A total amount of Rs.1.00 crore was released in 1994-95 to benefit 2336 SC students in 11 States. In 1995-96, an amount of Rs. 22.17 lakhs was released to five States only. The scheme has a great deal of potential provided it is properly utilised by the States/UTs.

Preparation Schemes

The Government of India sanctioned the scheme in 1958-59 to improve the intake of the SCs/STs in various government services in cadres like IAS/IPS/Allied Services under the Public Sector Undertakings by providing pre-examination training to candidates appearing in examinations held by the Union Public Service Commission, State Public Service Commissions, Banking Service Recruitment Boards and other recruiting bodies.

The Ministry of Welfare has been administering the scheme since the Fourth Plan (1969-74). The Ministry finances: (a) Pre-Examination Training Centres (PETCs) established by the State governments and the universities and (b) private coaching institutions. The State run PETCs are financed by the Centre and the State Governments on a matching basis over and above the committed liability of the State Governments in the terminal year of the previous Five Year Plan. The committed liability is borne by the State Governments from their own resources. The Centres run by the Universities and the Union Territory Administrations are reimbursed the actual expenditure incurred. Private coaching centres are paid on a contractual basis. The coaching is given to the SC/ST candidates in three broad categories of examinations. These are Central Civil Services, Medical and Engineering Entrance Examinations and other service examinations including the State Civil Services. The scheme offers a monthly stipend of Rs. 400 for the hostellers and Rs. 100 per month for the day scholars. The norms for payment of remuneration to the teachers in the training centres have been fixed for some of the examinations. Teachers coaching candidates for civil services examinations are paid an honorarium up to Rs. 500 for a lecture of two hours duration.

Benefits of the scheme have accrued to a large number of students, approximately 11,000 students each year. At present, 131 PETCs run by 22 States/UTs, 18 universities and four private coaching institutions of Delhi have been receiving grant under the Scheme.

However, a review of the Scheme as implemented has revealed glaring imbalances both in terms of the geographical spread of these centres as well as in terms of the coverage of examinations/ vocations. For example, in the States of Arunachal Pradesh, Mizoram and Sikkim and the UTs of Andaman & Nicobar Islands, Chandigarh, Dadra and Nagar Haveli, Daman & Diu and Lakshdweep no coaching centres are opened. Similarly in large States such as Bihar, West Bengal, Karnataka, Tamil Nadu there are no institutes providing coaching for Medical and Engineering Entrance examinations. The disciplines of management, chartered accountancy, cost accountancy providing a great employment potential are also not covered in any of these centres. The PETCs under the aegis of State Government provide coaching mainly for the clerical grade and other Group 'C' examinations. However, the need for more centres for Medical and Engineering, Central Civil Services and other professional courses is of great significance as the shortfall in eligible SC/ST candidates in Group 'A' and 'B' posts of Central Government, Public Sector Undertakings and Banks is much higher.

Apart from a few centres such as Guru Nanak Dev University, Amritsar, Punjab University, Patiala and private coaching institutes (Rau's Studey Circle, S.N. Das Gupta College and Sachdeva New P.T. College) the results from other centres are extremely poor. Most of the PETCS have been functioning from rented building. The PETCs have failed to provide hostels/library facilities to the candidates.

In order to remove the shortcomings identified, the scheme was modified in 1994 to bring within its umbrella coaching institutes of repute on the one hand and pre-examination coaching for new disciplines such as management, hotel management, accountancy, armed forces examinations on the other. The States have been urged to recommend names of the reputed private coaching institutes which could be selected for sponsoring candidates under this scheme. A committee under the chairmanship of Secretary, Ministry of Welfare (now Ministry of Social Justice and Empowerment) has been set up to make decisions the inclusion of new centres under this scheme.

The Committee has set certain norms for including institutes under this scheme. These are:

(1) The institute should be a registered trust or society and/or recognised by the concerned State/UT's Education and Social Welfare Departments or should be affiliated to the nearest University.

(2) The institute should have at least three years of successful experience in imparting coaching in the courses for which inclusion under the scheme is proposed.

(3) A minimum 15 per cent success rate in the relevant examination in previous three years has been stipulated as the bench mark for inclusion.

(4) The institute should have reasonable accommodation, teaching equipment as also library and hostel facilities.

(5) The institute should have qualified and competent teaching staff.

At the recommendation of the Planning Commission, a Task Force has been set up by the Ministry to review and suggest suitable modifications to the scheme. An All-India meeting with the Heads of State Welfare Departments and Universities was organized by the Welfare Ministry on 29.6.1996 to review the implementation of the scheme. Some of the recommendations are:

1. Spreading out of the coaching centres where concentration of SC/ST population is high and facilities for coaching do not exist;
2. Careful selection of students;
3. Coaching to be provided in relation to the availability of reserved vacancies; and
4. Constitution of Monitoring Committee at States/District level and award to the best PETC.

During the Eighth Plan Period, central assistance of Rs. 8.00 crores was provided to the State Governments/universities/private institutions.

Facilities for Foreign Education

The Government of India initiated a scheme in 1954-55 for the award of national overseas scholarships to the SC/ST, Denotified, Nomadic and Semi-Nomadic Tribes, SC converts to other religions and the children of Landless Agricultural labourers/Traditional Artisans for advanced Degree and Post-Doctoral studies abroad. Weightage is given to studies in Engineering Technology, Medicine, Agriculture and Science. At the Bachelor's and Master's degree levels also specific courses have been approved recently for award of scholarships. Selected candidates are allowed a period of three years after the year of selection within which they are required to obtain admission in foreign institutions, for which assistance is also provided by the Indian Missions abroad. The scholarships are given to the students by the Indian Missions during their stay abroad, which include the payment of tuition fees, maintenance and contingency allowances, and travel expenses. The rates of scholarships are other allowances under the scheme are given below:

1. Maintenance Allowance:

    (a) Bachelor's Degree Course — US $ 5940 p.a.

    (b) Postgraduate Course — US $ 6600 p.a.

    (c) Post Doctoral Course — US $ 7700 p.a.

2. Contingency Allowance — US $ 385 p.m.

3. Equipment Allowance — Rs.1100

4. Poll Tax — US $ 150

5. All compulsory fees of the University/Institute, such as Tuition Fee, Admission Fee, etc. and the Health/Medical Insurance premium, if any.

6. Cost of economy class air fare both ways up to destination and back by the shortest route.

7. IInd class rail fare from place of residence to the airport, and back.

The number of scholarships which was six initially, was raised to 12 in 1955-56 and to 21 in 1972-73, 25 in 1990 and to 30 in 1991. These awards are provided to candidates belonging to the Scheduled Castes (17 awards), the Scheduled Tribes (nine awards) the Scheduled Caste converts to other religions or their dependants (two awards), Denotified, Nomadic and Semi-nomadic Tribes (one award) and Children of landless agricultural labourers and traditional artisans of communities other than above (one award). Since the inception of the scheme in 1954-55, a total of 732 candidates have been given the scholarships and 525 candidates took benefit of it.

In addition to 30 National Overseas Scholarships, Passage Grants are also given to students who are in receipt of a merit scholarship from a foreign Government or Institute, in case such scholarship does not include the costs of passage. Passage Grants are available each year to the Scheduled Castes (four awards), the Scheduled Tribes (four awards) and Denotified and Semi-Nomadic Tribes (one award).

Special Programme

The scheme which is in operation from 1996-97 provides a package of educational inputs through residential schools for Scheduled Caste girls in areas where very low Scheduled Caste Female Literacy prevails due to traditions and environment not being conducive to learning. The schools would supplement existing measures to impart and consolidate literacy and promote quality education among Scheduled Caste Girls of first generation learners in areas of low literacy. The scheme is implemented by the Zila Parishad of the concerned District.

Such schools function in suitable hired premises. Such premises should have sufficient space accommodate Classrooms, Hostels, Kitchen and Staff Quarters and should preferably allow for expansion of school, if subsequently needed. All inclusive, grants-in-aid will be provided under the scheme to the Zila Parishad @ Rs.11,340 per annum per student in Class 1 split in two components (Rs. 4900 for direct facilities to students and Rs. 6440) for infrastructural and other running cost, including staff). No fees, charges or contributions will be collected from the students. Each school will have 25 girls in Class 1. The intake will be from among girls who are first generation learners from families identified for the purpose of the Integrated Rural Development Programme, as being below the poverty line. Priority in intake is to be given to the particularly disadvantaged amongst the Scheduled Castes such as the children of scavengers, flayers, and tanners.

The 1981 Census identified 48 districts situated in Bihar, Madhya Pradesh, Rajasthan and Uttar Pradesh where the literacy of Scheduled Caste Girls was below two per cent. The scheme accordingly covers only these districts. As against the target of 21 residential schools for the year 1996-97, 14 residential schools have so far been sanctioned in eight Zila Parishads of Madhya Pradesh and three residential Schools in three Zila Parishads of Uttar Pradesh. The total expenditure incurred up to 31.12.96 under the scheme was Rs. 19.84 lakh.

This is a very good scheme, if sincerely implemented. This scheme may be extended subsequent to other States as well, to cover those Scheduled Castes whose literacy rate is much below the State average.

Supporting Organizations

The objective of giving grants-in-aid to Voluntary Organizations of All-India character engaged in the welfare of the SC/ST and other Backward Classes, is to improve the educational and socio-economic conditions of these communities through voluntary efforts of various non-official agencies. Under this scheme started by the Government of India in 1953-54, only those voluntary agencies which have been registered for a year and have given some evidence of voluntary involvement in adult education and social upliftment are entitled to financial assistance. Grants-in-aid to the extent of ninety per cent of approved costs on several schemes are provided to the eligible voluntary organizations. Programmes for social upliftment of the SCs are also given for financial assistance under the scheme. To ensure active participation of these organizations, they are expected to contribute ten per cent of the grant. It is also desirable to have SC members in the managing Committee in adequate number and capacity. The Government of India has also issued detailed guidelines on Aid to Voluntary Organizations. The various schemes for which grants-in-aid are provided to the voluntary organizations include residential schools, day schools, hostels, child welfare centres, etc. and training in various disciplines like typewriting and stenography, computer application, tailoring and embroidery, motor driving, electronics and other industrial trades. More than 400 organizations are being financed under this scheme.

To ensure that the grantee complies with the terms and conditions of the grants and that the welfare schemes are run on dotted lines, the officers of the Ministry of Welfare, Director of the Scheduled Castes and the Scheduled Tribes and the National Commission for the SCs and STs inspect the aided schemes and make their recommendations and send their inspection reports to the Ministry of Welfare. Steps to improve the working and effectiveness of this scheme of voluntary organizations have to be worked out in consultation with the representation of various voluntary organizations reputed for their sincerity, integrity and effective implementation.

Apart from these and other Centrally Sponsored Schemes, the State Governments/Union Territory Administrations have various other schemes like scholarships including pre-matric scholarships, merit scholarships, special scholarships for very backward communities, attendance scholarships for girls, freeships, hostel facilities, residential schools (Ashram Schools), remedial and special coaching schemes along with other incentives like free mid-day meals, textbooks, uniforms, etc. for boys and girls belonging to the SC/ST communities only for primary section but also for higher education. There are also provisions for reservation of seats in educational institutions including professional and technical education for the SC/ST students. Relaxation in norms for admission in terms of minimum marks for selection, age limit, fees for admission/examination, etc. are also provided. The domain of their activities, however, varies from State to State.

Details of the facilities/schemes as on 1983-84 are given below: It is quite possible that the rates of stipends and other facilities have undergone a revision by this time and even the percentages of seats reserved for the SC/ST fixed on the basis of their population proportion in the State may have been refixed in many States/ UTs. Lack of latest data however, stands in the way of providing the latest information.

Reserved Seats

Insertion of Clause (4) of Article 15 by the First Constitutional Amendment Act, 1951 enables the State to make special provision for the advancement of (1) any socially and educationally backward classes of citizens, or for (2) the Scheduled Castes, and (3) the Scheduled Tribes. Since education, general as well as technical, is a potent instrument in the uplift of these communities, the Government of India considered it desirable that all possible facilities should be afforded and attempts be made to enable the students belonging to the SC/ST communities to gain admission in educational institutions including technical institutions.

The Ministry of Education, vide its letter dated November 23, 1954 had addressed to the Chief Secretaries of all State Governments suggesting that 20 per cent seats should be reserved for the SC/ST students in educational institutions and where admissions are limited to candidates who obtain certain minimum percentage of marks and not merely the passing of a certain examination, there a relaxation of five per cent may be provided for such candidate.

Further, on April 15, 1964 the Ministry of Education in another communication to all the State Governments and the universities suggested that 20 per cent of seats in all technical institutions should be reserved for the SC/ST candidates with a distinct share of 15 per cent for the SC and 5 per cent for the ST (since increased to 7.5 per cent from August 1982) and that this reservation is interchangeable between them. Five per cent reduction of marks to pass the qualifying examination should also be allowed to them. If upper age limit is fixed, it may be raised by three years for the SC/ST students.

Similarly, the Ministry of Health and Family Welfare, vide its letter dated December 12, 1972 addressed to the Vice-Chancellors of the universities having Medical Facilities, had urged that the universities might consider the feasibility of reserving 20 per cent of seats in Postgraduate Medical and Dental College, i.e. 15 per cent for the SCs and 5 per cent for the STs. It was also suggested in that letter that these students should also be given a concession of 5 per cent marks in the minimum percentage of marks needed for admission to such courses and that in case 20 per cent seats earmarked for them remain vacant, a further relaxation in the marks should be given to them in order of merit among themselves so that all the reserved seats are filled by candidates belonging to these communities only. The Ministry of Health and Family Welfare, having noticed that the State Governments/Universities/Medical Colleges, etc. were not giving due concessions in the matter of admission to postgraduate Medical and Dental courses to students of SC/ST, had again made a request to the concerned State Governments/universities to extend the above concession to the students belonging to the enlisted communities.

The UGC on its part as a follow up, directed the attention of the universities to the guidelines issued by the Ministry of Education and Social Welfare regarding reservation of seats for the SC/ST students in the universities/colleges. It was observed that according to the recent arrangements, 20 per cent of the seats were reserved for the SC/ST candidates who were also given a concession of five per cent marks in the minimum percentage of marks needed for admission in any course. It was later noted that even with these concessions some of the seats in the reserved quota remained vacant due to lack of SC/ST candidates with requisite marks. Accordingly, it was suggested that in case the 20 per cent seats earmarked for them remain vacant, a further relaxation in the marks may be given to them in order of merit amongst themselves, so that all the reserved seats can be filled by candidates belonging to these categories.

Kendriya Vidyalayas

Till 1976-77, no reservation of seats for the SC/ST students was available for admission to Kendriya Vidyalayas. The Kendriya Vidyalaya Sangathan, however, decided to reserve 15 per cent and 7.5 per cent seats for the SC and the ST candidates respectively, in respect of new admissions to Kendriya Vidyalaya with effect from the academic year 1976-77. The reservation quota was to apply to the total number of children given fresh admission in a Kendriya Vidyalaya at the start of a session and not to the fresh admissions made in each class. The Kendriya Vidyalaya Sangathan issued another instruction to all the Kendriya Vidyalayas in August 1978 to make sure that the quota reserved for the SC/ST students was utilized to the maximum extent possible and for that purpose, issued the following guidelines:

(i) The conditions of transferability of parents may be relaxed and children of even non-transferable SC/ST employees may be admitted, where necessary;

(ii) If any examination is held for admission to Kendriya Vidyalayas, candidate belonging to the SC/ST may be given a concession of five per cent marks in the standard fixed for other candidates from the academic session 1979-91.

Following the guidelines of the Central Government, almost all the State Governments/Union Territory Administrations have designed their own schemes for reservation of seats for the Scheduled Caste students in college providing general and professional education and in technical institutions. In States/UTs, like Orissa, Tripura, Andhra Pradesh, Karnataka,Tamil Nadu, Uttar Pradesh, West Bengal and Pondicherry, reservation of seats have been provided at school levels as well. In States/UTs like Arunachal Pradesh, Mizoram, Nagaland, Sikkim, Lakshadweep and Dadra and Nagar Haveli, having predominantly Scheduled Tribe population and negligible or no population of the Scheduled Castes, no seats have been specially reserved for the SC/ST students. The percentage of seats reserved differs from State to State, the highest being 20 in Haryana and the lowest is two in Manipur in relation to the Scheduled Caste students. This wide variation is due to the fact that different States/UTs have different percentage of SC population. In Central Government institutions, the percentage is, however, fixed and there is no variation.

Besides the reservation of seats in the educational institutions, many States/UTs have also relaxed the eligibility criterion. In most States/UTs a relaxation of five per cent marks is given. The actual position in respect of reservation of seats in the educational institutions as also the relaxation in marks in eligibility criterion for admission is different for each State/UT.

Elementary education up to Class VIII is free in all the States/UTs. Opening of educational institutions is enough to attract students from the general mass, but mere provision of schools and free education may not have similar impact on the SC/ST students on the educational front. To attract larger number of the SC/ST students to join their studies, apart from providing special incentives like supply of free uniform, books, mid-day meals, the scheme for providing stipend to the SC/ST students at pre-matric classes is in vogue in many States/UTs. The rate of stipend, however, is not uniform and in some States the scheme is meant for the SC girls only. Criteria of income has also been linked in some States/UTs. Some States like Madhya Pradesh, Punjab and Rajasthan claim that these stipends are given to all the eligible SC students. As a large number of States/UTs are still well below the target of universal coverage, the Commissioner for the SC/ST recommended in his 27th report (1979-81) that this scheme of pre-matric stipends should be made an open-ended one like the post-matric scholarships and all the eligible SC/ST students should be awarded scholarships. The Working Group on development of Dalits during the Seventh Five Year Plan (1985-90) also suggested that there should be provision of scholarship/stipend to all children belonging to the Scheduled Castes with 100 per cent coverage at all levels. They also recommended that the amount of scholarship should be a minimum of Rs. 40 per month. The Working Group on development and welfare of the Scheduled Castes during the Eighth-Five Year Plan (1990-95) also reiterated that all the Scheduled Caste children studying in pre-matric classes should be given scholarships. It also recommended to give Rs. 60 per month for ten months in a year to indigent SC/ST families as an incentive for sending their girls to the primary schools. The total cost for covering 51.41 lakh children would come to be Rs.308.47 crore annually. The total requirement of funds under the scheme during the Eighth Five-Year Plan was estimated by Working Group to be Rs.1542.37 crore or Rs.1550.00 crore.

In Arunachal Pradesh, scholarships are given to pre-university students of Rs. 100 p.m. for 10½ months in a year and Rs.175 p.m. for degree courses. The parental income ceiling is fixed at Rs 1000 p.m.

In Karnataka, the State Government provides scholarships in the range of Rs. 40 to Rs. 75 p.m. to students whose parental income is less than Rs. 10,000 p.a. This scholarship is admissible to those who are not eligible for the Government of India Post-matric scholarship. In Kerala, under the Post-matric scholarship scheme of the State Government the SC/ST students are provided a lump sum grant varying from Rs. 80 to Rs. 750, depending upon the course of study, plus a monthly stipend of Rs. 130 to those residing within eight kms and Rs. 150 to those residing beyond eight kms from the educational institutions. There is no income ceiling attached under this scheme. In case of hostellers, instead of stipend, actual boarding and lodging charges are paid under this scheme.

In Maharashtra, financial aid of Rs. 1000 p.a. is given to backward class students studying in medical and engineering courses. A maintenance allowance of Rs. 1200 p.a. is also given to backward class students residing in hostels attached to professional colleges. Under the Post-matric scholarship scheme of the Sikkim Government, scholarships of Rs. 300 p.m. are awarded to students whose parental income is below Rs. 1000 p.m. There is also a general scholarship in which 15 per cent of the scholarships are reserved for the SCs and 15 per cent for the STs.

In Andhra Pradesh, merit scholarships are awarded to top ten students for post-matric studies upto postgraduate level based on the marks obtained in the annual examinations since SSC. Rates vary from Rs. 2000 p.a. to Rs. 6,000 p.a. for boys and Rs.2500 p.a. to Rs. 7000 p.a. for girls.

In Arunachal Pradesh, merit scholarships of Rs. 50 p.m. are given in Classes IX and X to those who figure in first 30 positions in Class VIII; Rs. 75 p.m. in Classes XI and XII to those who figure in first 20 positions in Class X and Rs.100 p.m. for two years after Class XII for pursuing higher studies to those who have secured first ten positions in Class XII/PUC. The parental income ceiling for this scholarship is fixed at Rs. 1250 p.m.

In Haryana, merit scholarships are given at the rate of Rs. 40 p.m., Rs. 50 p.m. and Rs. 60 p.m. in Classes IX, X and XI respectively to the SC girls.

In Karnataka, the students who secure 60 per cent marks and above are given additional scholarships of Rs. 75 p.a. in Classes V to VII and Rs. 100 p.a. in classes VIII to X. Students who secure 50 per cent marks and above but less than 60 per cent marks are given additional scholarships of Rs. 50 p.a. in Classes V to VII and Rs. 75 p.a. in Classes VIII to X.

In Orissa, merit prizes are awarded to the SC/ST students based on matriculation examination results. A grant of Rs. 350 p.a. is awarded to Arts and Commerce students and Rs. 450 p.a. for Science students and students studying in diploma and degree courses in Engineering.

In Rajasthan, merit scholarships are given to one boy and one girl student from each *Panchayat Samiti* in the tribal sub-plan areas. Scholarship is awarded on the basis of marks obtained in class VIII examination. An amount of Rs. 1000 for the whole season is given to students admitted in select schools and Rs. 500 to students in other schools. Scholarships in special subjects (Mathematics and Science) are also awarded to students in schools located in the tribal sub-plan areas. The rates of scholarships are Rs. 40 p.m. in class IX, Rs. 50 p.m. in class X and Rs. 60 p.m. in class XI.

In West Bengal, special merit scholarship of Rs. 400 p.m. and Rs. 500 p.m. is awarded to the day-scholars and hostellers studying in Class IX to XII respectively.

In Andhra Pradesh scholarships to the SC students studying in Convent/Residential schools are pegged at the following rates: classes I to V @ Rs. 20 p.a., classes VI to VIII @ Rs. 25 p.a. and classes IX to XII @ Rs. 30 p.a. The income ceiling is Rs. 12,000 p.a. or Rs. 1000 per month.

In Orissa, students admitted to public schools are given scholarships of Rs.200 p.m. for ten months in a year.

In Sikkim, there is a general scholarship scheme for students in classes I to X in which four out of every ten scholarships are reserved for the SC/ST students. The rate of scholarship is Rs. 200 p.m. For the award of this scholarship there is an income ceiling of Rs. 1000 p.m.

In Andhra Pradesh, scholarships of Rs 100 p.m. are paid in addition to the stipend paid by universities or Government of India to students in Postgraduate courses like MD, MS, etc. Students pursuing M. Phil, Ph.D., etc. but not in receipt of any other scholarship, are given scholarship of Rs. 400 p.m. under this scheme.

In Gujarat, *Bhangi* students studying in Medical, BDS and Ayurvedic courses and whose parents' income is up to Rs. 15,000 p.a. are provided full scholarships from State Funds at the rates of the Government of India. In Mizoram, Ph.D. students who have completed M. Phil are granted fellowships of Rs. 700 p.m. with Rs. 3000 p.a. as contingency grant. Those who have taken Ph.D courses directly and those taking M. Phil course are awarded Rs. 600 p.m. as Research Fellowship and Rs. 3000 p.a. as contingency grant.

That the enrolment of girls in schools is much below than that of boys was revealed in all the All-India Educational Surveys, including the Sixth Survey (1993). Some State Governments have instituted scholarships for girls as an incentive to attract them to attend school. These scholarships are meant to bring the girls of school-going age to school and to retain them there. In 1986, only 47,111 (6.40 per cent) schools out of the total number of 7,35,771 schools in the country were awarding attendance scholarships to girls.

At all stages of school education 3,75,979 girls were availing the benefit of this incentive scheme. Of these beneficiaries, 70.44 per cent were studying in rural schools. Further 57.70 per cent of the beneficiaries belonged to the Scheduled Castes and 16.05 per cent to the Scheduled Tribes, which together accounted for 73.75 per cent of the beneficiaries. The break-up of the beneficiaries at various stages of school education can be seen in Table.

Loans without Interest

In Himachal Pradesh, interest free loans upto Rs. 2000 are give to those students whose parental annual income does not exceed Rs. 2000. The loan is recoverable in 20 instalments after four years from the date of disbursement of the loan.

In Tamil Nadu, loan scholarship is provided only to hostellers for pursuing their degree/postgraduate degree courses. An annual grant in the range of Rs. 500 to Rs. 970 is given under this scheme.

In Tamil Nadu, a lump sum grant of Rs. 300 is given to all SC/ST students who obtain an aggregate of 60 per cent marks in SSLC/Matric examination for continuning their study in recognized institutions. Bright Students Award is also given to two boys and two girls each from the SC (Hindu), STs, and SCs converted to Christianity in each district selected on the basis of the marks obtained in SSLC examination. Scholarship is given at the rate of Rs. 80 p.m. till the completion of Post-matric studies subject to a maximum of six years. Gandhi Memorial Award is given to one boy and one girl from the SC (Hindu) from each district based on the Higher Secondary marks. The rate of scholarship is Rs. 15000 for first year and Rs. 1000 per year for the remaining period, subject to a maximum period of 6 years for pursuing post-matric studies.

Break-up of attendance Scholarships for Girls According to Schools and Beneficiaries

Type of Schools	*No. of Schools*	*No. of Beneficiaries*	
		Scheduled Castes	*Others*
Primary	24,563 (4.65%)	97,071 (64.45%)	29,562 (19.63%)
Upper Primary	15,053 (10.83%)	80,533 (54.20%)	42,816 (28.81%)
Secondary	5,599 (10.65%)	25,228 (50.78%)	17,372 (34.97%)
Higher	1,896 (12.26%)	14,107 (52.07%)	8,963 (33.09%)

Source: Fifth All-India Educational Survey, pp. 185-88, 1986.

In Dadra and Nagar Haveli, cash awards for the top three students in annual examinations are given to the SC/ST students from classes V to VIII. The rates are: Rs. 70 p.a. for 1st prize, Rs. 60 p.a. for 2nd prize and Rs. 50 p.a. for 3rd prize.

In Delhi, merit scholarships are provided at the following rates: Rs. 10 p.m. for class VI, Rs. 15 p.m. for class VII and Rs. 20 p.m. for class VIII for all students securing 60 per cent marks or more, and Rs. 20 p.m. for class IX, Rs. 25 p.m. for class X, Rs. 30 p.m. for class XI and Rs. 35 p.m. for class XII to all students obtaining 55 per cent marks or more. There is another Open Merit Scholarship scheme under which some scholarships are reserved for the SC/ST students. The selected students get scholarships at the rate of Rs. 50 p.m. for ten months in a year from classes VI to VIII.

In Pondicherry, all those SC students who obtain more than 65 per cent marks in Xth standard examination are given a merit prize of Rs. 300. Dr. Ambedkar Memorial Award is given to one SC student from each region of Pondicherry on the basis of marks obtained of XII class examination. A lump sum of Rs. 1000 is paid to the selected student given that the student has secured at least 55 per cent marks.

No Tution Fee

The Scheduled Caste students are provided free education up to certain level in nearly all the States/UTs. Up to Class VIII in two States/UTs (Punjab and Chandigarh) education is free up to class X; in five States /UTs (Assam, Meghalaya, Nagaland, UP and Goa, Daman and Diu); it is free up to Class XII; in nine States, UTs (Gujarat, Himachal Pradesh, Sikkim, Tamil Nadu, West Bengal, Arunachal Pradesh, Andaman and Nicober Islands, Dadra and Nagar Haveli and Delhi); up to matriculation in one State (Orissa), up to intermediate in one State (Andhra Pradesh), up to degree level in one UT (Pondicherry); up to postgraduation level in one State (Jammu and Kashmir) and up to all levels in nine States/ UTs (Bihar, Haryana, Karnataka, Kerala, Madhya Pradesh, Maharashtra, Rajasthan, Tripura and Lakshadweep). Information is not available in respect of two States (Manipur and Mizoram).

In addition to freeships, as many as 21 States/UTs have also exempted the SCs from paying the examination fees as follows:

- upto class X in three UTs states (Chandigarh, Daman and Diu and Goa),
- upto class XII in six States/UTs (Gujarat, Madhya Pradesh, Sikkim, Tamil Nadu, West Bengal and A & N Islands),
- upto matriculation in one State (Orissa),
- upto all levels in seven States/UTs (Bihar, Himachal Pradesh, Kerala, Karnataka, Punjab, Tripura and Lakshadweep),
- Public examination in one State (Haryana), and
- Board examinations in four States/UTs (Jammu and Kashmir, Arunachal Pradesh, Delhi and Dadra and Nagar Haveli).

Ashram schools are opened in tribal areas providing free education, boarding and lodging facilities to the tribal children who inhabit inaccessible hills and forests without proper communication facilities. Apart from general education, the *Ashram* schools also give training in agriculture and crafts like blacksmithy, carpentry and weaving for boys and tailoring for girls. In Orissa, the residential schools for girls are called *Kanyashrams*, while the *Ashram* schools are meant for boys.These schools are run by State Government as well as by non-official organizations. The programme for the setting up and maintenance of *Ashram* schools is also included in the tribal sub-plan of the States in which sub-plans have been formulated. In some States *Ashram* schools have also been opened to fulfil educational needs of the Dalits.

The number of *Ashram* schools in various States/UTs catering to the needs of both the SC and ST students is shown in Table.

Considering the insufficient number of *Ashram* schools for the Scheduled Caste students, the Working Group on development and welfare of the Scheduled Castes during the Eighth Five-Year Plan suggested that in educationally backward regions, i.e. where the literacy rate among the Dalits is very low, there should be *Ashram* schools for the Scheduled Caste boys and girls at the primary level.

It has been noticed that generally the SC/ST students do not have the required facilities at home for studies, while the general students are far better placed in this regard. Most of the SC/ST students being first generation learners, also do not have the facility of proper guidance by their parents. Hostels, which provide environment for studies as well as facilities for coaching and guidance, therefore, play a very important role in the promotion of education among the SC/ST students. In this regard a study was conducted by the Government of Karnataka on the performance of hostellers in SSLC Examination held during April 1978, which shows that the performance of the SC/ST hostellers in the examination was far better in comparison to those who had no hostel facilities.

Number of Ashram Schools in Various States/UTs,

Sl. No.	*State/UTs*	*Level of Schooling*	*No. of Ashram Schools for SC*
1.	Andhra Pradesh	Primary level	9
		Middle level	46
2.	Assam	for SC/ST	
3.	Bihar		39
4.	Gujarat	Primary level	38
		Middle level	–
5.	Himachal Pradesh	Primary level for SC/ST	
		Middle level for SC/ST	
6.	Karnataka		63
7.	Kerala	Primary level	–
8.	Madhya Pradesh	up to middle level	31
9.	Maharashtra	up to class VIII	–
		up to class X	–
10.	Manipur	Primary level	–
		Middle level	–
		Secondary level	–
11.	Rajasthan	Primary level	1
		Middle/Secondary level	–
12.	Tamil Nadu		–
13.	Orissa	Residential Sevashrams (Classes I to V)	2
		Middle Education Standard (Ashram schools Kanyashrams for classes IV to VII)	3
		Residential High Schools (Classes IV to X)	3
		Residential Sevashrams (Primary School)	90
14.	Tripura	Classes I to VIII	–
		Classes I to X	–
15.	Uttar Pradesh	for SC/ST	
16.	West Bengal	Classes V to VIII for SC/ST	
		Classes I to XII	
17.	Arunachal Pradesh	Primary level	–
		Middle level	–

		Secondary level
		Higher Secondary level
18.	Dadra & Nagar Haveli	Classes I to X
19.	Goa, Daman & Diu	Classes I to VIII

Source: Educational Facilities to SC/ST, Ministry of Education, pp. 12-65, 1985.

In case of the SCs, while among day scholars, only 35 per cent of students who appeared for the above mentioned examination could pass, among the hostellers the pass percentage was as high as 53.5. Similarly, among the STs only 37.2 per cent of the students who appeared in the examination could pass, but the corresponding percentage among the ST hostellers was 68.00. As per the findings of the study, facilities in hostels like free boarding, lodging, supply of textbooks and stationery, special coaching, etc. were mainly responsible for the better performance of the SC/ST hostellers as compared to the day-scholars.

Hostels for the SC/ST boys and girls are Dalit under the Backward Classes Sector of the State Plans and Tribal Sub-plan. Non-Official organizations running hostels for the SC/ST students also receive grants-in-aid from State Governments/Union Territory Administrations and also from the Government of India.

The number of Government hostels for the SCs/STs is much less than needed in many States. In his 27th Report (1979-81) the Commissioner for SC/ST noted that the number of backward class hostels continued to be inadequate in Bihar, Rajasthan, Himachal Pradesh, Kerala and Uttar Pradesh and stressed that the Governments of the States with large SC/ST population, in which the number of Backward Class Hostels was inadequate, should take urgent steps to raise the number thereof adequately. The Commission for the SC/ST also suggested in 1980 that all the State Governments/Union Territory Administration should take immediate steps in providing hostels facilities for the SC/ST students in both pre-matric and post-matric classes. The Third All-India Educational Survey on Hostel Facilities for the Scheduled Castes carried out by the National Council of Educational Research and Training (NCERT) during December, 1973 also throws light on this problem. From the statistics available on 13 States (Andhra Pradesh, Bihar, Gujarat, Haryana, Karnataka, Kerala, Madhya Pradesh, Maharashtra, Rajasthan, Tamil Nadu, Tripura, Uttar Pradesh and West Bengal) and two Union Territories (Dadra and Nagar Haveli and Pondicherry), the report has pointed out the inadequacy of hostel facilities in different States. According to the survey, Uttar Pradesh with the highest Scheduled Caste population did not have the required percentage of hostels. With only 3.2 per cent of the total number of hostels, Uttar Pradesh ranked only eighth in the country in numerical strength of hostels, while Maharashtra having the lowest percentage of the Scheduled Caste population (six per cent) had the second highest number of hostels among all the States/UTs. Andhra Pradesh, with 14.51 per cent Scheduled Caste population had the highest number of hostels, i.e. 1036 hostels constituting 26.46 per cent of the total hostels. Surprisingly enough, Haryana having as high as 18.88 per cent of the Scheduled Caste population had only two hostels in the State for the Scheduled Castes. The position remained nearly the same even after a decade. Andhra Pradesh had the maximum number of hostels followed by Maharashtra. Uttar Pradesh remained in a bad shape, as also Punjab, Himachal Pradesh and Haryana.

The shortage of hostel facilities is to be met by construction of new hostels, expansion of the existing hostel buildings, opening of new hostels in rented accommodation and providing alternate accommodation facilities to the SC/ST students to run their own mess. It is, however, experienced that indiscriminate opening of hostels does not help in proper utilization of the hostel facilities. In some places, the hostels are overcrowded to accommodate boarders over and above the specified strength, whereas in many cases the seats continue to be vacant due to shortage of the SC/ST candidates. A number of studies were conducted by the field offices of the Commission for the SC/ST in 1976-79 on the working of welfare hostels in Karnataka, Orissa, Rajasthan and Chandigarh. In Karnataka, out of 27 hostels visited during 1978, full strength was achieved only in eight hostels and in one hostel the strength exceeded the sanctioned strength. Shortfall in attaining the full strength was observed in 18 hostels accounting for 66.7 per cent of the total sample. In Orissa, it was acknowledged during 1977-78 that hostels were opened indiscriminately without keeping in view the local demands, and such hostel buildings were utilized for the purposes other than that for which those were constructed. These were being made use of either as classrooms, teachers' quarters, office rooms and for other purposes. In one hostel in Jaipur in Rajasthan, it was found in 1978-79 that only one-third of the sanctioned strength of the hostel could be achieved and the rest of the seats were lying vacant owing to non-availability of suitable candidates. In Chandigarh, it was found in 1976-77 that all the three hostels run by the S.G.G.S Khalsa College, Mohilpur, Guru Ravi Dass Sabha, Ludhiana and Guru Nanak National College for Women were lying vacant for want of suitable candidates. The findings of the above studies suggest that due care was not taken to assess the local requirements before the new hostels were constructed. The Commission for the SC/ST, therefore, recommended that district authorities should annually review the capacity of seats in the hostels for the SC/ST and rationalize the facilities in view of the demand at block/*tahsil* level. As regards girls' hostels it was suggested that care should be taken to ensure that hostel buildings were not used for purposes other than girls' hostels. These hostels should have compound walls as also attached wardens' quarters. As far as possible, location of girls' hostels should not be in forlorn and isolated places.

It is often argued that setting up of hostels exclusively for the SC/ST students leads to isolation of the weaker sections who are not afforded opportunity to mix with the students of other castes from the beginning of their career-making. The Study Team on Social Welfare and Welfare of Backward Classes (Renuka Ray Study Team) in their Report presented in July 1959 made recommendation that there should be no separate institutions, hostels and colonies exclusively for the Scheduled Castes and that in all general hostels, controlled and assisted by the Government, at least ten per cent seats should be reserved for the Scheduled Castes.

The Department of Social Welfare of the Government of India was in agreement with this recommendation. As a policy matter, some States have taken steps in this direction for intermingling of the SC/ST students with those belonging to other castes in hostels. In order to avoid segregation on community basis and to promoting social integration of students of different communities, all the denominational hostels run by the Social Welfare Department, Karnataka, have been converted to non-denominational ones and 25 per cent of the seats in Welfare hostels have been reserved for admission of non-SC/ST students. In case, sufficient number of students belonging to other castes are not available, the vacant seats are taken up by the SC/ST students. In Tamil Nadu, twenty per cent of the seats in Welfare hostels are reserved for the students of Backward Classes and five per cent for the Forward Class students. Similarly, in Kerala, in all the hostels run by the Directorate of Harijan Welfare and Tribal Welfare, ten per cent of the seats are reserved for admitting the students other than SC/ST. In Bihar, in the SC hostels, 85 per cent seats are reserved for SCs and 15 per cent for others. In Rajasthan, in the hostels set up for the SCs, STs, etc. sixty per cent of the seats are reserved for the backward classes, for whom the hostel is meant and ten per cent for the other backward classes excepting the TAD hostels which are meant exclusively for the STs. In Pondicherry, in the hostels meant exclusively for the SC/ST students, 20 per cent of the seats are reserved for students from other communities.

The Basumatari Committee on the Welfare of the SC and ST in their 17th Report presented on December 16, 1970 suggested that Government's administrative machinery should be geared up to ensure the benefits of hostels built and maintained at States expenditure for the SC/ST students are availed primarily by students belonging to such communities. The Committee also suggested that Government should also ensure that all general hostels constructed with financial assistance of the Governments at the Central and State levels or maintained by non-official agencies with grants given by the Government make suitable provision for the SC/ST students and that efforts were made to attract them in larger numbers.

In the light of these recommendations, the Government of India in the Ministry of Education and Youth Services under Memo No.

F. 19-6/71. T.5 dated February 5, 1971 asked all the State Governments-all Engineering Colleges and Polytechnic Institutions to make sure that the existing hostel facilities are made available to the SC/ST students in accordance with recommendation made by the Parliamentary Committee on the Welfare of the SC/ST and efforts made to attract them in larger number to these hostels. The Ministry of Education and Youth services in its Memo No. F. 16-6/70-U.I. dated February 27, 1971 addressed to all State Governments/UTs/all Universities/and the University Grants Commission asked them to implement the recommendation of the Parliamentary Committee that all general hostels built with funds made available by the Government at the Central and State levels or maintained by non-official agencies with grants given by the Government make suitable provision for the SC/ST students and that efforts are made to attract them in larger numbers.

In order to avoid segregation and instilling a sense of social equality amongst the SC/ST students by improving their intake in general hostels, it was recommended in the 21st report (1971-73) of the Commissioner of the SC/ST that 25 per cent seats should be reserved for the SC/ST students in all general hostels. The matter was also discussed in the eighth meeting of the High Power Committee on October 20, 1978 in which it was recommended that necessary steps should be taken to ensure that the facility of admission to hostels was not denied to the SC/ST students and it was recommended that there should be reservation for the SC/ST in respect of allotment of seats in these hostels. In pursuance of this recommendation, the Union Ministry of Home Affairs issued instructions in January 1979 to all States/UTs, that necessary steps should be taken to reserve accommodation for the SC/ST students in all general hostels run by them or, by Voluntary Organizations receiving grants-in-aid, in proportion to the population of these communities in the respective States, UTs and also to give them due weightage over and above this proportion in the light of their educational and economic backwardness. The University Grants Commission has also gave necessary instructions to all the institutions assisted by it to reserve 20 per cent of the seats in such hostels for students belonging to the SC/ST. The University Grants Commission also took decision that its assistance for construction of hostels in backward areas would be at the rate of 75 per cent of the total expenditure as against 50 per cent available for other areas. The response of the State Governments/Union Territory Administrations in this regard is encouraging. A good number of the State Governments/Union Territory Administrations have taken steps in accordance with the instructions issued by the Ministry of Home Affairs. Some State Governments/Union Territory Administrations have fixed a definite percentage of reservation in general hostels for the SC/ST students as indicated in Table.

Percentage of Seats Reserved in General Hostels for the SC/ST Students

Sl. No.	*State/UT*	*Percentage of Reservation for*		*Remarks*	*Source*
		SCs	*STs*		
1.	Andhra Pradesh	20	5		
2.	Assam	6.5	8.5 in plains 4.5 in hills	7 per cent seats are reserved for SCs and 10 per cent for STs in Plains and Hills, respectively, in the hostels run by voluntary organizations.	a
3.	Delhi	10		for both SCs and STs.	a
4.	Gujarat	15	5		a
5.	Karnataka	25		For both SCs and STs	a
6.	Madhya Pradesh	15	20		a
7.	Manipur	50 for SCs and STs in Central Valley district		More than 90 per cent pre-matric and post-matric students district in Govt. as well as in aided hostels in the Hills district are SCs and STs.	
8.	Orissa	10 for both SCs and STs			a
9.	Pondicherry			It is reported that adequate accommodation facilities are available for SC hostellers	
10.	Tamil Nadu	18 for both SCs and STs			a
11.	Uttar Pradesh	18	nil		a

12.	West Bengal	15	5		a
13.	Himachal Pradesh	15	7		b
14.	Kerala		25	3	c
15.	Tripura	29	15	In hostels attached to colleges	d
16.	Goa, Daman and Diu			All SC/ST students are provided hostel accommodation	e

Sources: (a) p. 199 of 27th report of the Commissioner for SC/ST.
(b) p. 24 of Educational Facilities to SC/ST, Ministry of Education, 1985.
(c) p. 28, *ibid.*
(d) p. 51, *ibid.*
(e) p. 62, *ibid.*

Students living in hostels run or subsidized by the State Governments are provided with facility like furnitures, bedding and linen, textbooks, stationery, library books, newspapers, indoor and outdoor games, hairacuts, fares or passes for commuting to their schools and colleges, clothes to wear and washing soap, etc. These are free of cost, in addition to free lodging and boarding with food as per nutritional standards well spelt out and defined. The actual provision of facilities, however, differ from State to State.

In spite of these impressive investments in the hostel scheme, not many of the hostellers seem to be satisfied with the facilities provided. According to a study, only 23 per cent of the school hostellers and 11 per cent of the college hostellers accept that they are "fully satisfied" with the hostel facilities provided. As many as 35 per cent of the school hostellers and 31 per cent of college hostellers are only "partly satisfied", and 38 per cent of the school hostellers and 54 per cent of the college hostellers say that they are not satisfied with the facilities.

In order to find out the source of their dissatisfaction, one is inclined to refer to the report submitted by the Basumatari Committee in December, 1970 to the Fourth Lok Sabha and to recall the many deficiencies in the functioning of hostels that were recorded therein. The Committee observed that some of the hostels were housed in totally unsuitable buildings and surroundings, and that the living conditions of the inmates were far from satisfactory. It complained about lack of interest and concern on the part of the people running these hostels. Besides describing the lack of facilities in the hostels, the Committee brought out the fact that the Scheduled Caste students were not always in sound financial position to reach out to hostel facilities. They are so poor that they did not even have the fare to reach the hostel for seeking admission.

But the position has not shown any significant improvement since the submission of the Basumatari Committee's report, rather it has declined further. The State Minister for Backward Class Welfare of Andhra Pradesh after visiting four Government-run hostels for backward classes and Scheduled Castes in Khammam district said on February 11, 1991 that the students lived in sub-human conditions. They had no plates or trays and food was served on floor. He saw many children eating in plastic glasses or rejected polythene sachets while keeping the pigs and dogs at bay. Similarly, most of the children he saw did not have a shirt and the half-pants and they were wearing were often in tallers. He said at least 50 children he met were suffering from different skin ailments and other diseases. At least two dozen children had ugly patches of scabies on the faces and bodies. The children told him that no doctor had visited them for months. They complained to the hostel warden many times but nothing happened. The Minister said that he was afraid that many children might be suffering from serious ailments but could not be sure unless a medical check-up was done. He said the latrines were overflowing and a foul smell pervaded the entire atmosphere. What was worse, he did not find any trace of studies for which purpose the children were kept in hostels. Since the wardens absconded for months, the children never cared about studies.

If this is the state of affairs in hostels in Andhra Pradesh which boasts of having established the largest number of hostels for backward classes in the entire country, the conditions of hostels in other States/UTs can very well be imagined.

Schemes for Coaching

In order to overcome difficulties at the earlier stages of education and improve the performance of the SC children in the schools and colleges as well as in medical, engineering and other professional courses, the scheme of providing preparatory training, remedial teaching and special coaching to SC/ST students have been operational in many States/UTs. Some State Government also provide coaching for State/Central Services competitive examinations. The details of the Schemes in vogue in various States/UTs are given below.

In Andhra Pradesh, coaching is given to students in classes VIII and X to prepare them for Board Examinations. The scheme is being implemented in 23 districts with 15 centres per destrict for class VIII and ten centres per district for class X. In Assam, grants of Rs. 1000 p.a. per school are given for coaching the SC/ST students at high school level. During 1984-85, 400 schools were provided with grants for this purpose.

In Gujarat, additional coaching is given in subjects such as science, English and Mathematics to backward class students studying in classes VIII to X and residing in grants-in-aid hostels. Three part-time teachers specializing in these subjects are engaged in each centre and are paid an honorarium of Rs. 50 p.m. for coaching the students. These classes are held thrice in each week. Each centre gets Rs.1650. In Haryana, remedial coaching is provided at selected centres for students in classes IX, X and XI. In Jammu and Kashmir, seven coaching centres are operational providing special coaching for preparing students for examinations at pre-matric level. In Karnataka, remedial coaching is given to all SC/ST students who have fallen in SSLC examination. In Kerala, remedial coaching is made available to students appearing in SSLC and college examinations.

In Maharashtra, the directorate of Tribal Development running a scheme of conducting coaching classes to teach students who are poor in English, mathematics and science at school level. In Manipur, remedial coaching is provided to the SC/ST students in mathematics and science from classes VI to X. In Orissa, remedial coaching is provided to students of Class X studying in Harijan and Tribal Welfare Department High Schools.

In Rajasthan, remedial coaching facilities in subjects of science and mathematics are made available to students at the SC/ST hostels.

In Sikkim, remedial pre-examination coaching is provided to students appearing in classes X and XII examinations. In Tamil Nadu, a scheme of remedial coaching in English, Mathematics and Science for about one and a half hours a day after the school hours was started for the benefit of SC/ST students in classes VIII to X in selected High/Higher Secondary Schools, numbering 500 in the year 1981-82. This scheme was extended to classes XI and XII from 1982-83 in about 300 schools where special coaching is given in English, mathematics, physics, chemistry, zoology, botany, commerce and accountancy. The heads of the institutions and teachers participating in the programmes are paid an honorarium of Rs. 50 p.m.

In Tripura, remedial coaching is available for the inmates of hostels in English and mathematics for Middle/Secondary/Higher Secondary examinations. In Uttar Pradesh, remedial coaching is given to students of classes X and XII in Science, English and Mathematics for the preparation of Board examinations. This scheme is being run in 28 districts. Pre-entrance examination for medical and engineering is also provided to the SC/ST students. In West Bengal, there are 385 schools with 1785 coaching units with the maximum intake capacity of ten SC/ST students per unit which provides remedial coaching to students studying in classes V to X. In Arunachal Pradesh, special coaching is arranged for students appearing in the Board examinations.

In Chandigarh, remedial coaching is provided to the SC children for Classes I to V. In Pondicherry, coaching facilities are provided to the SC students in middle and secondary level classes by appointment of qualified part-time teachers for a strength of minimum 50 Scheduled Castes students in a particular stage.

In Andhra Pradesh, remedial coaching was provided to degree and intermediate students in 519 degree and junior colleges during 1984-85. Spoken English in also taught to students coming from non-English medium schools.

In Gujarat, remedial coaching is provided in Medical and Engineering courses for the SC/ST students. The lecturers are paid an honorarium of Rs. 25 per lecture. Lectures are given thrice in a week. In Karnataka, in all Government colleges remedial coaching is provided to the SC/ST students. In the engineering and Polytechnic courses, the SC/ST students are given special coaching for the first six months to bring them upto the level of the rest of the students.

In Madhya Pradesh, remedial courses have been introduced in 15 colleges situated in tribal areas. In Engineering colleges and Polytechnics also, remedial coaching is given to the SC/ST students. Pre-examination coaching is given in hostels attached to higher secondary schools for appearing in Medical and Engineering courses. In Tamil Nadu, SC/ST students studying in degree courses in all Government and Aided Arts Colleges numbering about 190 are provided remedial coaching. For covering all the courses at degree level, these coaching classes are held for a period of not less than two months. A lump sum grant of Rs. 1000 is provided to each college for this purpose. Remedial coaching is also given to the SC students in engineering colleges. In Delhi, remedial coaching is made available in Engineering, IIT and Polytechnic courses.

In Andhra Pradesh, the coaching centre at Osmania University gives coaching for IAS and Allied Services. It is proposed to extend this facility for providing coaching for competitions like Staff Selection Commission, Andhra Pradesh Public Service Commission Examinations, Medical and Engineering Entrance Examinations, etc. The Assam Administrative College imparts coaching for competitive examinations to the SC students. In Bihar, the University of Ranchi has developed coaching centre for preparing the SC students for the All-India competitive examinations. In Gujarat, in pre-examination coaching, the SC candidates are given training for examinations conducted by the UPSC, Gujarat Public Services Commission, Gujarat Panchayat Services, Banks, etc. A stipend of Rs. 85 p.m. is paid to day scholars and Rs. 125 p.m. to those residing in hostels. The lecturers are paid an honorarium of Rs. 20 per lecture. These training courses are conducted for a period of two to three months.

There are three centres in Haryana which provide coaching for various competitive examinations. In Himachal Pradesh, coaching is imparted to the SC students at the H.P. Institute of Public Administration for HAS/IAS/pre-medical competitive examinations. In Karnataka, five pre-examination coaching centres are there for preparing students for various competitive examinations. In Kerala, three centres are providing pre-examination coaching for the SC students.

Pre-examination training centres at Imphal (Manipur) provides free coaching to all candidates including SC for All India Civil Service Examinations. In Meghalaya, pre-examination coaching for competitive examinations (IAS/Central Services) is given at North-Eastern Hill University for the SC students.

In Punjab, training is provided for Central/State Services Examinations in the Training Centre at Patiala. Training is also given in stenography to both unemployed and employed SCs. A stipend of Rs. 100 p.m. is given to those who are unemployed.

In Rajasthan, the State Government is running a pre-examination training centre for the SC candidates for All-India Civil Services Examinations. It has capacity for forty students. Free accommodation and coaching facilities are provided during the four months of training. A stipend of Rs. 150 p.m. is also given to the trainees.

In Chennai, coaching is given to the SC/ST candidates appearing for Group IV Services Examinations conducted by the Tamil Nadu Public Service Commission. Seventeen centres have been set up for this purpose. Pre-examination coaching for National

Defence Academy/Indian Military Academy Examination is given to the SC candidates in the Special Training Institute, Chennai.

In Uttar Pradesh, coaching is imparted for higher level competitive examinations like Civil Services Examinations/ Provincial Civil Services Examinations. In Pondicherry, pre-examination training is given to the SC students for appearing in different competitive examinations. In West Bengal, the Scheduled Castes and Tribes Welfare Directorate runs courses for preparing candidates from the SC communities intending to appear at competitive examinations for jobs. For the West Bengal Civil Services Examinations the Directorate is running two Pre-Examination Training Centres (PETC) located at Maulana Azad College, Calcutta and A.C. College, Jalpaiguri. It also conducts a PETC for Miscellaneous Services and Clerkship Examinations at Bikash Bhavan, Salt Lake. At Suffee Commercial College, Calcutta, the Directorate offers courses for typing and stenography.

Availability of Textbook

The distribution of free textbooks and even stationery to students is one of the incentives provided by the State Governments/Union Territory Administrations to attract children to school and to retain them there. In 1984-85, all States/UTs except Kerala, Manipur, Uttar Pradesh and Delhi had some scheme of making available free textbooks, stationery, etc., to the students including the SC students at different levels of school education. It is found out by the Fifth All India Educational Survey (1986) that 416,730 (56.54 per cent) schools covering all stages of school education have the provision of free textbooks to students. According to findings of this Survey, 33,524,152 students of all stages of school education are receiving benefit of this incentive scheme. Of these beneficiaries, 77.16 per cent are studying in rural schools and the remaining 22.84 per cent in urban schools. Among the beneficiaries 41.27 per cent are girls. Further, 24.82 per cent of the beneficiaries are from the Scheduled Castes, which together comes to 36.53 per cent of the total number of beneficiaries.

The position is indicated in Table.

Beneficiaries of Free Textbooks in 1986

Type of School	*No. of Schools*	*Number of beneficiaries SC*	*Others*
Primary	315,213 (59.62%)	5,159,161 (26.50%)	11,722,537 (60.22%)
Upper Primary	70,872 (50.98%)	1,888,652 (18.59%)	7,249,287 (71.36%)
Secondary	23,529 (44.77%)	932,323 (34.55%)	1,529,556 (56.69%)
Higher Secondary	7,116 (46.01%)	341,121 (28.43%)	777,219 (64.77%)
Total	416,730	8,321,157 (24.82%)	21,278,599 (63.47%)

Source: Fifth All India Educational Survey, pp. 183-85, 1986.

The scheme differs from State to State. In West Bengal, there is no upper income limit for the SC/ST students for availing of the Book Grant. The rates are as follows:

Class V	Rs. 20.00
Class VI	Rs. 50.00
Class VII to VIII	Rs. 150.00
Class IX	Rs. 200.00
Class X	Rs. 100.00

Free Uniform

It is a fact that the children from weaker sections of the society generally do not go to schools due to economic incapacity. One of the reasons is the lack of suitable clothing for going to school. Though it is an uneasy task to provide a school uniform to every student, all States/UTs except Kerala, Manipur, Mizoram, Nagaland, Punjab, Sikkim, Uttar Pradesh and Lakshadweep have attempted to provide free uniform at least in a limited number of schools.

The Fifth All India Educational Survey (1986) reveals that out of 735,771 schools in the country, 308,201 (41.89 per cent) covering all the stages of education have some scheme or the other for providing the incentive of free uniform to students. As shown during the Fifth Survey, 16,067,242 students are being benefited by this incentive scheme at all stages of school education. Of all the beneficiaries, 77.44 per cent are studying in rural schools and 22.56 per cent in urban schools. Among these beneficiaries, 33.04 per cent are the Scheduled Castes. Further, among the beneficiaries, 49.98 per cent are girls.

The number of beneficiaries in different stages of school education is indicated in Table.

Beneficiaries of Free Uniform in 1986

Type of School	*No. of Schools*	*Number of beneficiaries*	
		SC	*Others*
Primary	247,588 (46.83%)	3,774,269 (36.06%)	5,435,633 (51.94%)
Upper Primary	48,050 (34.56%)	1,068,706 (25.62%)	2,578,648 (61.83%)
Secondary	9,548 (18.17%)	294,152 (33.87%)	504,835 (58.12%)
Higher Secondary	3,015 (19.50%)	172,799 (30.40%)	373,774 (66.81%)
Total	308,021	5,309,926 (33.04%)	8,892,890 (55.36%)

Source: Fifth All-India Educational Survey, pp. 180-183, 1986.

Free Meals

Schemes to provide mid-day meals for school children have a positive impact not only on nutrition of the child but also on school attendance. Started in 1982 by the M.G. Ramachandran regime, the Tamil Nadu Government's pioneering programme on nutrition of the child in socially disadvantaged communities in rural and urban areas has not only won the acclaim of international agencies like the UNICEF and World Bank, but also attracted other States attention to launch similar programmes to bring children to schools and retain them there. All State Governments except Bihar, Gujarat, Jammu and Kashmir, Kerala, Maharashtra, Manipur, Mizoram, Nagaland and Uttar Pradesh have been running mid-day meals scheme in schools for the students including the SC students. The Fifth All India Educational Survey (1986) shows that out of 735,771 schools in the country, 187,016 (25.42 per cent) covering all the stages of school education have the provision of mid-day meals for children. As per the finding of the Survey, of the 22,553,505 beneficiaries 78.41 per cent are studying in rural areas. Among the beneficiaries, 59.02 per cent are boys and 40.98 per cent are girls. 20.05 per cent of the beneficiaries are the Scheduled Castes, which together makeup 32.86 per cent of the beneficiaries.

The number of beneficiaries in different stages of school education is given in Table.

The Working Group on Development and Welfare of the Scheduled Castes during the Eighth Five-Year Plan recommended that mid-day meals should become compulsory in the school education system to ensure full enrolment and continued attendance of the SC children, particularly of girls from the community. As primary education is highly emphasized, the Government of India has decided to extend this scheme in phases from the financial year 1995-96 to improve enrolment, attendance and retention of school children in primary schools. The first Centrally Sponsored mid-day meal programme was launched on August 15, 1995 in a Government school near Delhi under the National Programme of Nutritional Support to Primary Education (NPNSPE) as part of the Centre's ambitious social welfare programme. The programme was projected to cost Rs. 610 crores in 1995-96, Rs. 1474 crores in 1996-97 and Rs. 2226 crores in 1997-98.

Number of Beneficiaries in Different Stages of School and Education

Type of School	*No. of Schools*	*Number of beneficiaries SC*	*Others*
Primary	147,647 (27.92%)	2,997,849 (21.93%)	8,394,675 (61.41%)
Upper Primary	33,757 (24.84%)	1,077,902 (15.24%)	5,448,007 (77.02%)
Secondary	3,784 (7.20%)	237,101 (23.84%)	708,563 (71.24%)
Higher Secondary	1,824 (11.82%)	208,347 (25.54%)	592,721 (72.64%)
Total	187,016	4,521,199 (20.05%)	15,143,966 (67.14%)

Source: Fifth All-India Educational Survey, pp. 178-80, 1986, Vol. I.

These Central and Centrally Sponsored Schemes and the Schemes in the State Sector, detailed above, primarily target at creating a congenial atmosphere for promotion and development of education for such weaker sections of population known as Scheduled Castes so that they do not remain in a disadvantageous position in comparison to other sections in the matter of availing educational opportunities. So far, governments have clearly stressed upon granting financial and material assistance to the Scheduled Castes for attracting them towards education. In quantitative terms, the range of schemes evolved and implemented for the benefit of the Scheduled Castes appear doubtlessly impressive. But, considering the magnitude of the problem of bringing these entire communities within the fold of education, these measures seem to have touched only a fringe of the problem.There are several shortcomings in the nature and *modus operandi* of these schemes, like lack of financial or material assistance, i.e. scholarships, stipends, book grants, uniform or mid-day meals, delay in grants of stipends/scholarships, book grants or books, stationery and equipments etc. cumbersome and bureaucratic procedures followed in granting financial assistance, poor hostel facilities, lack of awareness of the facilities, etc.

In theory, any Scheduled Caste child, if he or she wishes to pursue higher studies, can do so without any let or hindrance. Seats are reserved for him or her at all levels of education including technical and professional education. A specific number of fellowships/overseas scholarships are also available to him. There are about 5000 hostels for backward class and another 3500 SC girls'/boys' hostels for their free boarding and lodging, in addition to other ancillary facilities including free food, and if one wants, one can get accommodation in any general hostel where seats are reserved. There are provisions for stipends as well as free special coaching in specific subjects for preparing them for competitive services examinations. A set of books for Medical /Engineering/ Agriculture/Polytechnic courses is provided to each SC student of such courses. Apart from freeships in educational institutions, the post-matric scholarships scheme covers almost all the SC students in post-matric stage of education. About 12.6 lakh SC students were covered by the post-matric scholarships scheme in 1992-93 and the number of beneficiaries in 1996-97 was more than 15 lakh. Compared to the importance given to the post-matric education of the SC children, the pre-matric education did not receive equal importance and attention from the Planners and Administrators.

Though almost all the States/UTs grant pre-matric scholarships to the SC children under different schemes and there are special schemes for children of those engaged in unclean occupations and for girls of indigent SC families in pre-matric stage, get the quantum of financial assistance in pre-matric stage of education is grossly inadequate and hence the coverage is highly inadequate. As in the case of post-matric scholarships scheme sometimes the instalment may not be received even till the middle of the session and in some cases at the fag end of the session. As a result, only those who can afford or get some support from the voluntary organizations can continue their education. While those who do not have such a benefit have to go without education even though they are eligible. The policy of attaching higher weightage to post-matric education than pre-matric education has been anomalous and akin to the act of drawing a cart by putting it before the horse. It is here that the major loophole lies and is the reason why bulk of the students belonging to the Scheduled Castes not being able to move up the education ladder. As this creates a situation in which those students who have been able to cross the initial hurdle at the primary and secondary level are able to move up with ease but those who fail to cross the first hurdle are doomed for the life. The proposal to include all the children of 6-11 year age group in the scheme should be given a serious thought, as it is at this crucial age that incentives are needed to compensate the opportunity costs and to attract the students to school. One, however, feels that if the constitutional obligation of providing free compulsory elementary education to all children up to the age of 14 was scrupulously and meticulously followed, not only would illiteracy have been completely erased by this time but other concomitant advantages like, fall in the rate of growth in population, better living conditions, etc., would have ensured, making the country richer. It is generally alleged that the schemes of financial assistance have failed to live up to the expectations of helping the poorer sections of the Scheduled Castes.

The financial concessions and other facilities have been availed of, more by the privileged groups amongst the Scheduled Caste communities, than the poorer and needy as the quantum of assistance has seldom been sufficient enough to induce the 'really poor' to go in for education. It is held that free tuition does not mean free education to the majority of SC as the opportunity cost of education for poorer sections is much higher than the well-to-do groups. It has been rightly stated that equal access for unequal groups is not true equality.

There has been a large scale expansion of access to schooling but the quality of inputs and management of rural schools leaves much to be desired. This has led to rural-urban differentials which is manifested in regional inequalities. All steps need be taken to ensure that the quality of rural schooling is the same as that of urban schools and those who are enrolled are able to complete the required cycle of education without frequent repetitions.

It will not be right to assume that the mere provision of educational facilities, financial and other incentives would automatically ensure utilization of these benefits. Various studies indicate that such facilities are availed of only by the 'elite' section of the Scheduled Caste population and these benefits have failed to trickle down to the needy masses who do not even know what they are entitled to. The real problem lies in bringing this vast deprived groups within the fold of education and ensure that they are equally benefited, if not more.

7

Societal Factors

The story of the social origin of the Dalits or what is traditionally known as *sudras* or the untouchables is age old. Hindu epics like *Dharmashastras* and *Smritis* dealing with the origin of *varna* system, the *Rigveda* is the oldest one which tells us that all the four varnas, i.e. Brahmin, Kshatriya, Vaishya and Sudra are originated from the different limbs of the Almighty. According to the *Rigveda* the origin of *Brahmin* is supposed to be from the mouth, *Kshatriya* from the arms, *Vaishya* from the chest and *Sudra* from the feet of the Almighty. According to *Gita* the origin is supposed to be done by the Creator himself on the basis of *Guna* (quality) and the *Karma* (action). Ancient epics make it clear that the untouchables owe their origin in the traditional *varna* and caste system. It can, therefore, be noted that the untouchables and the untouchability are by-products of Hindu caste system. According to the code of Manu, all those who were born out of the pratiloma marriage were assigned the lowest rank in the *varna* hierarchy.

Ghurye (1961) notes that when the Indo-Aryans came over to India and established their social organization, they made four-fold division. The original Indians were discarded from their social, cultural and religious context of social organization and were assigned the fourth and the bottom status in the *varna* hierarchy which constituted the *sudra varna*. He further divides sudras into two groups viz., (i) clean *sudras* and (ii) unclean *sudras*. These unclean *sudras* were known as untouchables and were assigned such degraded and spiteful tasks as sweeping, scavenging, removal of the skin of dead animals. They also used to eat leaf, pork and other such things. Their entry to religious places of their movement on the common roads or places generally used by the upper three varnas, were strictly prohibited on account of their being polluted. Their sheer touch or even shadow polluted a *Brahmin* or *Kshatriya* or a *Vaishya.* In this way the practice of untouchability contained to prevail as they were below the level of ritual purity. In the medieval period due to the Mughal invasion, the then Brahmin priests fortified the caste system with socially unelastic taboos, customs and norms in order to maintain their religious and racial purity and pollution became rigid and untouchability became a mythical reality with practical implications. According to Majumdar (1958) the untouchable castes are those who suffer from different social and political disabilities, many of which are traditionally prescribed and socially forced by higher castes.

Hutton has also given a similar view. During the age of *Dharmashastra,* the idea of purity and pollution became so stiff that it was not even thought in dreams by a higher caste to maintain any kind of social contact with the untouchables or low castes.

During 800 B.C. the idea of religious purity was quite clear in practice which was not only applied to *Chandals* or the untouchables but also on the fourth *varna.* Kautilya also acknowledges the views of *Dharmashastras* in a similar way. According to *Manusmriti,* the untouchables had not only religious and cultural disabilities but they were simultaneously barred from possessing wealth since a wealthy *sudra* could torture a Brahmin. From the above description it is clear that the sudras did not suffer only from the religious, cultural and educational disabilities but they were posed with economic disabilities as such. Thus, as regards the genesis of the Dalits or as commonly called the untouchables, there is a lot of discussion about them in the traditional Hindu epics and the shastras. Particularly the early antiquarians and the *Dharmashastra* writers have explained their origin in their writings by the names of *Chandals, Svapachas* and *Mritapas.* In the *Chhandoyogyopanishad* there is a description of *Chandal* denoting a degraded group of humanity and is ranked alongside cat and dog, which according to Ghurye formed the fifth order of the varna hierarchy, i.e., even below that of *sudra,* who represented the fourth and bottom of the hierarchy. The *Chandals* according to Dharmasutra writers, were the progeny of the most hated of the reverse order of mixed unions; that of a Brahmin female with a Sudra male. Kautilya, the practical administrator, agrees that if the *chandals* treat themselves as *sudras,* he has no objection, but he too considers the *chandals* so low that he advises all other mixed castes to avoid mixing with chandals. It is interesting to note that he accommodates the sons born of miscogenation in his law of in heritance. Similarly Baudhayan and Vashistha mention a degraded caste called *Svapaka.* Baudhayana once declares the group to have come into being from the union of an Ambashtha male with a Brahmin female, while at another place he attributes it to the union of an Ugra male with a Kshatriya female. Manu makes Svapaka the progency of Kshatriya male and an Ugra female i.e. he gives a derivation which is just the opposite of Baudhayana's second derivation. It should be noted here that Manu in his description uses the term "Svapacha" in place of "Svapaka" in describing its occupation as hangman or caneworker. Kautilya also mentions the groups as Svapaka and derives it from the union of an Ugra male and a Rshatriya female. In his derivation in respect of progency he, thus, agrees with Baudhayana. Similarly Patanjali, the great grammarian who lived about 150 B.C. and who is generally considered to be a meticulous observer of contemporary usage, has given us his grammatical explanation for the female of Svapacha group being called a "Svapacha" and not "Svapachi". What exactly were the avocation and status of a Svapacha in Patanjali's time we do not know Patanjali further talks of "Mritapas" in combination with "chandals". While Kautilya rigorously excluded *Chandals* from all social contacts, he does not prescribe similar treatment with Svapachas. But Manu is very explicit and insistent that the *Svapachas* and *Chandals* should be grouped together. He prescribes them residence outside the village, and the use of the shrouds of corpses as their clothing, broken, pots for meals, iron for ornaments and dogs and donkeys for their wealth. They were to be the hangman who were denied entry in the villages and towns during day time. There was restriction that the food vessels used by

Chandals, Mritapas and *Svapachas* should not be used by others, as there was no means to purify them. They were the "apapatras".

Thus, on the basis of above description of the *Dharmasastras* and *Smritis,* it is clear that there were several groups of people called Chandals, Svapachas and Mritapas formed the fifth order of the hierarchy, that is, below sudras and who slowly and surely declined in their social position between the time of Panini and that of Manu. In the age of Manu their social and cultural position deteriorated beyond description and were looked upon as vile specimens of humanity. In Buddhist birth stories called *Jatakas,* we find again the reference of Chandals as the lower caste. Before 800 B.C. as has already been mentioned, we find the idea of ceremonial purity almost full-fledged and even operative with regard not only the despised and degraded group of people called Chandals but also the fourth order of society, the sudras.

On the basis of the above description it can be concluded that there existed many groups of sudras and even of those who were below the sudras and were socially unseeable and untouchable, and the ideas of purity whether occupational or ceremonial which were found to have been a factor in the genesis of caste are the very soul of the idea and practice of untouchability. Although no consensus of opinion is found about the progeny of these groups, it is evident from the above description that they were the most despised groups of humanity, who were later treated into one order of the untouchables which included the *sudras* also and are presently known as Dalits which is a collective name for all such so called untouchable classes bearing different sub-castes names. Thus, the historical survey reveals that the practice of untouchability started in the Vedic period and became more rigid during the *Manusmriti* and the mediaeval period. In the time of Manu the untouchables were not only treated as out-castes but they were not even allowed entry into villages. It is surprising to note here how paradoxical ideas and social sanctions are inherent in ancient Hindu epics about the untouchables. On the one hand, according to *Manusmriti* they are prohibited from all social, cultural, religious and economic activities because they are born in the families below ritual rank and caste purity, while on the other hand the *Yagyabablkyasmriti* approves that every one is born *Sudra* by birth and becomes purified by sacraments and that a *sudra* can also be regarded equally important as *Brahmin, Kshatriya* and *Vaisya.* Jones points out that as a food grain which is grown out in a fertile soil and is, therefore, good in all respects, so also a man who is born out of respected parents can only be entitled to utilize all the institutions of the twice borns. It clarifies how Manu approves and gives social sanctions to the social and economic exploitation of the Sudras. And more so by the doctrine of "Rarma" their scope for social thinking and doing have been confined since the present according to the doctrine of "Karma" is the result of the past deeds and therefore, one should abide by his duties of his varna, (*Varna* Dharma), assigned to him for getting a good future life. The activities beyond the *Varna* Dharma are despised in his world according to Karma theory. Therefore a sudra cannot undertake the professions and activities of upper varnas to improve his socio-cultural conditions which are traditionally assigned to twice borns only. In such a scenario a sociological enigma arises before the social scientists as to how can the sudras or the untouchables improve their socio-economic and cultural statuses in a society like India whose traditional seat of action is based on fatalism *Karmabad,* birth and re-birth and transcendentalism. Of course, when we trace the age old history of culture in our country, we find that there were avenues and ways for social and occupational mobility during Rigvedic period and even in the period of *Mahabharat* but it was confined to *Brahmin, Kshatriya* and *Vaisya varnas* only. This concession for the change of occupation, status and even inter varna marriage was a special sanction to those three *varnas.* The *Sudras* were strictly prohibited from such concessions.

From the above description it is evident that the origin of untouchability lies in the traditional varna and the caste systems. The social scientists do not hold consensus of opinion about the origin of untouchability. It is still an ambiguous matter. Thus, whatever, be the base of untouchability, whether racial and cultural according to Majumdar of social and religious according to Hutton, it is clear in itself that untouchability originated due to the strict observance and long prevalence of the taboos, customs and rigid hierarchical gradiation of the caste system. In this connection Srinivas (1956) notes that untouchability is more than just a ritual rank and the pollution it carries, there is a congruence of economic, ritual and political statuses in the case of Harijans.

Similarly according to Ambedkar (1948) who is known as a giant ghost of untouchability, this type of untouchability among the Hindus stands in a class by itself. There is nothing that can make the untouchables pure... They are born impure, they are impure while they live, they have the death of impure and they give birth to children who are born with the stigma of untouchability offered to them.

From the above description it is evident that there is no scientific base of untouchability. Its origin is irrational, non-social and tyrannical. Therefore, it is a sin of Hindu religion and culture. Towards the end of the nineteenth century the social conditions of the untouchables became so grave that they had to be totally deprived of the touch of Hindu social organization. The *savarna* Hindus rejected them to be the members of Hindu society. As a result of the so-called uprooted, dejected and tyrannically oppressed untouchables began their conversion into Christianity and Islam and in doing so, thousands and thousands of untouchables got relief in Christianity and Islam where they felt solace of mind, co-operation of catholic generosity and Islamic brotherhood. It seems that for the hundreds of years they have suffered from inferiority and lack of co-operation from the higher Hindus and were forced to live a life of downtrodden, depressed or what in Marathi convention is called the 'Dalit Panthers.' It is clear from the historical tradition of social attitude to untouchables. Thus, to the untouchables, Hinduism seemed to be a veritable chamber of horrors. The sanctity and infallibility of the *Vedas Smritis* and *Shastras,* the iron law of caste, the disgusting doctrine of *Karma* and the irrational sanction of ascribed status by birth are to untouchables the veritable instruments which Hindu social organization has forged to torture them. These very instruments which have mutilated, blasted and blighted the life of these downtrodden castes are the real reasons for the untold social and economic miseries of the untouchables.

During British rule, Dalits were known as 'depressed class' and by this name an organization of them was established by

Ambedkar who became the champion for the cause of the untouchables. During 1931 the Census Commission of India, employed use of term 'Exterior Caste' for them, when some people raised objection to call them the depressed class. Hutton (1913) has also made use of word exterior caste for the untouchables in his book. When Mahatma Gandhi came in the field of liberation movement, he put strong protest against such social discrimination for them and was not willing on any ground to achieve freedom by depriving scheduled castes of their social, economic and cultural advantages of society. As a result, of his efforts, all of the then social and political reformers and workers accepted them as members of Hindu social organization. In 1929 the British Government held three Round Table Conference to discuss the problems of a new constitution and a system of Government for India. Ambedkar was nominated as representative of the depressed classes and attended all the three conferences. The Congress and Gandhiji, however, chose to boycot the first conference in 1930 but agreed to attend the second in 1931. It was in the second conference that bitter and life-long enemity between Gandhiji and Ambedkar first developed. Thus, Gandhi's philosophy and his programme for the removal of untouchability were understandably an anathema to Ambedkar. For him the question of political safeguards for untouchables came first. He felt that the upper castes had made and kept the untouchables a community separate and unequal from other castes and that in reality they did not form part of the Hindu community. Unlike Gandhi, he saw no possibility that the untouchables would either be assimilated into Hindu community or be granted rights equal to those of upper caste Hindus. Therefore, he stressed that separate elections alone would protect the untouchables from upper caste dominance and disenfranchisement. The result of this conflict was that from that time of Round Table Conference until Gandhiji's death Ambedkar considered the Mahatma an enemy, not a liberator of the untouchables. In 1935 St. Simon Commission was set up which first used the word "scheduled caste" to refer to this section of Hindu society. The word scheduled caste, thus, is a collective term to refer to all the untouchable castes. And, all the untouchable castes belonging to different states of the country put under this category were accepted by Indian Constitution in 1950. Ghurye (1961) constitutionally defines scheduled castes as those groups whose names are included in the Scheduled Castes Order in force for the time being. According to article 341 of the Indian Constitution, there is a provision for the President of India that he after discussion with the governors of all states in this he would declare the list of the scheduled castes of each state. Mahatma Gandhi, in an attempt to attach more prestige and respect introduced them as 'Harijan' which literally means the son of God. As regards the number of scheduled castes in India, we find nearly five hundred of castes in different states known by their different caste names, who are on the list of scheduled caste. In Uttar Pradesh alone there are 66 castes. But prominent among these known as scheduled castes, is a larger group of castes known as *Chamar* (Camar). The word Camar is derived from the Sanskrit *Charmakara* which literally means leather worker.

During Rigvedic times, the leather workers do not appear to be an object of approbrium and, indeed their services were of great importance to the warriors of those days. In the ancient Indian epic, the *Mahabharat*, the *chamar* was the maker of shields, breast plates and body armour, as well as of drums and various parts of chariots. Many mythical and legendary conceptions have been put forth to explain the social origin of the *chamars*, though none has been established.

It is said that chamars are the off-springs of the mixed intercaste marriages, or the despised and menial occupations of leather tanning relegated them to the periferies of respectable society. A legendary tale goes that they are part of a race conquered by Indo-Aryans. At most, there appears to be reason to believe that the *chamars* are a heterogenuous group of people who have received from time to time recruits from castes higher up in the caste hierarchy. Similarly Crooke observes that mythical accounts of chamar origin match the ocean sands for number and variety. For example, there is a legend of five brothers. While on a walk, five Brahmins brothers stumbled upon the carcass of a dead cow. Four of them walked on, but the fifth stopped and pulled the carcass off the road. For this act, his brothers ex-communicated him and ever after it became his lot and that of his descendants, the *chamars*, to remove polluted and polluting dead cattle.

Thus, the position of *chamars* as well as the other scheduled castes specially *Dhobi, Dharkar, Dusadh, Dom* and various others in India is very low indeed. In the villages they work as menials for some traditional payment of food grains and clothes. They were, and in some places still are, subject to forced labour, are landless recently have had little hope of improving their impoverished condition. The traditional occupations assigned to them are tanning hides, making shoes and working as farm labourers removing the carcass of dead cattle which they eat (*chamars*) washing of dirty clothes (*Dhobis*), cattle rearing and working on the farm (*Dusadhs* and *Dharkars*) wood gathering and vegetation (*Passis* and *Khatiks*) and so on.

Since leather is considered a polluting object and beaf is the most polluting of foods, the *chamars* who engage in such acts, and by association all other chamars, became polluted. Because of this pollution *chamars* are generally forced to live on the periphery of a village or in separate hamlets.

Lillington (1913, 351) quotes a proverb about *chamars*, who are "supposed" to be dark in complexion, while the upper castes (The Brahmin specially) are "supposed" to be fair in complexion.

Karia Brahman, Gora Chamar.
Inke Saath na utariye Par.

It means that if the Brahmin be black, if the chamar be fair, let the wise beware, if cross the river he dare. The meaning is that a fair skinned Chamar is such a rarity that something must be wrong and an upper caste person ought to be on his guard.

A similar description of colour is mentioned in *Puranas* and *Manu Smriti* regarding the four *varnas*, i.e. *Brahmin* to be represented by red complexion, *Kshatriya* by white, *Vaishya* by yellow and *Sudra* by dark. But to the present situation, in the study of the scheduled castes of Varanasi the above proverbial conception seems presently irrational and baseless as a large number of scheduled castes are fair skinned having a good personality traits, highly educated and well placed in manners and style of life are observed.

As regards the eradication of untouchability and amelioration of the conditions of Scheduled Castes, it can be described under three stages. At first stage the untouchables began their movement in South regarding their entry into temples in Travancore in 1924. The leader of this initial phase of movement was Jyotiba Phule of Poona. After that Shashi Bandopadhyay and V.R. Sinde started the reform movement and set up a commission of depressed classes in Bombay. Later on the insatiable greed for emancipation of scheduled castes was evoked in Ambedkar who in order to consolidate and nationalise his leadership championed the cause of the scheduled castes unto the last and an All India Depressed Class Federation was formed under his patronage in 1942. In this way, the first attempt of movement to achieve religious rights to enter the temple and other religious places came to be launched in Travancore in 1924.

In the second stage, attempts made by the *savarna* Hindus can be mentioned. In this direction the reform movements for annihilation of caste system and removal of untouchability made by the Arya Samaj in U.P., *Brahmo Samaj* in Bengal and *Prarthna Samaj* in Bombay were significant. The Ramkrishna Mission also rendered vulnerable services. These missions tried to uplift the socio-economic conditions on the basis of individual freedom and equality, as a result of which many of the social disabilities were removed from Hindu society and the untouchables got the scope for their education in government schools, entrance to temples and use of the public properties and amenities—such as wells, ponds, roads, etc. In this connection, many of the social reformers, thinkers, poets and educationists like Ramanand, Kabeer, Tulsi, Raidas, Dadu, Namdeo were active in discarding the practice of untouchability. Other noted thinkers and educationists like Rabindranath Tagore, Ishwar Chandra Vidhyasagar, Gokhale and many others were bearing the torch of social reform.

At the third stage, the work and services of *Harijan Sevak Sangh* and Mahatma Gandhi can be mentioned. Gandhi being inspired with the zeal of *Swaraj*, launched the Harijan reform movement in an effort to improve their lot by evoking a consciousness and unity in the diversified socio-cultural climate of Indian society.

Similarly the Congress Governments of different provinces also began a planned movement to ameliorate their conditions in 1937. After independence the Government of India made certain provisions and rules in the Constitution to remove the practice of untouchability and the disabilities of the scheduled castes and consequently Untouchability Offences Act (1955) and the caste Disabilities Removal Act (1955) were passed according to which any form of caste discrimination and practice of untouchability in any form is subject to judicial punishment.

Educational Growth

Scheduled Castes in Indian Population represent a sizable chunk as there has been a rapid growth in their population in recent years. According to Census of India, 1981, the total number of the members of scheduled castes is 8,24,80,251 out of the total population of 68,39,97,512 which constitutes above one-seventh of the total population. Population of the country, in general, and that of scheduled castes, in particular, has enormously increased. According to 1981 census, the State (Uttar Pradesh) has 11,08,85,874 persons belonging to scheduled castes out of the total scheduled castes population of 1,90,95,413. It reveals that it constitutes 23.2 per cent of the total scheduled castes population. The percentage of scheduled caste population to total population in India is 12.20. In comparison, the percentage of the scheduled caste population in total population in U.P. is 17.22. It clearly shows that every fifth person in the state is a scheduled caste person. This ratio is much higher in comparison to their population at the national level where it is above one-seventh.

As we have already discussed in the preceding pages that there are around five hundred scheduled castes in different states of India enlisted on the order of scheduled castes. In U.P. alone there are 66 scheduled castes. The *Chamars* are in majority and most common among them. As a group, the *Chamars* are most numerous in North India, specially in the States of Uttar Pradesh, Punjab and Bihar. Same is the case in south, specially in Maharashtra, Mysore and Andhra.

The Census of 1901 showed them to be numerically the largest group of castes in the former North-Western provinces and Oudh, while the Brahmins ranked second (India: Census Commission, 1902: 180-229). The Census of 1961 and that of 1971 also maintained *Chamars* as the largest group among the scheduled castes. There are numerous cases (*Jati*) of *Chamars* the Census of 1891 listed 1156 of them (Briggs, 1920:21). Other major groups who come next are *Dhobi, Dom, Passi, Dusadh, Dharkar* and *Khatik* who are in large majorities compared to other scheduled castes all over the country.

As regards the growth of education among the scheduled castes it can be stated that the traditionally rigid hierarchy of *varna* and caste systems did not assign any importance to their educational achievement and learning. They had nothing to do with education, religion and rituals in society. It was during the British period and after independence that modern education open up to all irrespective of caste, creed and colour differences. Initial efforts at spreading modern education in India were made by the non-official agencies such as missionaries, private societies and individuals. But it was not a systematic approach to provide educational opportunities to Dalit students. The scheduled castes were not given admission even in state-owned institution. After a lot of consideration, the government school in the Presidency of Bengal having the matter discussed with the Court of Directors announced that the educational institutions of government department would provide equal opportunities to all the citizens irrespective of any social discrimination. In this way, during the British rule in India some concrete work started between 1813-1816 under the supervision of the East India Company and Lord Macaulay began with the Herculian task of organizing modern eduation system in India whose purpose would be to educate Indian masses making any distinction on the basis of caste, so that the required knowledge of science and technology be spread in society. It should be observed that the traditional education of India was indigenous in nature and was mainly based on religious literatures. The modern education had objective to impart the knowledge of science, technology, religion and philosophy to improve the social conditions of society. But since there were no special provisions for providing educational facilities to the scheduled castes, their number in schools and colleges were very few and they were suffered social discrimination as the children of high castes being conscious of their caste status, did not want to sit together on equal terms with the children of low castes.

It was only after independence that the development of education among the scheduled castes found a firm declaration in the Constitution of India by abolishing untouchability. The Untouchability (Offences) Act of 1955 (Amended in 1976 as Protection of Civil Rights and Other Provisions Act) provides punitive measures against the practice of untouchability and discrimination in any form and the Constitution lays down the goal of establishment a society based on equality, liberty and secularity. In Article 29 of the Constitution, the provision was made to eliminate discrimination based on caste, creed or colour in any government aided schools. Similarly Article 16 is devoted to special reservations regarding educational facilities of scheduled castes. Thus the facilities regarding free education, books, and boarding were provided to attract and facilitate the rising number of the scheduled castes. The egalitarian outlook and a 'common culture' presented by the educational institutions has created a necessary precondition for the increasing enrolment of students of all sections of society in general and that of scheduled castes in particular.

The increasing number of scheduled castes in educational institutions has also subsequently led to an increasing literacy rate among them.

Traditional Gap

The Hindu society has been so much a rigid system of ascriptive hierarchy with the polarity principles of pollution and ritual purity that a lot of social and cultural inequalities were inherently built in society which led specially the "low" castes to be the subject of torture, oppression and all sorts of exploitation by the higher caste Hindus. It evidence can be found in the restrictions of social, cultural, economic and political spheres of activities approved by the taboos and customs of caste system for the low caste people. The hierarchical gradation projected such a structural configuration of caste system in which the best recognized position was that of Brahmins on the top and that of *Sudras* (now the scheduled castes) on the bottom and by this way the amount of community feelings has been restricted and that the citizens owed moral allegiance first to their caste rather than to the society as a whole which the segmental division connotes. In the middle region of the hierarchy the intermediate classes profess to think that their caste is better than their neighbours. The restrictions on feeding and social intercourse on occupation and marriage and so the civil and religious disabilities meant specially for the scheduled castes (*Sudras*) and the special privileges and sanctions for the higher castes. In different parts of the country, specially in south, the *Sudras* were forced to live outside the village. In Maharashtra, Madras, Andhra, Travancore and Gujarat, the untouchables were prohibited from walking on the roads, entering the temples and such other places. The *Mahars* and *Mang* (a sub-caste of *Chamar*) had to hang over earthen Pan within their neck in which to spit, otherwise their spit on roads will pollute a Brahmin or Kshatriya when touched with their feet. They had also to affix a thorny branch behind their back in Maharashtra and Gujarat while walking on roads so that their foot-prints may be wiped off by that otherwise this will pollute the higher castes when touched with their feet. Thus, we see that the cruel and iron law of caste system prescribed such a blend of paradoxical situations of inequalities, which restricted the *Sudras* from social, economic, educational, cultural and religious fields of activities on the one hand, while encouraged privileges and monopoly of the higher caste Hindus in such fields on the other hand.

To sum up, it can be said that the traditional social order is so replete with inequalities that it did not impart any humanitarian rights to the scheduled castes.

It would be useful to discuss here the major areas of disabilities which led to create the broad gap of inequalities in the traditional social system of Indian society as it has been already frequently discussed. The most significant of all disabilities, were the social disabilities, traditionally prescribed to scheduled castes, leading to restriction on their social contacts and relations with higher castes, use of the public properties such as wells, roads, ponds, etc. and in the spheres of housing, education, recreation, entrance into schools. The other was the economic disabilities banning scheduled castes (the *Sudras*) from entering into higher occupations, possession of wealth and landed property. This led to their economic exploitation by the high castes as they were not given a chance to exercise their skill and efficiency in the handling of neat, clean and fair occupations generally occupied by the higher castes, even if they be more intelligent and efficient than them. Hence it has rebuked and abused the dignity of labour and efficiency.

The third major area of disabilities leading towards social inequalities was that of religious sphere. *Sudras* were strictly prohibited from making entrance to religious places and temples, touching of the religious books and reciting of the religious hymns usually made by the higher Hindus. They were not allowed even to pray before the idols of deities or God heads as they were considered equals of cats and dogs and treated as social excrements of Hindu social system. They were not allowed to observe any ritual rites. Thus, they were merely destined to degraded, despised and do menial tasks in society. The most in human disabilities imposed on them were their exemption from political participation, exercise of enfranchisement and restriction from entering political spheres of activities which caused the scheduled castes ultimately to revolt against the hierarchy of caste system and to overthrow Hinduism. In doing so, history took a serious turn during the first quarter of the 20th century when Ambedkar jumped into the social arena as a 'culture hero' of the scheduled castes to trample down the tyranny, oppression and despotic supremacy of the traditional Hinduism. As a special nominee and national leader of the scheduled castes, he struggled throughout his life to abolish the inequalities, social discriminations and the hierarchy of the caste system in order to provide an equal status to scheduled castes and other backward classes. After independence, the Indian Constitution in 1950 prescribed a number of legal provisions to abolish social discriminations and to secure to all its citizens equality and liberty.

Law as Guard

The Indian Constitution in 1950 made a number of provisions

for the eradication of social inequalities, discriminations and the practice of untouchability in an effort to improve the social and economic conditions of Dalits and also to maintain an order of equality and liberty in society. The Government has provided some special reservation or in other words the "protective discrimination" especially in the field of education, occupation and political representation which aims at the elimination of social, economic and educational inequalities. The main reasoning behind the government's policy of reservation was and is the removal of great and undesirable inequalities exist between the scheduled castes and non-scheduled castes. By temporarily creating conditions of unequal and favourable treatment for the scheduled castes, the Indian Government hopes eventually to bring about conditions of equality in the society at large. The provisions for "protective discrimination" or special reservation, thus, might be grouped under three headings; education, government job and political representation. This provision of reservation was originally scheduled to be in effect for ten years from 1950 to 1959, however, it was extended for another ten years and as achievements are not upto the level of government expectation, it, therefore, being extended time and again for a period of ten years which was to end in 1980 but it has been again extended to ten years. In the educational sphere, the government at the Centre and the States have various schemes for providing Matric, Post-graduate and Graduate scholarships, free remissions, books, boarding grants and so forth, to the members of the scheduled castes. There is also provision for a few overseas scholarships.

In the field of government jobs, a certain percentage of jobs at the Centre and the State levels are reserved exclusively for members of the scheduled castes. At the Centre 15 per cent of the posts recruited by competitive examinations and 16.7 per cent of the posts recruited by appointments, are reserved for the scheduled castes. In the States, reserved government jobs are equal to the percentage of scheduled castes in the total population of the state. In U.P. it is 18 per cent. Over and above reservations, extra-concessions and relaxations of age limit and qualifications are granted to them so that they may fully utilize their rights in their interest. In the political sphere according to Articles 330, 332 and

334 of the Indian Constitution a certain number of seats are reserved for the scheduled castes in the Parliaments, State Legislatures, *Panchayats* and other local bodies. At present 7 seats of M.P.'s (Member of Parliament) out of the total seats of 544 of the Parliament and 557 seats of M.L.A.'s (Member of Legislative Assembly) out of the total seats of 3997 State Legislatures in the country are reserved for them.

In addition to above reservations, the Government of India as well as the State Governments sponsor various welfare schemes from time to time to evaluate the rate of progress among the scheduled castes and campaign for the eradication of untouchability and casteism. Among other welfare programmes undertaken by government, are free acquisition of land for housing and agriculture, loans from the nationalized banks to meet their requirements, etc. are given to them. During the First Five Year Plan, the government invested 5.97 crore of rupees on the scheduled castes under various programmes. A strong emphasis was given in the Third Five Year Plan in which the government invested Rs. 37.94 crores. In Fourth Five Year Plan, it was Rs. 66 crores which was spent with a view to expedite their socio-economic progress. Thus, the Constitution of India includes many articles meant for the abolition of all sorts of disabilities. At the very outset the preamble in the Constitution says, "We, the people of India, having solemnly resolved to constitute India into a sovereign Democratic Republic and to secure to all its citizens, justice, social, economic and political, liberty of thought, expression, belief, faith and worship, and equality of status and opportunity, and to promote among them all fraternity assuring the dignity of individual and unity of the Nation." The important articles of the Constitution are:

Basic Rights

(14) equality before the law,

(15) no caste discrimination by government or private persons in regard to use of public facilities, special provisions in favour of the untouchables and backward classes permissible,

(16) no caste discrimination in government services; reservation of places permitted for untouchables and 'backward classes',

(17) untouchability abolished and enforcement an offence,

(19) right to conduct all sorts of occupations and industries by the untouchables,

(23) forced labour abolished; no caste discrimination in regard to compulsory public service (amended and enforced in 1976),

(25) (2-b) freedom of religion qualified to serve temple entry laws and state power to legislate social welfare and reform,

(29) no castes descrimination in admission to state aided educational institutions.

Directive Principles

(44) personal law to be replaced by uniform civil code,

(45) state shall protect and promote interests of 'weaker sections of people' specially untouchables.

More Provisions

(325) no caste electorate,

(330) reservation of seats for scheduled castes in Parliament and State Legislatures,

(335) claims of untouchables to be considered in appointment in government services.

The Untouchability (Offences) Act 1955, outlaws all the kinds of discrimination on the ground of untouchability in virtually all fields of activity except home life, private religious ceremonies and private employment. Article 17 as already discussed above is also meant for the abolition of untouchability and in particular in section I, II, III, VI and VII of that, provisions have been made for each and every individual irrespective of caste discrimination to utilize all public properties such as well, tank, religious places, river bank, cremetorium ground, shops, restaurants, hotels, rest houses, public vehicles, hospitals, educational institutions and so on.

Despite all these provisions and policies of government, the most wretched part is its failure to undertake studies of the effectiveness of laws and policies. The Government is conscious of everything about its goals and institutions it has set up under the programme of reservations of "protective discrimination" special privileges and abolition of untouchability among the scheduled castes. There has, however, been no evaluative studies of the programme except, it seems, one attempt by the Commissioner for scheduled castes and scheduled tribes. In 1961 the Commissioner sent an enquiry to all the State Governments asking for information along these lines, but as of 1963, he had received not a single reply.

The pieces of informations received and informations available lead to the conclusion that such programme of "protective discriminations" have been variously effective. In the sphere of political representation, the scheduled castes are elected to all the reserve seats but it is still debatable whether or not they properly represent the interests of their constituency men. Some progress on concrete level has been made in the field of education. In fact, it appears to be the most successful part of the policy.

In the sphere of reserved jobs and government services however, the position in relation to the actual representation of scheduled castes and scheduled tribes on post under the Government of India and their attached and sub-ordinate offices is satisfactory. The effectiveness of the legal abolition of the practice of untouchability and other forms of discrimination is quite poor, as the picture remains somewhat the same in the villages. In a circular issued to all District Magistrates by the Government of the State of Uttar Pradesh, it was noted that: "The practice of untouchability continues unabated... such occurrences bring a bad name to the government and show that the provisions of Untouchability (Offices) Act 1955, are being disregarded on a large scale. At present, in spite of all efforts to remove untouchability and caste disabilities, it is observed that casteism and untouchability have taken a different shape, and at the same time they gained new social, economic and political significance (Issacs, 1950; Srinivas, 1966; Galanter, 1968; Lynch, 1969).

Facilities for Education

The history of educational growth among Dalits is almost the history of last fifty years. After independence the education among the scheduled castes has been marked by a firm declaration in the Indian Constitution by abolishing untouchability. The fundamental rights include the principles of justice, equality and fraternity to all and charge the state with the responsibility of undertaking special steps for removal of discriminations on the basis of caste and birth. The placement of the scheduled castes under one schedule has stressed the special responsibility of the government with special regard to their education and occupation.

During the first, second and third Five Year Plans, the total number of scholarships of all kinds were 5,17,511. In the first Five Year Plan a sum of Rs. 1.58 crores were spent on in the form of scholarships, while in the Third Plan Rs. 14.21 crores were spent. From 1969 to 1973 the government invested Rs. 35.38 crores of rupees to award 6 lakhs and 62 thousand scholarships to Dalit students. There more than 18 overseas scholarships meant for the scheduled castes for their abroad studies.

During the first 18 years of planning, about Rs. 277 crores were spent on the special programmes for the welfare of the Dalits out of which Rs. 110 crores were spent for the scheduled castes. Rs. 117 crores were spent on the schemes of educational development among them and other backward classes and various steps have been undertaking for the removal of untouchability through legislation, publicity, educational schemes, organization of special programmes and expansion of opportunities for social and economic betterment. The provision of Untouchability (Offences) Act 1955 has been vigorously enforced. An outlay of Rs. 3 crores was provided during Fourth Plan at the Centre for improvement in living conditions of those working in unclean occupations. Since voluntary organizations play an important role in extending welfare activities among the backward classes and the scheduled castes, assistance is given to them for running projects like publicity and propaganda for removal of untouchability, running the hostels and educational institutions, organizing welfare ard community centres, social education and conducting training and orientation courses.

Thus, the outlay of special programmes for the welfare of the scheduled castes and backward classes is ever increasing having rise from Rs. 30 crores in the First Plan to Rs. 79 crores in the Second Plan and to about Rs. 102 crores in the Third Plan and of the total amount of Rs. 211 crores spent during the first three plans, about Rs. 72 crores were spend on the scheduled castes. Of these 72 crores, Rs. 34 crores have been devoted to educational programmes, Rs. 11 crores to economic upliftment schemes and Rs. 27 crores to health, housing and other schemes. During the Fourth Plan a sum of Rs. 66 crores was spent for the social, economic and educational uplift of the scheduled castes. The Fifth Plan was also devoted to achieve the above target. Special programmes were initiated by the Central and State Governments and Rs. 296.16 crores were spent. The Sixth Five Year Plan (1980-85) was landmark in this direction. During the period 1980-85 an outlay of Rs. 600 crores was provided to the social, economic and educational welfare of the scheduled castes with a joint venture of central and state sectors and special central assistance was given for component plants for the development of the Scheduled Castes. The Sixth Plan strategy for the socio-economic development of scheduled castes, scheduled tribes and other backward classes was designed to ensure a higher degree of devolution of funds through the Special Component Plans (SCPs) and through special central assistance than in earlier plans with the overall objectives to see that atleast half of them were provided substantial assistance to enable them to move to the other side of the poverty line.

In order to increase education among the scheduled castes and scheduled tribes and scheme of Post-matric Scholarship was started in 1945-46 with the objective of providing financial assistance to the scheduled caste and scheduled tribe students studying at post-matriculation stages in various schools and colleges in the country, so as to enable them to complete that education starting with only 144 awards to scheduled caste and 89 for scheduled tribes in 1948-49, the number of awards to scheduled castes and scheduled tribes had reached 8.33 lakh in 1983-84 and crossed 9 lakh in 1984-85. In the context of rising cost of buying and other such factors the rates for all courses and income limits of parents /guardians/wards for eligibility of the scholarships was also revised with effect from 1st July 1981. From 1980-81 the employed students with a total income of Rs. 750 per month are made eligible for scholarships, restricted to reimbursement of compulsory non-refundable dues/fees, etc. Restrictive conditions of scholarships to only two children of the same parents have also been relaxed in the case of girl students from 1980-81.

Financial aid on matching basis is given to state governments and union territories for the construction of new hostels and to expand existing ones at any place where the facilities for girls belonging to these classes are inadequate.

The Government provides cent per cent financial assistance to reputed and competent organizations/institutions to undertake short duration action oriented studies on problems concerned with the formulation and evaluation of programmes for economic, social and educational uplift of scheduled castes.

The book bank scheme is initiated for scheduled castes and scheduled tribes students studying in the medical and engineering degree courses in the country so as to provide text books to those who cannot afford expensive education without state support. One set of text books is given to three students and life period of a set is fixed for three years.

The pre-matric scholarship scheme began in 1977-78 is intended for development of children who are involved in the so called unclean occupations, viz., scavenging of dry latrines, flaying and tourning studying in classes VI to X. A scholarship of Rs. 145 per month is given to each student under the scheme.

Thus the achievements during the Sixth Plan with regard to socio-economic development programmes for scheduled castes and scheduled tribes are: stipends and scholarship were given to 115 lakh children belonging to scheduled castes and scheduled tribes and another 113 lakh children belonging to these categories were covered by educational incentives like freeships, supply of uniforms, stationery, books, etc. Post-matric scholarships were awarded to nine lakh scheduled castes and scheduled tribes students and 300 hostels and 900 Ashram Schools were established in the country. In order to improving the representation of scheduled castes and scheduled tribes in several posts and services under central and state government and also in public sector undertakings, bank services, Life Insurance Corporation of India, pre-examination coaching centres have been set up in different parts of the country for preparing scheduled castes and scheduled tribe candidates for different competitive examination held by UPSC/State Public Service Commissions and other recruiting bodies. The number of such centres sanctioned/established by the end of March 1985 was over 62.

In the economic field the scheme have been more in the nature of the provision of inputs for the generation of income among beneficiary families. About three lakh scheduled castes and scheduled tribes were given financial help for sustaining activities in production sectors like agriculture, animal husbandry and cottage industries.

A significant programme taken up was the liberation of scavengers from their demeaning occupation through conversion of dry (service) latrines into water closets under a centrally sponsored scheme in towns and municipalities covering a whole town at a time. This was taken up as a pilot project in 14 states and 37 towns were covered. Against the target of 8.65 million scheduled caste families to be brought above the poverty line, it is estimated that by the end of 1984-85, 8.71 million scheduled caste families have been benefited. It is, however, by no means certain that all those families assisted have, in fact, moved above the poverty line and for the Seventh Plan it is possible that some families assisted in the Sixth Plan may yet receive some assistance to take them permanently above the poverty line.

A noteworthy feature of the Special Component Plans (SCPs) drawn up by the states for the socio-economic development of the

Scheduled Castes is that the quality of the schemes and their implementation has shown marked improvement over the previous plans. However, much still need to be done towards organizational improvements. Co-ordination among many implementation agencies and proper linkage between programmes and schemes aimed at the same target groups need to be strengthened and revitalized. Some of the major obstacles observed relate to a lack of decentralization from the state to the Block level, of adequate communication between them and of a proper reporting and monitoring machinery at the ground level. Another development that can have a favourable effect on the future programme for the uplift of these backward communities has been the increase in the number of scheduled caste Development Corporations in various states which make available margin money for accelerating economic and income generating activities among the scheduled castes. Their role in catalysing development and in mobilizing additional credit should not be underestimated and there are 195 Scheduled Caste Development Corporations working in 17 states and two union territories with a total capital of over Rs. 173 crores. The corporations have enabled some 27 million families of scheduled castes to get benefits through assistance by themselves and through bank loans which they helped the families to receive. In aggregate subsidies, margin money loans and bank loans amount to Rs. 635 crores.

Another important achievement of the Sixth Plan is the distribution among Scheduled Caste families of land declared surplus under the ceiling laws. During this plan period 806143 acres of land declared surplus under ceiling laws were distributed among 688175 scheduled caste families. Out of a total of 43 lakh acres of surplus land distributed, the total area distributed to scheduled castes accounted for 13.33 lakh acres. Out of the total beneficiaries of 32.48 lakh who were granted surplus land 12.47 lakh beneficiaries (38 per cent) are the scheduled castes families.

The aim of the Seventh Plan (1985-90) was to continue the thrust towards the socio-economic development of the scheduled castes and to impart them occupational mobility and economic strength. Special attention is given to this segment of population to cross the poverty line. The Scheduled Caste Development Corporations which were laid down during the Sixth Plan constitute one of the instruments of economic development of the scheduled castes. Total elimination of scavenging was one of the objectives of the Seventh Plan. For this purpose low cost housing are sanctioned and whole town approach for conversion of dry latrines into waterborne latrines will be adopted. The children of scavengers were to be given special incentives and financial assistance for their education.

Thus the basic approach of the Seventh Plan in regard to social up-life of the scheduled castes is to conduct programmes of socio-economic and educational development among them based on the evaluation of the achievements made during the Sixth Plan and to review the critical situations and obstacles which hinder the implementation of these programmes. The special central assistance has been increased for socio-economic programmes for scheduled castes. Rs. 830 crores have been proposed for this purpose. Basic facilities like, drinking water, housing facilities, electrification, link roads and fair price shops will be provided for the scheduled castes in their localities by the end of the Seventh Plan. This will the endeavour of the Central and State governments to decrease the gap between the general level of social and economic development and that of scheduled castes. During this plan period a three pronged strategy has been evolved to speed up the development of the scheduled castes: (a) special component plans of the Central Ministries and State Governments, (b) special central assistance to the special component plans for the scheduled castes of the states, and (c) scheduled castes development corporations in the states. The percentage distribution of the scheduled caste students to the total students population reveals that in 1950-51 the figure stood at 0.32 per cent, in 1955-56 it moved to 2.5 per cent in 1960-61 it was 5.3 per cent and by 1970-71 it had moved to nearly 10 per cent and in 1985 to about 15 per cent.

The families, thus, offered by the Central and the State Governments in lowering the qualifying marks for entry to higher posts in the government services has had influence on increasing the number of the members of the scheduled castes in different occupations, it undoubtedly lead them toward occupational mobility and change in status. In this way education opens many possibilities for a number of secular occupations. According to 'India' 1985, the number of officers under Central Government belonging to scheduled castes and scheduled tribes as on 1st January, 1983 was Class I-3574, Class II-6368, Class III-311070 and Class IV (excluding sweepers) 255053. Their numbers in IAS and IPS as on 1st January, 1983 was 404 and 330 respectively.

They get their children educated by the modern convent public schools which suits to their call of the time. Many studies conducted in this regard show the evidences how modern education is an effective mechanism to elevate their socially degraded status in society. By getting education in engineering, law, medicine, they enter those occupations which are prestigeous for present society. Thus they emerge as doctors, engineers, civil contractors and administrative officers in government and thereby improve their social position in society by these remunerative jobs and adopt a Westernized style of life. In this concern the studies made by Harper (1968), Rowe (1968), Damle (1968) and Lynch (1969) confirm the idea of their changing status through education. Whereas modern education is a tool for achieving upward mobility and thereby change in social position outside the framework of the caste system, it is important to note that two mechanisms of social mobility—Sanskritization and Westernization—are not mutually inclusive. The scheduled castes specially take part in both these frequently without feeling the logical contradiction. They try to make the best of both the worlds. Westernization gives them a chance to move up in the modern status system having an occupational base. But they do recognize their obligations towards their castemen who have a low level of education and economic status. Often the elite within the caste form an exclusive group and attempt to move upwards by seeking marital alliances among equals or higher ones, and by developing contacts in the desired social circle. While the status change of a section of caste is related to the process of Westernization, the part it plays in raising the status of fellow castemen is related to that of Sanskritization.

But as regards the treatment and behaviour of the higher castes towards the scheduled caste employees specially in urban community, it is noticed that they are enjoying a privileged status and are accorded treatment equal to employees of higher castes.

In this way, the spread of education among the scheduled castes and their entry into secular occupations may have the result in creating social classes among them on lines parallel to those obtaining in the wider society. The degree of the acceptance of the scheduled castes by the prevalent higher castes of the Indian society and the ability of the scheduled castes to act as equals in that status would determine and be determined by the extent to which modernization has occurred in the country. It can be also discussed that in the process of acquiring modern education and entering highly paid and prestigious jobs, they are developing their contracts with urbo-industrial set up of society which gives them a new style of life as well as changes in status and which is almost free from the strong clutches of ascriptive hierarchy of caste. In this process there is a development of an 'elite section' among the scheduled castes which provides a reference group of imitation or what Friedl (1964) said 'lagging emulation' for the rest of the scheduled castes.

Fundamental Problems

The scheduled castes have been currently much more conscious toward education and social status and the government is providing necessary steps to improve their educational and social standards. But, despite the reckless facilities given to them, their remain some major educational and social problems and difficulties. The problems arising before the scheduled castes in the present Indian situation are mainly of two types: (i) those arising out of their unimportant enrolment and, (ii) those arising out of their traditionally lower social position in the caste hierarchy. Even if the first set of problems may be overcome due to government measures, the nature of the second set of difficulties are subject for further studies and illustrations. The studies in this concern show that in spite of their educational achievement and better occupational status they are not accorded equal recognition in terms of prestige by the higher caste Hindu as the sentimental and psychological attachment of higher Hindus with their caste traditions have not died out. The practice of untouchability with slight change in use remains more or less the same specially in rural areas. Of course, in urban and industrial areas the picture is much more changed because of the modernizing forces.

As regards the school atmosphere, it is observed that the scheduled caste students feels much secure in the hostel where he is every one's equal than in the general hostel. There are still conflicting situations regarding social contacts and interpersonal relations. The effects of education among the scheduled castes linked to student-parent relationship have been diverse in nature due to the prevalent differences of attitude and values. From the angle of the family, education in the younger generation makes a larger gap in the knowledge of the parents and the children. This gap is widening due to the conflict between tradition and modernity as the young educated ones form very radical attitude against the prescribed caste norms while the older generations of the scheduled castes are still bearing the backlog of traditions in terms of purity and pollution, superiority and inferiority. This would mean greater problems of adjustment among the uneducated parents and their educated children, but this gap may be less conflicting for the third generation of the scheduled castes.

Having been aware of social status, higher education and political participation, they themselves maintain a hierarchical gradation among their castes which hinders their integrated approach to fight against the social shortcomings imposed by the higher castes. In this direction, the education among the scheduled castes has not brought much effective result to eliminate their own disabilities. For instance, a *Dhobi* considers himself superior to a *Chamar* and a *Chamar* considers himself superior to a *Hela*. Such a consideration can bring a further change among their own castes by leading to a gradation among themselves.

The concessional provisions as sanctioned by the government in qualifying tests is also affecting the majority of the scheduled castes by permanently cultivating the conception in the minds of the members of the scheduled castes that they occupy their positions not based on merits but because of the concessions accorded to them. This is psychologically making their motivations and serious consciousness to achieve educational competence very narrow and limited while socio-economic improvement in a caste based society like India needs a strong commitment, serious orientation and strong intellectual potentialities to acquire educational performance so as to develop the capacities and efficiencies with which they can equally compete and come up with the higher castes. The reservations in the field of education and jobs cannot provide an open scope as the reserve quotas will always be below the expectation of the scheduled castes. The most silly aspect of the educational and job reservations is lying with government itself as no sufficient surveys have been carried out by the government to check the effectiveness of these reservations in the interest of the scheduled castes.

Problem of Mobility

Although there are a number of forces or causes of social mobility and status changes among the scheduled castes but for the present the following factors are functionally more important in connection with the change of status and social mobility among the scheduled castes in Indian society.

Open Field

Since independence the Government of India has made some serious efforts to raise the literacy level of society in general and that of the scheduled castes, in particular. Education, today, is the main source for the understanding and application of Science and Technology in society in order to increase the economic and social standard. The Government of India has made special provisions under its constitution to spread education among Dalits whereby they can raise their standard of living by entering into secular jobs and improving their socio-economic status in society equally according to higher castes. It is hoped that the expansion of modern education will eliminate caste system and social discrimination. The studies in this regard made by Srinivas (1962), Rowe (1968), Cohn (1955), Damle (1968), Rao (1970) support the fact.

The Differenciation

Special reservations by the government under the constitutional provisions regarding occupation, education and political representation as well as the welfare programmes sponsored by the Central and the State Governments for the abolition of untouchability and socio-economic uplift of the scheduled castes have been major incentives which have served and are serving the positive function of social mobility, economic improvement and changing of the status of Dalits in India.

Migration to cities and towns provides new avenues to the scheduled castes for change of occupation and a particular style of life marked with secular social living against the ascriptive ranking of the caste system. During the last few decades the process of migration has been very much enhanced due to the prevalent landlessness, poor economic conditions, and lack of wage paid jobs in the rural areas. Consequently, the scheduled castes all over India have moved to cities and towns in search of jobs on cash payment. This process is also followed by a subsequent decline of the cottage industries and the breakdown of the traditional *jajmani* system in rural India.

Modern Problems

Industrialization and urbanization have created new economic roles, releasing a wider spectrum of occupational choice, spatial mobility and migration leading to change in occupational pattern. The growth of industrialization in India is marked with an accelerated growth of occupations and has improved the chances of factory employment. On the other hand urbanization has provided a lure for sophisticated social living for different sections of society in general, and for the scheduled castes in particular. The urban and industrial contacts and mutual interaction with various organizations have consequently increased inter-cultural and inter-caste relationships among the scheduled castes and in doing so it has reduced the importance of ascriptive hierarchy of caste system and its customs by promoting new motivations and values for achievement orientation.

In the Name of Democracy

The Indian democracy is constitutionally committed to promote the values of equality of opportunities, liberty of thought and expression, fraternity and social justice to all its members irrespective of caste discriminations. This has broadened the outlook on life as the scheduled castes in particular, as a result of growing education and status awareness among them are tended to adopt and inculcate these values for improving their position as equal to other higher castes in Indian social structure.

Caste Factor

Relations and contacts in modern society are marked at the same time with awakening of the associations of different castes. This feeling of caste associations is very strong among the scheduled castes who think their associations as an effective force before government and public both to press for their demands for social recognition and acceptance. The caste associations, thus, serve as integrated approach to fight against caste based social evils which hinder their growth.

Generation to Generation

Intra-generational mobility is also one more factor linked to the changing status of scheduled castes in India. The interchanges of occupation within the same generation, and education and industrialization have encouraged such mobility. Therefore, a clear-cut movement is perceived from manual to non-manual and caste based to secular occupations.

The phrase literally implies the gradual imitation and contests for equal status where one chases the other in the context of imitation. The theory of "Lagging emulation" tries to explain the Sanskritization of lower castes and concurrent Westernization of the upper castes or the 'elite section' of their own castes in India through the notion of imitative reference group. The low castes with little mobility and very less urban contacts imitate the local dominant castes or the elite section, while the dominant caste or the elite section of the same caste having greater mobility and urban contacts imitate the urban and more westernized prestige model. The theory can be translated into the theoretical framework of reference group and observability in order to examining the changing status and social mobility among the scheduled castes. It is more useful and inclusive of Sanskritization and Westernization both specially in Indian context as it goes even beyond the limits of Sanskritization and Westernization with logical and critical explanation of the situation by releasing a wider scope of adaptability among them.

The history of the genesis of scheduled castes or commonly known as untouchables is age old and seems to be by-product of the traditional varna system and the caste system. In the works of antiquarians and *Dharmasastra* writers specially Baudhayan, Patanjali, Kautilya and Manu, there are references of the existence of *Chandals, Svapachas* and *Mritapas* who were supposed to be the vile specimens of humanity and thus were denied entry to villages and towns in the day time. Not only this, but they suffered from a number of socio-cultural and economic disabilities and inequalities. They were placed even below the rank of *Sudras* and thus formed the fifth order of the hierarchy according to Prof. Ghurye, Manu permits them that they may treat themselves as equal to Sudras.

It seems from the historical traditions of attitude to untouchables that for hundreds of years they have suffered from inferiority and lack of co-operation from the higher castes and were subjected to a life of downtrodden and depressed. For a long time during British rule in India, they were known as the "depressed class" and by this name an organization of them was established by Ambedkar who championed the cause of untochables. During 1931 the Census Commission of India employed the term "exterior caste" for them. Hutton has also used the same name in his description of caste in India. When Mahatma Gandhi came in the field of liberation movement, he preached for the social justice of these untouchables and used the term "Harijan" for them in order to give them respect and sympathy. In 1935, Saint Simon Commission was set up which finally used the word "scheduled castes" to call whole of this section of human society. It is a collective term referring to all the untouchable castes which was finally accepted by the Indian Constitution in 1950.

As regards the eradication of untouchability and amelioration of the conditions of the scheduled castes, we find that first of all in Travancore a movement was started under the leadership of Jyotiba Phule regarding entry to temples in 1924. Later on, many leaders such as Bandopadhyaya, V.R. Sindhe started the reform movement. After this Ambedkar came to the scene and in order to consolidate and rationalize his leadership, he strongly advocated for the emancipation of the untouchables during 1942. Despite that a number of saints, poets and social observers like Ramanand, Kabir, Tulsi, Chaitanya, Bhartendu Harishchandra and many others whose working ground was Varanasi, from where they spread their messages for eradication of untouchability were already active since long.

After independence the Government of India provided certain constitutional safeguards for protecting the interest of the scheduled castes and abolishing the practice of untouchability. The Untouchability (Offences) Act and Caste Disabilities Removal Act were passed in 1955 and special provisions were made for them regarding their education, job and political representation by reservation of seats. In many articles of the constitution, specially 15, 17, 25, 29 and several provisions have been made to abandon all sorts of discrimination based on caste, creed and colour regarding entry to schools, temples, river banks, shops, restaurants and use of water tanks, crematorium, roads, wells, etc. On the whole, the Scheduled Castes constitute one-seventh of the total population of India. There are about 500 castes in the scheduled castes list and in U.P. alone there are 66 castes belonging to the list.

It was after independence that a systematic growth of education has been possible due to enforcement of constitutional provisions. Article 16 of the constitution is devoted to special reservations regarding their educational facilities. The facilities given under the Five Year Plans in the form of scholarship and other aids have brought much more changes in their status by increasing the level of literacy among them. The Sixth Plan had a special stress for improvement of education and employment of the scheduled castes. The Seventh

Five Year Plan is specially designed to remove the shortcomings of the community and also to provide maximum educational development by increasing the number of scholarships, hostel facilities and other amenities. Simultaneously the democratic values and urban influence have motivated them enormously towards socio-occupational mobility.

Thus, in contemporary Indian society the educational opportunities, "protective discrimination," special privileges, migration to cities as a result of urbanization and industrialization, democratic values, caste associations are some of the main forces for upward mobility.

8

Protection under Constitution

Indian society has for centuries been horizontally and vertically split and stratified on the basis of caste. People are born into a caste or sub-caste many of which have traditionally suffered from various kinds of social discrimination and disabilities. These traditionally backward and deprived sections of society are so weak that they have not been able to take equal advantage of equal opportunities compared to the educationally and socially stronger castes or classes. Thus the weaker sections of society have suffered from getting social justice. Social justice denotes overall development of weaker sections. Overall development includes educational development, economic development, political representation, social empowerment at all levels of institutions. The constitution provides benefits to weaker section of society under Article 15(4) and 16(4) mainly related to educational development and employment opportunities in Government services. It is the responsibility of the State to provide educational opportunities and employment opportunities to all including weaker sections of the society on the principle of equality. It was the enormity of inequality that gave rise to various low-caste movements, particularly in the south, right from the beginning of this century. As a result of sustained agitations, specific quotas of seats had been ear marked in medical and engineering colleges in the state. Travancore-Cochin, Madras, Mysore before independence. In post-Independence India, the first important step to remedy this situation was taken with the incorporation of clause 4 under Article 16 of the Constitution which empowered the states to reserve posts in favour of backward classes of citizens. After Independence, Scheduled Castes and Scheduled Tribes have been Constitutionally recognised as groups under the category of weaker sections. They have started getting benefits in educational institutions and employment. Backward castes (OBCs) got recognition in 1993. The present chapter focuses on Constitutional provisions related to various benefits available to these groups.

Social justice is a means to achieve the aim of establishing an egalitarian society and eradicating distribution of power in its several social sections. To achieve the goals of distribution of political, administrative and economic power, the Constitution of India was amended eighty-five times during the last fifty years. The democratic, secular and liberal Constitution of India is doing well under the ethos of social milieu and it is playing a major role in shaping its policies and competing to gain and control political power.

The Indian constitutional law is a unique social document which accepts social pluralism and makes provisions for safeguarding the interests of different social sections. It has been aimed at bringing social equality, social justice and distribution of power along with protection of right to equality. However, in the last few years, it has become imperative for the defenders of the exploitative social order and monopolizers of social, economic and political power to take to the streets and approach the judiciary to create hinderances in the way of social legislation for distribution of power. On the other hand, the leaders of the deprived and disadvantaged social sections have been trying to get benefit of the special provisions made for bringing social justice to the poor and deprived social sections, in order to have a share in the distribution of state power.

The expression 'backward classes' has not been defined anywhere in the Indian Constitution. Backward classes includes Scheduled Castes (SCs) and Scheduled Tribes (STs) and other backward classes (OBCs). The OBCs are other than SCs and STs, and who are also socially and educationally backward in comparison to the other advanced sections of the society.

Articles 15(4) and 340 use the words 'socially and educationally backward classes', It may be mentioned that whereas Article 16(4) refers to "any backward class citizen", in clause (4) of Article 15, the reference is "any socially and educationally backward classes". As Pt. Nehru explained before the select committee, this departure was made to bring the language of Article 15(4) in line with that of Article 340, which provides that Backward Classes Commission may be set up for "socially and educationally backward class citizens."

Perusal of the Parliament debate on this amendment clearly shows that irrespective of the criteria for the classification of backward classes there had to be a list of castes and communities. Pt. Nehru observed, "we want to put an end to ...... all those infinite divisions that have grown up in our social life. We may call them by any name you like, the caste system or religious divisions, etc....." (B.P. Mandal, 1980, p. 24, Vol. I)

Article 16(4) speaks of just 'backward classes', and Article mentions the 'weaker sections of the people'. Even now, the term 'backward classes' is defined differently in the reports of the different backward classes commissions and the judgments of various High Courts and the Supreme Court of India.

Legal Safeguards

As leader of the Congress Party in the Constituent Assembly of India, Jawaharlal Nehru moved a historic resolution on the aims and objectives of the Constitution. It was regarding provisions for adequate safeguards to the minorities, backward and depressed sections of society. The resolution stated that: "Wherein shall be guaranteed and secured to all the people of India, justice, social, economic and political, equality of status and opportunity before the law, freedom of thought, expression, belief faith, worship, vocation, association and action, subject to law and public morality, and wherein adequate safeguards shall be made available to minorities, backward and tribal areas, and depressed and other backward classes.

The problems of backward classes including the issue of distribution of political and administrative power through policy of reservation and other benefits enjoyed by them till the attainment of independence and the future of these policies were thoroughly debated before appropriate Articles and provisions were incorporated in the Indian Constitution. Despite the divergent views expressed as to the meaning of the term 'backward classes' there was a consensus that the term would include not just the Scheduled Castes and Scheduled Tribes, but also others who were economically, educationally and socially backward. In India, there are some communities, apart from the Scheduled Castes and Scheduled Tribes, which give a definite impression of social and educational backwardness and inferiority and powerlessness in comparison to the monopoly of social, economic and political power by the traditional upper castes.

The sub-committee on Fundamental Rights had discussed the question of other backward classes in detail. It, however, did not provide reservation and any other special measures to them. It was left it for the State Governments to identify the backward classes in their respective territories and to assist them. Thus, the chance of OBCs to share power in the central services became futile but they became important power brokers at the state level.

Positive Attitude

The Constitution of India made certain provisions for the welfare of deprived social section, known as affirmative action, reservation policy and positive discrimination. The aims and objectives of the Constitution, the general agreement and the compromises reached in the Constituent Assembly are reflected in the different Articles and provisions relating to backward classes, e.g., the Preamble, Articles 38 and 46 of the Directive Principles of State Policy, Articles 14, 15 and 16 of the Fundamental Rights and Articles 338 and 340 of the Constitution of India. The Preamble to the Constitution expresses the determination and aspirations of the people of India in the following terms:

> "...Justice, Social Economic and Political,
>
> Liberty of thought, expression, belief, faith and worship:
>
> Equality of status and of opportunity; and
>
> to promote fraternity among them all assuring the dignity of the individual and the unity and integrity of the Nation."

The two objectives: justice—social, economic and political; and equality of status and opportunity of the Preamble are specially relevant and linked to the advancement of the weaker sections and backward classes. In short, the Constitution of India promises not only political democracy, but also social democracy as described by Ambedkar in his speech in the Constitution Assembly: "It means a way of life which recognizes liberty equality and fraternity which are not treated as separate items in a trinity. They form a union of trinity in the sense that to divorce one from the other is to defeat the very purpose of democracy. Liberty cannot be divorced from equality and cannot be divorced from liberty. Nor can liberty and equality be divorced from fraternity.

The Constitution of India includes a number of Articles which deal with compensatory preference for the backward classes. The most important among them are Articles 15(4) and 16(4). Articles 46, 325, 338, 340, 341, 342, 366(24) and 366(25) also have an influence on the subject.

Effect of Directive Principles

The Directive Principles of State Policy enshrined in the Articles 38 and 46 of the Indian Constitution make it the duty of the State to strive to promote the welfare of the people in general and weaker sections, including the backward classes, in particular. Article 38 of the Constitution reads thus:

(1) The State shall strive to promote the welfare of the people by securing and protecting as effectively as it may a social order in which justice, social, economic and political, shall inform all the institutions of national life.

(2) The state shall, in particular, strive to minimize the inequalities in income, and endeavour to eliminate inequalities in status, facilities and opportunities, not only amongst individuals but also amongst groups of people residing in different areas or engaged in different vocations.

Thus, the Directive Principles along with the Preamble embody the socio-economic ideals which the nation had set before itself during the freedom movement. It points out to the political mind of the makers of the Constitution who visualized the creation of a new social order in India on the basis of social, economic and political justice, eliminating the evils of the existing socio-economic system. Though the nature of the 'social order' is not defined in the Constitution, but is interpreted to mean a 'welfare state' and 'socialistic pattern of society'. As a part of this objective, the State is directed to remove the existing inequalities of income, status, facilities and opportunities among the individuals and groups in India. Further, Article 46 directs that: "The State shall promote with special care the educational and economic interests of weaker sections of the people, and, in particular, of the Scheduled Castes and Scheduled Tribes, and shall protect them from social injustice and all forms of exploitation."

As can be seen, Article 46 makes the State duty bound to take action to ameliorate the conditions of the weaker sections including the backward classes. They are two-fold: (i) to promote with special care the educational and economic interests by taking 'positive measures'; and (ii) to prevent social injustice and all forms of exploitation by taking 'preventive measures'.

Protection against Discrimination

The issue of equality and inequality, the theory that no two persons are equal and the belief that equality of opportunity could do away with the drawbacks which many faced due to their social inferiority have occupied the minds of eminent philosophers such as Locke, Rousseau, Huxley and many others. As Andre Beteille has said "the distinction between natural inequality and social inequality is inherently ambiguous."

However, there was no doubt about the arbitrarily hierarchical and social and economic exploitation through caste system that had guided Indian society till date. At the base of this pyramidal structure lay the masses of economically suppressed, politically disabled and socially deprived Depressed Classes of India. For ages, they had been victimised and at the dawn of freedom, the time had come to begin, an extraordinary phase of the upliftment of the masses of humanity from the state of animals like social existence, deep poverty and inhuman economic exploitation.

Equality for All

The new constitutional and legal environment emphasized equal participation by every citizen in the functioning of the state. Founding fathers of the constitution tried to eliminate the discrimination of centuries by ensuring universal adult franchise. To reverse the age old oppression of backwards, special constitutional measures were enacted for the SCs who had traditionally been the sufferers of socio-economic oppression. Arnold Toynbee writes "Law's weakness is that its range is not co-extensive with social life. There are many kinds of social relations that cannot be regulated by legislation." Nevertheless, it showed the sincerity and moral commitment of the Constitution makers that they sought to establish a secular democratic set up based on equality for all before the law. Article 15 of the Constitution prohibited discrimination on grounds of religion, race, caste, sex or place of birth and Article 17 sought to abolish untouchability while Articles 330 and 332 ensured the reservation of seats for Scheduled Castes in the Lok Sabha and the Legislative Assemblies of the States. Responding to the needs of the hour, the Constituent Assembly members opted for the policy of reservation or "protective discrimination" towards the Scheduled Castes and Scheduled Tribes.

With the objective of improving the economic and social conditions of the Depressed Classes spread all over the country, the Government of India decided to list them in a Schedule in 1930, in so that accurate estimate of their numbers can be sought and special benefits to them can be provided through legislative and executive action. There was no absolute definition to establish the criteria that branded a particular group or caste as belonging to the "Scheduled Castes", hence the *Census Report of 1931* gave a nine-point test in order to distinguish the Scheduled Castes from others :

From the point of view of the State, the important test is the right to use public conveniences—roads, wells and schools and if this is regarded as the primary test, religions disabilities and the social differences indirectly involved by them may be considered contributory only. Some significance must be attached to them obviously if an ordinary person regards the persons of certain groups so that he wants to keep away from them. Certain persons of those groups do suffer under a serious disability. The list of castes was first released in the Schedule appended to the Government of India Act, 1935 and was later included in the Constitution of India (SC and ST) Order, 1950.

Regarding the tribal population in the country, there were mainly concentrates in the North-Eastern Himalayan Belt, Orissa, Madhya Pradesh, Gujarat, Rajasthan, Bihar, Maharashtra and Himachal Pradesh. The British adopted policies which were designed to keep them separate the tribals from the mainstream as part of their deliberate policy of not developing communications in the tribal areas. This isolation resulted in exploitation by non-tribal moneylenders, contractors, zamindars and middlemen. The few roads that were constructed were only helping contractors to exploit forest produce.

Jawaharlal Nehru suggested that their development be along the lines of their own culture and thoroughly disagreed with the idea that tribals should be considered primitive while the rest thought of themselves as civilised.

Article 46 contains a very significant directive to the state. It says:

"The State shall promote, with special care, the educational and economic interests of the weaker sections of the people and in particular, of the Scheduled Castes and the Scheduled Tribes and shall protect them from social injustice and all forms of exploitation." It is evident that "the weaker sections of the people do include the "backward classes of citizens contemplated by Article 16(4). Article 46 aims at their educational and economic development, Article 164 makes for the appointment of a Minister to look after exclusively tribal interests while Article 224 provides special administration of Scheduled Areas and Tribal Areas ; grants by the Centre to certain States come under Article 235. Reservation of seats for tribals is provided in the Lok Sabha under Article 330 and in the State Assemblies under Article 332. Article 334 grants reservation of seats and special representation, Article 335 grants special claims to service and posts. Article 342 of the Constitution is exclusively about Scheduled Tribes. Many more constitutional provisions were granted subsequently also. Constitutional enactments were followed by administrative structure suitable for safeguarding the interests of the tribals, thereby initiating the age of social and economic change. Interaction between national and tribal leaders as well as social workers and anthropologists helped to the present set-up for tribal upliftment.

The President of India has been constitutionally empowered to appoint a Commissioner for Scheduled Castes and Scheduled Tribes at the national level with the special responsibility of protecting the interests of the tribal population. The Director General of Backward Classes, with the help of Regional Deputy Directors assists in all the tribal welfare acivities, and the Commissioner for Scheduled Castes and Scheduled Tribes submits his annual report to Parliament through the President. At the State level, the Governor and Chief Minister supervise and implement welfare schemes for STs through the Welfare Minister. The Welfare Ministry in turn is advised by the Tribes Advisory Council and the Tribal Research Institutes in formulating policies and programmes for their upliftment. Many religious and academic agencies are also engaged in the act of improving the socio-economic conditions of the tribals in various parts of India.

Although it is blamed that more work for tribals has been done on paper than in the field, it would be wrong to say that very little has been done for tribal upliftment. Alongwith legislation and socio-economic and educational schemes, the most important feature has been the willing effort of both the Central and State governments to provide all assistance in their endeavour to improve the living conditions of the tribals. The 20-Point Economic Programme and the subsequent rural rehabilitation schemes such as IRDP, ITDP, ERRP, abolition of Bonded Labour etc. were clear manifestations of this intentions and acts. Irrespective of whether or not critics, politicians and the tribals themselves feel that not much has been done, it cannot be denied that the government has been determined in its efforts to integrate the tribals into social set up even while enabling them to retain the intrinsic advantages of their own cultures. They have not been thrust within the confines of "Reservations" as the Red Indians in North America and turned into objects of tourist curiosity.

The establishment of Ashram schools, such as those in Orissa, encourage the tribal culture and traditions and creative arts. At the same time at every level of recruitment right from teachers and class IV employees to the Civil Services and Legislatures, seats are reserved for tribal candidates. Four decades after Independence, the system of reservation or affirmative action continues.

After more than forty years of its introduction, the question being asked again and again today is—has the reservation policy achieved its objective and should it now be done away with altogether?

The idea of having 78 and 38 seats in Parliament and 540 and 282 seats in the State for SC and ST candidates was to help them to voice the grievances and rectify the injustices done on them. Whereas there has been no systematic study of the role of reserved candidates in the legislatures, it has been seen that their capacity for decision-making is often marginalised, that they are used by political parties to secure votes and that they have hardly used their status to secure personal benefits. If they are intended to promote the cause of their community they get branded as *Dalit* or *Adivasi* leaders. If they ignore themselves they are accused of betraying the community and adopting elitist attitudes.

Justice for All

The Constitution of India gives right of equality before law to all citizens of the country irrespective of caste, creed, religion, sex, etc. Article 14 of the Constitution provides rights to citizens of the country. The other Articles of the Constitution, e.g., 15 and 16 provide right of admission to any educational institutions and employment respectively. The question does arises: Are all citizens getting equal opportunity, and enjoying benefits enshrined under various Articles of the Constitution of India? If the answer is yes than why large number of population is still educationally deprived and without any job. If the answer is no, then do they have no right to get social justice under the constitution of India, like those who 'have'.

B.P. Mandal (1980, p. 21, Vol. I) quotes Justice K. Subba Rao's views from "Social Justice and Law" (National, New Delhi) as follows:

> "In a limited sense, the right to social justice may be defined as the right of the weak, aged, destitute, poor, women, children and other under-privileged persons to the protection of the State against the ruthless competition of life. It seeks to give the necessary

> adventitious aids to the underprivileged so that they may have the equal opportunity with the more advanced in the race of life. It is a bundle of rights; in one sense it is carved of other rights; in another sense it is a preserver of other rights. It is the balancing wheel between haves and havenots."

The doctrine of equality has many facets. It is a dynamic, an evolving concepts. Its main facets relevant to Indian society, have been referred to in the Preamble and the Articles under the sub-heading "Right to equality"—(Articles 14 to 18).

Our Constitution makers were fully conscious of the need for providing safeguards to the weaker sections of society. Whereas Articles 15, 16 and 29 create the overall impression of according equal access to all citizens to educational, employment and other facilities, Clause (4) of Article 16 lays down.

> (4) Nothing in this article shall prevent the State from making any provision for the reservation of appointments or posts in favour of any backward class of citizens which, in the opinion of the State, is not adequately represented in the services under the State.

Subsequently as a result of the Constitution (First Amendment) Act, 1951 a similar clause was added to Article 15 also. Thus, it will be seen that Clauses (4) of both Article 15 and 16 provide special provisions for the advancement of any socially and educationally backward classes. Further, Article 46 enjoins upon the State the obligation to promote with special care the educational and economic interests of the weaker sections of the people.

From the above, it may appear that special safeguards have been provided to weaker sections under Articles 15(4) and 16(4) as fundamental rights to education, employment, etc. But the real power lies with the State and individuals are beneficiaries entitled to take benefits under these articles.

The Fundamental Rights are primarily concerned with the rights of the individual. Claims of society do not have the same sort of immediately and urgency as the claims of individuals. Wrongs suffered by individuals stick out much more pointedly than the wrongs suffered by the society. In the light of this the exceptions contained under Articles 15(4) and 16(4) appear to confer a privileged status on backward classes which seems out of line with the overall scheme of Fundamental Rights. It is only under Directive Principles of the State Policy that the claims of society in general are given due recognition.

The issues of Fundamental Rights of individuals and Directive Principles of the State Policy became a very common theme of Parliamentary debates and judicial pronouncements in early 1950s. Pandit Nehru during the Parliamentary debates on the Constitution (First Amendment) Bill, 1951, stated:

> "...The Directive Principles of State Policy represent a dynamic move towards a certain objective. The Fundamental Rights represent something static, to preserve certain rights which exist. Both again are right. But somehow and sometime it might so happen that dynamic movement and that static standstill do not quite fit into each other."
>
> "...The result is that the whole purpose behind the Constitution which was meant to be a dynamic Constitution leading to a certain goal step by step is somewhat hampered and hindered by the static element being emphasised a little more than the dynamic element and we have to find out some way of solving it."
>
> "...If in the protection of individual liberty you protect also individual or group inequality, then you come into conflict with that Directive Principle which wants, according to your own Constitution, a gradual advance or let us put it another way, not so gradual but more rapid advance, wherever possible, to a State where there is less and less inequality and more and more equality. If any kind of an appeal to individual liberty and freedom is to mean as an appeal to the continuation of the existing inequality, then you get into difficulties. Then you become static, that ideal of an egalitarian society which I hope most of us aim at."

The dilemma observed by Pandit Nehru is very real and has been faced repeatedly in the course of implementing legislation aimed at creating of a more just social order. Whereas we can take legitimate pride in having set up a Democratic Republic in India, the elitist and unequal character of Indian society cannot be considered as a matter of great satisfaction.

The core issue is to consider the implication of 'Equality in the light of human societies' in the book 'More Equality' (1973). H.G. Gans in his book has observed that three alternative outcomes of 'Equality' are often considered: (i) Equality of opportunity, (ii) Equality of treatment, and (iii) Equality of results. He further elaborate these three alternatives of equality. Equality of opportunity promised under Article 16(1) of the Constitution, is actually a libertarian and not egalitarian principle as it allows the same freedom to everybody in the race of life. "People who start their lives at a disadvantage rarely benefit significantly from equality of opportunity, because, unless they are distinctly superior in skills or upward mobility techniques; they can rarely catch up with the more fortunate and most disadvantaged people never even get access to the supposedly equal opportunity. . . Equality of opportunity is also an asocial principle, because it neglects the several invisible and cumulative obstacles in the way of disadvantaged in fact, unless the children of the poor are taken from their parents at birth and brought up in middle-class homes, most are condemned to inequality of opportunity."

Gans says equality of treatment, notes Gans, may be interpreted in two ways. "On the one hand, it means treating people as roughly equal in impersonal social intersections . . . On the other hand, it means providing people with the same resources regardless of their current resources of socio-economic position; used in this sense, equality of treatment suffers from the same drawback as equality of opportunity for to treat the disadvantaged uniformly with the advantaged will only prepetuate their disadvantage. Even in the courts which pride themselves on equality of treatment before the law, the defendent who can afford only a poor or overworked lawyer will not often obtain equal treatment from the judge."

In the light of the above considerations, Gans observes "Consequently, the only truly egalitarian principle is equality of results, which may require unequal opportunity or treatment for the initially disadvantaged so that they eventually wind up equal in resources or rights."

In fact the spirit of Fundamental Rights itself remains unrealised unless proper conditions are created for protecting the legitimate rights of the under-privileged. Soon after Independence every State enacted land reforms legislation, providing security of tenure to tenants and tillers, placed a ceiling on land holdings, etc. As the weak and poor tenants and cultivators did not have the means to enforce their rights and the powerful land owners had the resources and influence to evade ceiling laws, our land measures have fallen far short of their aims. Stronger sections of society keep perpetrating all sorts of atrocities against Dalits and other backward classes and they are often able to get away without any puinishment. Our entire legal apparatus is so expensive and time-consuming that under-privileged sections of society mostly do not have the means or stamina to get justice from law courts. Under these circumstances, the claim of 'Equality before the law' does not carry much conviction with the weaker sections of Indian society. Equality of results being the real acid test of effective equality, there is no running away from the fact that our sovereign democratic republic will remain seriously affected without a fair share of the fruits of freedom. Equality of opportunity and Equality of treatment are also made available to the backward sections of our people. In this connection, Justice K. Subba Rao has noted:

> "...unless adventitious aids are given to the under-privileged people, it would be impossible to suggest that they have equal opportunities with the more advanced people. This is the reason and the justification for the demand of social justice that the under-privileged citizens of the country should be given a preferential treatment in order to give them an equal opportunity with other more advanced sections of the community."
>
> *(Ibid.)*

In this connection nothing generates so much heat and genuine indignation as the concept of 'merit'. Whereas no body objects to the grant of special educational facilities and several other concessions to the backward classes, the provision of a reserved quota in educational institutions or services for members of Scheduled Castes, Scheduled Tribes or other Backward Classes gives rise to sharp reaction. This argument can be strongly supported by the well known historical fact when the Janta Dal

Government headed by shri V.P. Singh issued order for reservation to OBCs in service in 1990 there was country wide agitation against this decision.

This kind of reaction is based on two considerations: First, it hurts a person's sense of fair play to find that a more 'meritorious' candidate has been omitted in preference to a less 'meritorious' person on purely extraneous grounds. Secondly, it is argued, that by selecting candidates with lower merit against reserved quota vacancies, the nation is being deprived of the services of the best talent that is available to it.

Right to equality—one of the fundamental rights enshrined in the Constitution of India—guarantees every citizen, under Article 14, equality before law or equal protection of laws, and under Article 16(1) equality of opportunity in matters of public appointment. The Constitution prohibits any discrimination that is common to any traditional hierarchical and compartmental society in India. This is explained and specified in Articles 15(1), 16(2) and 29(2). All these are the steps towards the realization and protection of the right to equality. The relevant Articles are mentioned as follows:

As per Article 14 "the state shall not deny any person equality before the law or the equal protection of laws within the territory of India". Similarly, Article 16(1) says that "there shall be equality of opportunity for all citizens in matters relating to employment or appointment to any office under the State".

The Constitution prohibits discrimination, to ensure the equality before law and equality of opportunity and to secure social justice to every citizens. Prohibition of discrimination is the first step towards the realization of the right to equality. This is explained and made specific in Articles 15 and 29. The Constitution, under Article 15(1), prohibits discrimination against any citizens on grounds of religion, race, caste, sex or place of birth either by the State or by any of its citizens. Article 15 reads:

1. The State shall not discriminate against any citizen on grounds only of religion, race, caste, sex, place of birth or any of them.

2. No citizen shall, on grounds only of religion, race, caste, sex, plae of birth or any of them, be subject to any disability, liability, restriction or conditions with regard to:

(a) access to shops, public restaurants, hotels, places of public entertainment, or

(b) the use of wells, tanks, bathing ghats, roads, and places of public resort maintained wholly or partly out of State funds or dedicated to the use of the general public.

Article 16(2) prohibits discrimination on grounds only of religion, race, caste, sex, descent, place of birth, residence or any of them with regard to any appointment or office under the State. It lays down that "no citizen shall on grounds only of religion, race, caste, sex, descent, place of birth, residence, or any of them shall be ineligible for or discriminated against in respect of any employment or office under the State".

Article 29(2) also prohibits discrimination on grounds only of religion, race, caste, language or any of them in respect of admission into any educational institution maintained by the State or receiving aid from the State funds. It reads as follows: "No citizen shall be denied admission into any educational institution maintained by the State or receiving aid out of State funds on grounds only of religion, race, caste, language or any of them."

Various Provisions

Along with the Right to Equality, the Constitution of India provides separate and special provisions for the advancement of backward classes. It is often called compensatory discrimination, protective discrimination and discrimination in reverse. These provisions permit the government to undertake special steps for the upliftment of the backward classes. Article 15(4), which was incorporated into the Indian Constitution under the Constitution (First Amendment) Act, 1951 declares: "Nothing in Article 15 or in Clause (2) of Article 29 shall prevent the State from making any special provision for the advancement of any socially and educationally backward classes of citizens or for the Scheduled Castes and the Scheduled Tribes."

Article 15(4) provides the ground to the State to make special provisions for the backward classes in all the areas within its jurisdiction. The expression 'class' in Article 15(4) means a homogeneous section of the people ground together on account of certain common traits and by being identifiable by some common attributes such as status, rank, occupation, residence in a locality, race and religion. In defining whether a particular section forms a class, caste cannot be totally excluded. At the same time, a test based upon only caste or community cannot be accepted. Article 16(4) which is relevant to government jobs, says: "Nothing in this Article shall prevent the State from making any provision for the reservation of appointments or posts in favour of any backward class of citizens which in the opinion of the State is not adequately represented in the services under the State."

When the Constitution of India came into force with effect from 26th January 1950, Article 15 did not have the Clause (4). Later on, in the light of the judgment of the High Court of Madras and the Supreme Court of India in the famous case Champarkam Dorairajan versus The State of Madras, the Constitution was amended. The Government of India felt that some special provision must be made for the educational advanement of the backward classes, as they could not get any benefit under Article 16(4) of the Constitution. Hence, an amendment to the Constitution was made to reserve seats for the citizens of the backward classes, the Scheduled Castes and the Scheduled Tribes in public services and educational institutions and also undertake other measures for the advancement of the other backward classes. Accordingly, Clause (4) was added to the Article 15 by the first amendment to the Constitution. By this amendment, Article 15 and 29 were brought to become consistent with Articles 16(4) and 340. According to the Supreme Court of India, the above special provisions of the Constitution are in the nature of an enabling provision' and a 'discretionary power' of the State under Articles 15(4) and 16(4) to take any measure for the advancement of socially and educationally backward classes.

For a long time it had been regarded that Articles 15(4) and 16(4) are 'exceptions' to Articles 15(1) and 16(1). According to this view, the claims of the backward classes could be projected only through exceptional Clauses and not outside them. But, in the case of State of Kerala *versus* N.M. Thomas, the Supreme Court by majority rejected this notion of exception and held that the State was free to select any 'means' to achieve equality for these backward classes. It is evident that the Supreme Court has discarded the old way of thinking that Articles 15(4) and 16(4) are exceptions to the equality guaranteed and declared that these Articles are themselves aimed at achieving the goal of equality broadly proclaimed and guaranteed by Articles 14, 15(1) and 16(1).

The prevailing view now is that Article 15(4) of the Constitution authorizes the State to make 'special provision' for the uplift of the socially and educationally backward classes of citizens. So also, Article 16(4) authorizes the State to make 'any provision' for the reservation of appointment in favour of backward classes of citizens, which, in the opinion of the State, are not sufficiently represented in the services under the State. It also permits the government to readily identify a backward class with reference to a person's caste. It is also clear from the decisions of the Supreme Court in the case of Balaji *versus* State of Mysore (1963) and Indira Sawhney *versus* Union of India (1992) that the action envisaged by the Articles 15(4) and 16(4) can be taken either by the Union or the State Government. The policy of reservation subsequently adopted in many States in India is connected to the need for the maintenance of efficiency in administration. This is clear from Article 335 which reads: "The claims of the members of the Scheduled Castes and the Scheduled Tribes shall be taken into consideration, consistently with the maintenance of efficiency of administration, in the making of appointments to services and posts in connection with the affairs of the Union or of a State."

This Article, thus, makes it clear that to get the benefit of reservation a candidate on a post in the government or in a public undertaking would have to fulfil the minimum educational and other qualifications required for the post in consonance with the nature and requirement of that post, so as to maintain efficiency of any organisation.

Educational Reservation

Under Articles 15 (4) and 29, it is compulsory for educational institutions and universities to reserve 20 per cent, i.e., 1/5th of seats for SC and ST candidates, for whom qualifying marks are considerably relaxed. Despite the relaxation, the quotas often remain unfulfilled and many institutions try to avoid reserving seats. At the post-graduate level, number of SC and ST candidates in Engineering and Medical courses remain very low. Moreover, the Report of the Commissioner for Scheduled Castes and Scheduled Tribes 1978-79 reveals that 83 per cent general as against 75 per cent and 66 per cent of SC and ST Children between the ages of 6 and 11 were enrolled in Primary Schools. In addition, the dropout rate at the Primary level of these children was 79 per cent.

Educationally, the SC and ST children face financial problems, hostile social backup, an supp;ortive atmosphere for studies at home and inadequate guidance for academics. Despite the obstacles, the outstanding students among the SC and ST have increased and many occupy positions of power in the buraucracy and elsewhere because of the policy of protective discrimination which enables them to compete, no matter how small the number and how difficult their path to success.

Job Reservation

Under Articles 16(4), 320(4) and 333, 15 per cent and 7 per cent respectively were reserved for SCs and STs at all levels of the public sector. Qualifications for both recruitment and promotion were relaxed in the cases of such candidates. Between 1959 and 1979, the number of SC and ST candidates in Class-I services has risen from 1.18 per cent to 4.75 per cent. At the lower levels, however, they occupy many positions but have little or no scope in the private sector. If a society is to be judged not only for what it is but what it aspires to be, and if the Constitution is considered as the expression of a society's desire to have an ideal set up for all its citizens, then the Indian Constitution is remarkable for its stress on the idea of equality. Not only is the principal of equality incorporated in the Preamble and the Directive Principles of State Policy and Fundamental Rights, but it has also been protected judicial decisions and legislations enacted over the years. Jurists agree that in its commitment to equality, the Indian Constitution has gone beyond any contemporary Constitution including that of America.

Past Experience

The disharmony and turmoil which is presently prevalent is due to the paradox of equality versus the reality of inequality and injustice which still have not vanished from our society. In order to ensure equality under unequal circumstances and in order to discriminate in favour of those who in the past had been discriminated against, a policy of "affirmative action" or protective discrimination was necessary. The factor behind the idea of protective discrimination was that certain sections, castes or groups have special claims on society which cannot be ignored for mere individual excellence. The compensatory principles in which redressal is made for wrongs of past whole classes and groups of people may not always succeed in reversing past injuries and care has to be taken that in destroying old inequalities we do not create fresh ones. Discrimination is a disastrous, no matter how good the intentions are of those who use it and how careful we have to be in using it even for a desirable end.

In adopting, retaining and even extending the range of the policy of protective discrimination, the individual claims as against those of the group, of the reward given to merit as against those of need are important to be balanced. It would be wrongful to think that by making concessions to communities and castes, the needs of every individual is fulfilled. Classification of castes and communities incorporates in itself the concept of discrimination as does classification of individuals into slots and niches. The SCs and STs have already been classified as such and everyday there is further clamour from other backward or economically deprived groups for a portion of the State's resources as recompense for past injuries and/or present needs.

Communal politics, minority politics and the politics of backwardness were encouraged by the British to the freedom movement and they are a fact of life in contemporary Indian politics, which is heavily dependent on the concept of "vote banks" for the major political parties and their partisan goals. There is no perfect correlation between the ritual status of a caste and their actual material condition. There are many forces which come into play presently which have reduced the association between caste and income, occupation and education. Keeping in mind that the interests of the Scheduled Castes and Scheduled Tribes have been given constitutional protection, it seems anachronistic to increase the scope of positive discrimination to such an extent that an individuals caste become a determining factor in his entitlements.

While including an individual or a community in the list of backward classes in India, one would have to consider both the economic and sociological factors. While the stigma of caste and the isolation of the tribals may continue, even hardened cynics would agree that the feeling of distance and discrimination between castes today has been decreased. However, economic inequality and poverty have not started much decrease, so that visible and glaring evidence of poverty can be seen in both rural areas as well as in urban slums. Poverty, illiteracy and health problems are not the exclusive problems of the SC and ST but for as Jagjivan Ram they are the problems of a poor Brahmin and a poor Harijan are the same.

In many cases, protective discrimination has become a "crutch" for both activating the state and the affected persons themselves, who take little initiative and instead depend on official programmes and policies for advancement and social mobility.

Since the ideology underlying the division of castes into high and low, proved "negative discrimination", reservation in educational, economic and legislative institutions were aimed at removing both gaps and discrimination, with education serving as the important tool of an improved lifestyle. Reservation in jobs and monetary incentives were also designed to both social and financial standing, while political reservation ensured that they shoud be given an adequate participation in the formulation of state policies.

Reasons for Extension

Why has the policy of reservation which had initially been given for a period of twenty years been again and again extended and why is there at present a clamour to redefine the criteria for reservation ?

With the Scheduled Castes and Scheduled Tribes being an important vote bank, vested political interests could never terminate the policy or end the period of reservation. Despite many economic and educational surveys and studies being undertaken, the observations have not shown that the reservation policy alone has set right all previous hardships and difficulties faced by the "weaker sections". The efforts of the state policy cannot be written off for them has had a psychological impact on the Scheduled Castes and Scheduled Tribes making many of their capable members to come forward. Seeing the benefits of reservation which have reached the SCs or STs an amorphous group of so-called "other backward classes/castes" have used political character and to secure reservation for themselves, e.g., in southern states Karnataka and Andhra Pradesh, where approximately 55 per cent and 45 per cent of the seats are reserved.

Analytical Views

With the rapid rise of India's population from the time of Independence to the present, the pressure on the sufficient, educational and job opportunities have been heavy. Competition has become hard in the educational and professional institutions and the increasing demand for employment opportunities have not kept pace with the growth of the population. Again, a new generation has grown up with a secular, liberal education and for them the existence of caste-based reservation in every sphere seems to be a irrational to the concept of equality and individual capacities.

Caste prejudices may be a reality especially in rural areas but the systematic increase in the percentage of reservation in different states presents a shrinking opportunities to those who are not the so called disadvantaged. In addition, the benefits of reservation are hardly reaching the needy. There is no denial to the children of the reserved category bureaucrats and politicians to continue availing privileges under the quota system. In fact, the reservation policy has given rise to new pejorative terms such as "quota wallah" SC or ST etc. It is not be wise to view all criticism voiced against reservation as merely the cries of the privileged sections who are scared of losing the upper hand. Rather it should be seen as the mind set that when the country is supposed to be entering into the 21st century, political pressures force the fragmentation of society, yet again into high and low Scheduled Castes and Scheduled Tribes, women and handicapped persons all trying to ease themselves into comfortable slots with the minimum of effort by virtue of birth and through the medium of reservations.

At the same time it would be unjust to attribute the decline in efficiency in the government and the lowering of educational standards to the reservation policy. Initially, lower percentage was reserved for Scheduled Castes and Scheduled Tribes who are still heavily outnumbered by general candidates. It is the increasing reservation to various pressure groups for political expediency which is causing disappointment amongst those who have to sacrifice their chances for members of other sections of society who are not necessarily either the most disadvantaged or deserving candidates in the competitions for the few seats and jobs available in open market. Protective justice for the deprived is a legitimate aim of society but mollycoddling those who are already ahead constitutes an injustice which has to be handled with political will rather than political expediency, if caste rivalries are not to be tended and hatred perpetuated to new generations of Indians.

While the Constitution of India bars any form of discrimination among citizens, yet protective discrimination becomes legal in the context of "reservation". While the Constitution was categorical in reservations for the Scheduled Castes and Scheduled Tribes, it was vague about the other Backward Castes or OBCs. This was due to the ambiguity at that time in identifying the beneficiaries, specifying the type of benefits that would be required as well as implementing this policy of preferential treatment. Several autonomous Commissions and Committees have therefore looked into the issue of reservation under Articles 15 (4) and 16(4) appointed by the State and Central Governments. While various State governments have appointed nearly seventeen Commissions and Committees, the Central Government form the Kalekar Commission in 1953 and the Mandal Commission in 1979 for deciding the quota of reservation as well as identifying those who needed such protective discrimination. The recommendations are divided in two categories: one adopted caste as the basis for reservation (both the Mandal and Kalekar Commission) and the adopted economic criteria (the State Committees adopted by J & K, West Bengal, Karnataka and Gujarat).

The Mandal Commission focussed on the aspects of reservation—namely, the criteria and percentage of reservation among others. Eleven indicators were grouped under three heads—social, educational and economic indicators were fixed in order to ascertain the socio-economic backwardness of the people. It acted on the principle that economic backwardness was the result of socio-educational backwardness and thus poverty was the result of caste-based handicaps.

Whereas caste has now disappeared in its ritualistic form, it has gained new importance and secured a fresh existence on the political front. This has increased, rather than decreased casteism in the country, as caste-based pressure groups vie with each other to secure certain privileges for themselves. Since a government job carries with it a great deal of social prestige and financial security, it has been thought that caste-based proportional reservation should be provided in the government, the public sector and educational institutions. As the Supreme Court does not favour raising the percentage of reservation beyond 50 per cent, the Mandal Commission was constrained to recommend a 27 per cent reservation for 3,743 castes.

Justice Rane on the other hand, in his report presented before the Gujarat Assembly in March 1985 clearly stated: "It will not only be totally unrealistic but also unpatriotic to make any attempt to assess social backwardness on the basis of caste." Many fact that caste-based reservation would create gaps in society and it would eliminate non-Hindu communities. Already in the fifty years of independence the higher echelons all castes have progressed, due to reservation or otherwise, so it is inevitable to bring in those who are the poorest and most deprived within the ambit of reservation. To meet the need for fixing new criteria in determining backwardness, the Commission suggested that family income and occupation to be the only criterion for determining socio-economic backwardness. In Gujarat, 63 occupations with incomes below Rs. 10,000 per annum were determined as backward.

According to Ishwari Prasad, there must be two conditions in a modern day reservation policy, one, identification should be secular and rational and, two, there should be an in-built mechanism for its dissolution in the course of time.

Financial criteria is acceptable because of its social neutrality. Instead of entering into the controversial issues of the respective positions of the four thousand castes of India, the lone criteria of income will determine the question of special treatment while at the same time eliminating the question of caste and its corresponding social position altogether.

Thirdly, economic criteria will and must be self-abolishing as the increase of income will obviously uplift a person from the purview of reservations. The policy of reservation must have inbuilt deservation which is possible only if economic criteria is the parameter.

Where caste is taken as the factor determining socio-economic backwardness, there will never be any dereservation, as this is a Indian caste society. The phenomenal rise of India's population makes impossible social parity with regard to jobs and education as the resources have not increased sufficiently to absorb this gigantic mass of people.

In the past it was a generally accepted fact of life that different lifestyles were appropriate to different castes of society. With the increase of literacy and education to the Scheduled Castes and Scheduled Tribes, western way of living and a government job are seen as ideals to which they aspire. There is strong desire for white collar jobs among Scheduled Castes and Scheduled Tribes, as in any sphere of Indian society there is great respectability attached to them. Hence a white collar job, whether that of a clerk or a peon, a mark of respectability. For this reason, studies reveal that since these classes were, until recently, excluded from such professions they aspire all the more zealously for government or clerical posts. Due to such state of affair government-run craft training schools do not attract as many students as they should, despite the fact that a manually skilled job would give greater monetary benefits than a clerical one. Westernised education, expansion of caste-free occupations and geographical mobility have all combined to give a thrust to individual social mobility. Urban and semi-urban centres which have become overloaded due to an ever increasing number of people, strains and constraints of caste and hierarchical pressures are missing normally seen in the villages.

Caste politics and pressure groups have formed an unholy combination for getting ahead without due efforts have given voice to the plea for increased reservation. However, reservation may be a prominent method for ensuring social justice and equality, but it cannot and should not be an obstacle for the very urgent needs for concerted economic action, which alone can bring succour to millions in this country.

The Report of the Commissioner for Scheduled Castes says, "Even though recommendations were made for extending the scope of the principle of positive discrimination, greater emphasis was placed on basic structural changes in the economy through formulation of equitous policies and their effective implementation, besides attending to the immediate problems" regarding wages, protection of traditional occupations and equal distribution of land. The Commission regarded that the Central Government's decision not to dereserve, but launch a special drive for filling vacant posts in reserved quotas was a measure with limited scope. Two national level bodies namely, The Tribal Cooperative Marketing Development Federation of India Limited and the National Scheduled Castes and Scheduled Tribes Finance Development Corporation have also been formed to fulfil the needs of the SCs and STs.

Since new generation is hardly aware of the extremely humiliating status of the Scheduled Castes and the isolation of the Tribals, the willingness of the government in distributing largesse to them arouses in the intermediary Backward Classes. The clamour for State-sponsored social mobility and economic and educational security by means of reservation is being asked by OBCs in every state. Politicians are buying peace by extending the scope and percentage of reservations in OBCs every State while the actual task of forming the nation's economy, extending educational facilities and improving the quality of life for the every increasing population remains a dream.

With the reservation policy being routinely renewed so frequently, other "dominant" caste groups such as Kurmi, Yadav, Koeri, Lingayats, Vokkaligas etc. all over the country are demanding backward status and reservation. Due to the benefits which are the outcome of reservation to various communities, each vies with the other in the race for backwardness.

A frequently given argument is that Backward Classes have a low social status, even if they are comparatively well-off. In his landmark work on the *Harijan Elite* Prof. Sachchidananda has included numerous case studies in which interviews were conducted with members of the harijan elite, who had given up their caste-based hierarchal occupations. By connecting themselves from their traditional occupations which had the brand of pollution, untouchability automatically vanished. It was found that status disabilities were mainly led to village only but here too, discrimination at public wells and in temples had decreased to a great extent. Moreover, legislators and public servants were ultimised thereby establishing a direct correlation between the politico-economic status of an individual and his social status. A well off harijan says, "Superior Brahmins come to my residence to conduct each and every family ritual. This privilege, however, is not available to other persons of my caste residing in the same village." Having given up the traditional caste occupation of toddy tapping , healthy social relations and being a vegetarian has made him "acceptable" even to diehard Brahmins in the village.

Eating with Harijans is no longer taboo and in bigger cities there is hardly any discrimination prevailing on this front. The entry of SCs in government or professional institutions is secretly disliked by colleagues because of contempt for Scheduled Castes, growing competition and jealousy because of their weapon of protective discrimination. Some harijan have an inherited inferiority and oversensitiveness so that they frequently infer discrimination or ill-treatment where it is not exercised.

Human nature being what it is, resentment towards those who have been offered special privileges or those who are considered interlopers, as Asian immigrants in the USA and England, are bound to surface.

With respect to the ability of the SC leaders to transform the social set up by virtue of their upgradation to positions of power and prestige, the study shows that large numbers of educated ones both in urban and rural areas and have little active concern with improving conditions of their less fortunate caste fellows. Alienated from traditional professions, their major concern appears to be that of meeting the needs of the immediate family and kin. Some of the leaders who have risen high in the social hierarchy have snapped their ties with their bleak past. While public servants were completely out of concern with their community, social workers and legislators had to work out dual roles of maintaining close relations with the wider community for their own ends, as well as achieving a hold over their own community whose support they required during elections.

The SC leaders perceived that by and large structural distance between the Scheduled Castes and others have reduced significantly especially in cities, where young and educated Scheduled Castes felt no blocks because of the role of education as instrument of change.

While caste Hindus have liberalised their attitudes towards dalits, it has been observed that so called middle range backward castes offer larger resistance to the rising status of the Harijan than the very highest castes. Not only do they perceive a threat to their own positions because of the growing power of the Scheduled Castes but they are also jealous of the benefits and advantages provided to the Scheduled Castes by the Constitution.

As far as politics is concerned, the Harijan leader has to maintain a delicate balance between an image as a receiver of benefits of their own community while ensuring that they do not isolate the rest of their constituency by being too radical or strident in promoting the cause of freedom from oppression.

If the goal of reservation was to integrate the Scheduled Castes and Scheduled Tribes with the rest of the population than the system of quotas in profession, education and politics have only strengthened their separate identity and caused jealousy to members of higher castes who are similarly deprived but are without reservation.

While political expediency has made reservations somewhat permanent. In fact, many members of the Scheduled Castes and Scheduled Tribes are now able to prove the gains of the reservation policy, which has protected them for the last five decades, catapulting many to positions of power, privilege and wealth. But if one looks at the number of SC/ST Secretaries in the government of India or the actual literacy rates and the data of those SCs/STs below the poverty line as compared to the rest, it will repeat the old saying "One swallow does not make a summer." The upliftment of a single individual member of the community does not enhance the economic condition of the rest. While there may be Jagjivan

Rams, B.R. Ambedkars, Karpoori Thakurs, Solankis, and K.R. Narayanans, their presence in the highest positions of political and administrative structure seemed to by only psychological strength. Whereas the rise of Indira Gandhi to the premiership of India may have been motivating to women all over the world, her presence did not enhance the status of women. There was no decline in evils pertaining to and atrocities committed on women during her term in office.

Two generations of Indians have tried to redress for the victimisation and low status given to Scheduled Castes and Scheduled Tribes in the past. Sincere efforts have been made to bring these communities on a par with the rest and to extent them socio-psychological support. It has been found that economic progress gets the maximum amount of social progress. The time has come when concrete steps to uplift all the Backward Classes must be taken in the form of free and compulsory education, vocational training, land, housing, health care, family planning and nutrition. A rural thrust such as the one given in the 20-Point Economic Programme, the abolition of bonded labour, the inclusion of tribals in the mainstream and other viable schemes for industrial and agricultural development must be initiated with great sincerity and commitement. What they need is a alternative to the problems of poverty, illness, shelter and illiteracy. Job reservations are only for the communities amongst SCs and STs and job reservations benefit only a handful minority of the downtrodden.

While the determination of one Indira Gandhi led to the withdrawal of a constitutional commitment on princely privileges and privy pauses, similarly the time has come to take political initiative to wish away rather than increase reservation. Reservations help a limited number of people and have no significant overall benefit to the most suppressed in that community.

The acceptance of the Mandal Commission suggestions would serve no purpose other than dividing society along caste lines and awakening caste awareness even where it was existent as in the metropolitan cities and rural areas in every state. The presentation of caste certificates at each platform would lead to further corruption and needless expansion of an already entrenched bureaucracy. By including more and more people within the purview of reservations there will be a mere expansion of nonproductive clerical and bureaucratic posts, for which there will be a little scope for individual progress.

Case for SCs and STs

The Constitution mentioned only the reservation policy. It did not fix any particular percentage of seats in professional and technical institutions and posts in government and semi-government jobs. In 1950, the Government of India reserved 12.5 per cent seats for the Scheduled Castes and 5 per cent for the Scheduled Tribes in all-India services to be recruited on the basis of open competition. It also relaxed the age limit in their case by three years. In 1952, it relaxed the age limit to five years more than the maximum prescribed for others. Now, in the central and state services, seats and posts are reserved in proportion to population. In 1970, the Central Government raised the reservation quota for the Scheduled Castes to 15 per cent, and that for the Scheduled Tribes to 7.5 per cent. As for reservation of jobs, the Constitution describes no fixed period. Naturally, the State is supposed to continue such preferential treatment until the SCs, STs and OBCs make substantial progress educationally and economically and reach a level of equality with the rest of the Indian citizens.

It hastened the process of socio-economic changes in India and specially of improving the conditions of the weaker sections and backward classes who constitute a majority of the population. The future of national progress and achievement of an egalitarian society depends on the rapid advancement of these backward sections of the people. The Constitution has set its goal to achieve this social justice and it can be explained in terms representation percentage of employees in the various categories of Central Government services.

RESERVATION OF OTHER BACKWARD CLASSES, SCHEDULED CASTES/SCHEDULED TRIBES IN CENTRAL GOVERNMENT SERVICES

Class	*Total*	*SC/ST*	*OBC*	*General*
I	174026 (100.00)	9891 (5.68)	8169 (4.69)	155966 (89.63)
II	912925 (100.00)	165982 (18.18)	97063 (10.63)	649880 (71.19)

III & IV	484687 (100.00)	118282 (24.40)	91975 (18.98)	274430 (56.62)
All Classes (excluding sweepers)	1571638 (100.00)	294155 (18.72)	197207 (12.55)	1080276 (68.73)

Source: Government of India Report on the Backward Classes Commission, First Part, Vol. I & II, 1980, Statement No. 1, p. 92.

This statement gives an interesting trend (i) there is decline in percentage of reservation of SCs/STs and OBCs from lower classes to higher class of posts. (ii) there is an increase in percentage of reservation of General Category. This shows a reverse trend, i.e., forward castes held largest share.

The positive impact of the affirmative action taken by the Indian Constitution can also be explained in terms of the educational progress and raising the level of literacy of the SCs and STs in India. At the time of India's independence in 1947, the literacy rate among them was below one per cent and in the last fifty years there has been considerable increase in their literacy rate. It is a fact that almost half of the world's illiterate population lives in India, but slowly the literacy level is going up. The position can be justified on the basis of Table.

The literacy rate in the case of SCs and STs has constantly gone up during the last five decades. The growth rate of literacy is higher among SCs and STs when compared to the total population. It is also clear from the data that the gap between them and rest of the population has increased. There are also considerable changes in literacy rates among different castes and different tribes. Again, wide interstate and inter-district variations exist in the context of SCs and STs. The special provisions in the Constitution led to the progressive realization of the creation of a new and just social order as visualized by the architects of the Constitution. Further, in view of economic development of the underprivileged section of the society, the Constitution of India has set goals for the eradication of poverty. The First Five Year Plan of India (1952-57) outlined its objects like this. The State shall, in particular, direct its policy towards achieving (a) that the citizens, men and women equally have the right to a fair means of livelihood, and (b) that the ownership and control of the material resources of the community are so distributed as to subserve the common good. In 1954, the

Government of India gave recognition to the socialist pattern of society as one of the objects of its economic and social policy. It was focussed to improve the living standards of the masses and provide gainful employment to those living below the poverty line. Many plans failed to end poverty, unemployment and economic inequality. Although there had been a perceptible increases in per capita income and some decline in percentage of the persons living below the poverty line, the magnitude of poverty in India is very high. In the context of SCs and STs, they continue to be socially and educationally backward and form the bottom of socio-economic pyramids. Table gives comparative picture of the decline of poverty during the period 1977-78 to 1987-88.

PERCENTAGE GROWTH RATE OF LITERACY AMONG SCs/STs IN INDIA IN 1961, 1971, 1981 AND 1991 CENSUS

Social Sections	*Literacy Rates*				*Growth Rates of Literacy*		
	1961	*1971*	*1981*	*1991*	*1991*	*1971-81*	*1981-91*
Total Population	24.00	29.45	36.23	52.21	22.71	23.02	44.10
SCs	10.27	14.67	21.30	37.41	42.84	45.74	75.76
	(3.29)	(6.44)	(10.93)	(23.76)	(95.44)	(69.71)	
STs	88.54	11.29	16.35	29.60	32.20	44.82	81.35
	(3.16)	(4.85)	(8.04)	(18.19)	(53.48)	(65.77)	

Note: Figures in parentheses show percentage of female literacy.
Source: Shymanand Singh, *Tribal Education in India*, Uppal (New Delhi), 1991, p. 7 and Census of India 1991 Series-I SC and ST, p. 14.

PERCENTAGE OF SCs AND STs LIVING BELOW POVERTY LINE

Year	*Total Population*	*Scheduled Castes*	*Scheduled Tribes*
1977-78	51.2	64.6	72.4
1983-84	40.4	53.1	58.4
1987-88	33.4	44.7	52.6

Source: Eighth Five Year Plan, 1992-97, Planning Commission, Government of India, 1992 (New Delhi), Vol. II, p. 420.

The data reveal that one-third of Indian population lives in the condition of poverty. They are denied access to the basic needs of life such as sufficient food, clothes, house and medicine. There is no provision of social security for the poor. Now, the process of liberalization and the new economic policy have created a market friendly atmosphere. It could lead to still wider disparities within Indian society. The underprivileged sections will not get benefit of the opportunities, and the competitive market system will wipe out special privileges provided to them. This will increase the gap between the rich and the poor.

In Article 334 of the Indian Constitution reservation of seats in legislatures (Lok Sabha and Vidhan Sabhas) was made initially only for ten years. It was later extended through a series of amendments to the Constitution. The 62nd constitutional amendment in 1989 had extended reservation upto January 2000. In proportion to the population of SCs and STs reservation in legislature provided to them in Indian Parliament and State Legislatures. Table presents number of reserved seats alongwith the total seats.

As is clear from the table that out of 543 seats in the Lok Sabha, 46 seats are reserved for the SCs and STs. It provided them an opportunity to take part in the decision-making process of the country and many strong leaders have emerged from amongst them. In the various State Governments reservation in legislature produced capable ministers from them. In absence of these provisions they might not have got opportunity to serve the people and get share in the political process. Thus, reserved seats in legislature became a boom for bringing social justice and social change in India.

STATEWISE NUMBERS OF SEATS RESERVED FOR SCs AND STs IN THE ASSEMBLIES AND PARLIAMENT

	Lok Sabha			*Assemblies*		
	Total	*SC*	*ST*	*Total*	*SC*	*ST*
States						
1. Andhra Pradesh	42	6	2	294	39	15
2. Arunachal Pradesh	2		2	60		59
3. Assam	14	1	2	126	8	16
4. Bihar	54	8	5	324	48	28
5. Gujarat	26	2	4	182	13	26
6. Haryana	10	2	0	90	17	0
7. Himachal Pradesh	4	1	0	68	16	3
8. Jammu & Kashmir	6	0	0	76	6	0
9. Karnataka	28	4	0	224	33	2
10. Kerala	20	2	0	140	13	1

11. Madhya Pradesh	40	6	9	320	44	75
12. Maharashtra	48	3	4	288	18	22
13. Manipur	2	0	1	60	1	19
14. Meghalaya	2	0	2	60	0	55
15. Nagaland	1	0	1	60	0	59
16. Orissa	21	3	5	147	22	34
17. Punjab	13	3	0	117	29	0
18. Rajasthan	25	4	3	200	33	34
19. Sikkim	1	0	0	32	1	15
20. Tamil Nadu	39	7	0	234	42	3
21. Tripura	2	0	1	60	7	17
22. Uttar Pradesh	85	18	0	425	92	1
23. West Bengal	42	8	2	294	59	17
24. Goa	2	0	0	30	1	0
25. Mizoram	1	0	1	40	6	38
26. Delhi	7	1	0	56	9	0
Union Territories						
1. Pondicherry	1	0	0	30	5	0
2. A&N Islands	1	0	0	-	-	-
3. Chandigarh	1	0	0	-	-	-
4. Dadra & Nagar Haveli	1	0	1	-	-	-
5. Daman & Diu	1	0	0	-	-	-
6. Lakshdweep	1	0	1	-	-	-
All India	543	79	46	4037	56	529

Source: *28th Report of the Commission of SC and ST*, Government of India (New Delhi) 1986-87, pp. 242-43.

The tenth Plan document (2002-07) brought out by the Planning Commission quoted representation of SCs, STs, at different level of political institutions (See Table).

PERCENTAGE GROWTH RATE OF LITERACY AMONG SCs/STs IN INDIA IN 1961, 1971, 1981 AND 1991 CENSUS

Category			*1991*			*1999*	
SCs	6	7	3,67,941	18,546	1,822	562	79
	(10.5)	(9.5)	(14.3)	(14.4)	(13.5)	(13.8)	(14.**)
STs	3	3	2,35,445	7,237	1,170	530	4**
	(5.3)	(4.1)	(9.1)	(5.6)	(8.7)	(13.0)	(7.5)
General	48	64	11,76,875	99,798	10,482	2,980	423
Total	57	74	2580261	1,25,581	13,484	4,072	543

1. National Informatics Centre, Parliament House, New Delhi. Figures within paranthesis indicate percentage to total.
2. Election Commission, New Delhi, Department of Rural Development, GOI, New Delhi. NIC, Parliament

Appointment of Commission

Article 340 is connected with the appointment of commissions for the investigation of the socio-economic considerations of SCs, STs and OBCs. It makes it obligatory for the appointment of commissions by the President (i) to look into and report on the administration of the scheduled areas and the welfare of the Scheduled Tribes, and (ii) to investigate the conditions of socially and educationally backward classes and to make recommendations as to the step that should be taken by the Union or State Government to ameliorate those conditions. So far two such commissions have been appointed by the President of India under the Article 340 of the Constitution.

The First Commission on Backward Classes under the chairmanship of Kaka Kalelkar gave extremely wide ranging recommendations for upliftment of the backward classes. Some of the most noteworthy recommendations of the Commission were:

(i) Undertaking caste-wise enumeration of population in the census of 1961.

(ii) Relating social backwardness of a class to its low position in the traditional caste hierarchy of Hindu Society.

(iii) Treating all women as a class as 'backward'.

(iv) Reservation of 70 per cent in seats in all technical and professional institutions for qualified students of backward classes.

(v) Minimum reservation of vacancies in all government services and local bodies for OBCs on the following scale:

Class I (25%), Class II (33.3%), Class III & IV (40%).

The report of the commission was not unanimous; five of its members recorded minutes of dissent. Shri Kaka Kalelkar in his forwarding letter to the President opposed inclusion of caste as a basis for backwardness.

About the caste-based reservations policy as recommended by the Kalelkar Commission, Govind Ballabh Pant, the then Home Minister, noted that the recognition of the specific castes as backward may serve to maintain and even perpetuate the existing distinction based on caste. The Central Government did not implement it and left it for the State Governments to adopt their own criteria. Again, in 1978, the claim of OBCs was referred to the second Backward Classes Commission, headed by B.P. Mandal. The terms of reference Mandal Commission were: (i) to determine the criteria for defining socially and educationally backward classes; (ii) to recommend steps to be taken for the advancement of the socially and educationally backward classes of citizens so identified; (iii) to examine the desirability or otherwise of making provisions for the reservation of appointment of posts in favour of such backward classes of citizens which are not reasonably represented in public services and posts in connection with the affairs of the Union or any State, and (iv) present to the President a report setting out of facts as found by them and making such recommendations as they think proper.

The Mandal Commission also settled upon the routine and ready tool of caste with which to identify backward classes. The research team, appointed to carry out a village level survey, chose family as a unit of observation. The team found as a horizontal segmental division of society spread over a district of a region or the whole state even beyond. In each village, a section of a caste exists largely in vertical relationship with other castes. The survey, thus, neglected the community aspect of caste. The Commission prepared one consolidated list of backward classes L.R. Naik, a Member of the Commission, while giving a dissenting note, recommended that a separate list be prepared for each state and that each list should be in two parts, one part listing the intermediate backward classes and other one the depressed backward classes. The Commission did not accept this suggestion. It even cited the judgment of the Supreme Court of India in Balaji *versus* State of Mysore case, which had *inter alia* stated that in introducing two categories of backward classes, what the impugned order, in substance, purports to do is to devise methods for all the classes of citizens who are less advanced compared to the most advanced in the state, this is not the scope of Article 15(4).

The Commission found that the representation of the backward classes (other than SCs and STs) in the central services in different categories was below that of the SCs and STs although the population of these backward classes was more than double of the SCs and STs. The better representation of the SCs and STs is entirely because of the reservation policy.

The Mandal Commission identified as many as 3,943 castes covering about 52 per cent of the total population of India as OBCs in its report in 1980. It, therefore, suggested reservation for these backward classes in proportion of their population. However, in the context of the legal constraint that total reservation should not exceed 50 per cent for all categories, it restricted this reservation to 27 per cent in government service and in educational institutions. It proposed the following overall scheme of reservation for the OBCs:

(i) Candidates belonging to these classes recruited on the basis of merit in an open competition should be excluded against their reservation quota of 27 per cent.

(ii) Reservation should also be provided in promotions at all levels.

(iii) Any reserved quota remaining unfilled should be carried forward for a period of three years and dereserved thereafter.

(iv) Relaxation in the upper age limit for direct recruitment should be given to candidates of the backward classes as in the case of the SCs and STs.

(v) A roster system for each category of posts should be adopted by the authorities concerned as in the case of the SCs and STs.

The report of the Mandal Commission was placed before Lok Sabha in 1982 for the debate. But the political will for implementation was lacking till the emergence of OBCs as a political force in 1989 parliamentary election. The Mandal Commission's recommendations were implemented by the Janata Dal government led by V.P. Singh on 13th August 1990. This was challenged in the Supreme Court and various High Courts. The Supreme Court issued a stay order on 7th November, 1990. The issue was then examined by the nine-member Constitutional Bench which, on 16th November, 1992, in its majority judgment (4 out of 9) permitted the Central Government to reserve 27 per cent for the OBCs subject to the exclusion of the creamy layer. After the identification of the creamy layer by the Ramanand Prasad Committee in March 1993 and their exclusion from becoming the beneficiary of OBCs the Central Government executed the V.P. Singh govenment order of 13th August, 1990 in September 1993. Thus, the constitutional validity of reservation for OBCs in central service was thoroughly examined by the Supreme Court which said that the list of OBCs can be made on the basis of caste as it represents an existing identifiable social group of the country's population. At present, for the three groups of backward classes—SCs, STs and OBCs, 15, 7.5 and 27 per cent of posts respectively are reserved.

The Indian social and political system is moving towards achievement of a trinity of goals of the constitution viz., socialism, secularism and democracy. Now, a situation has been created by the State that all sections of the society can take part in the State power equally, irrespective of their caste, community, race, religion and sex.

Although there are always some groups who conspire, some oppress, some manipulate and equally others expose conspiracy, fight oppression and resist manipulations. The different sides are not evenly matched. But the pluralist Indian society gives protection to all of its divergent interest, under its broad political spectrum and its law is committed to bringing distribution of power, social justice and eradicating poverty of its deprived masses. The economic development as well as the spread egalitarian values has generated a formidable challenge to the old social order and those who were at the bottom of the social and economic order are moving up and are in the process of getting power from the hands of traditional elite.

9
Conclusion

Dalits are backward in general, in all areas and they are backward in the field of Education is particular. The suffering and total marginalisation of a major portion of Indian society dates back to the time immemorial. Though even the perpetrators of Dalits concede to the fact that they were the earlier inhabitants of this land. The heap of insult and untold story of their miseries on all fronts still goes on unabated. The Aryan invaders, if any arbitrarily took possession of their land and wealth and ultimately spoiled their cultural heritage. Once the invaders had started inhabiting in this land which they encroached upon.

Unmindful of the emotion and senstivity of its original inhabitants, they started framing herms which were totally biased and drecommon. Hindus religion had been instrumental in exploiting and suppressing a large section of Indian Society. Thus Indian society has always been the religio-centric one. Realising the vulnerability of religious mythology in Indian society, the dominating and villainous Brahmin society left no stone unturned in cashing in on it. They established the varanashrams and divided the people according to their professions. Untouchables were not belonged to the either of these four varnashrams - Brahmins, Kshatriyas, Vaisyas and Sudras. Thus stretching over the millenia the original inhabitants of Indus valley have been undergoing all sorts of humiliation and even ostracisation at the hands of Aryan invaders. The works assigned to the untouchables were much humiliating and menial. They were not to be come in the view of an upper caste and they were not supposed to trend on the path, where an upper caste was supposed to traverse. The untouchables were not permitted into temples and institutions of learning. Hence millenia long suffering at the hands upper caste indian society created deep-rooted inferiority complex in them from which they are yet to be recovered.

As it is widely known inferiority complex retards one's mental growth, it gives one away from expressing his or her talents. Advent of the British to a certain extent proved to be a blessing in disguise for the untouchables. The British made them understand that the education can play a major role in freeing them from the shackles of slavery. This volume is a critically analysed coverage of the role education played in emanicipating Dalits in the last century.

Education is a means through which one inculcates knowledge, values, skills and attitudes. It is a major tool for socio-economic improvement of an individual and it also reduces social inequalities political assertation and income distribution. The education has been instrumental in defining and maping out the aims and objectives of an individual. In education the criteria is mere merit not the caste or creed of an individual. Thus it provides the right person with the oceanic opportunities in displaying his/her skill and intelligence. It has the potentiality for creating awareness of the difficulties and obstacles that may hinder the path of development. Such awareness in a better way helped the deprived groups to go in searach for alternative solutions of their problems for improving their lot and climbing the ladder of social hierarchy. In independent India the main objective of the education is to look after the needs and development of Dalit children who have remained isolated from the ambit of education for centuries. After the independence the changing governments at least took some means to raise the educational standard of the Dalits despite the result of the some has not been so satisfactory in the terms of its implementation and outcome. It has been found that the growth of the educational standard among Dalits are not uniform and educational facilities among backward castes are being distributed unevenly. In almost all the states in India certain prominent castes among the Dalits are dominating the educational facilities meant for the whole Dalit society.

This study provides the readers with an analytical and comprehensive coverage on Dalit Education. It focuses on the almost all the aspects of the Indian Educational system such as identification of Dalit; education and Dalits in India; schooling system and dalit children; dalit education and state responsibility; educatioon and identity formation; inequalities in education suffered by backward classes; debate development and dalit society; socio-cultural and dalit in higher education; and lastly social policy and social transformation. Almost all the historical evidences sourced out related to Dalits had pointed the identity of Dalits negatively. In Indian history Dalits had always been treated as object instead of as subject. By embracing other religions apart from Hinduism they put in all the efforts to regain their lost identity or status. In the present context two aspects of Dalit identity are discussed in better way. Firstly Dalit as object of history and secondly Dalit as subject of history. Thus, the major problem to be solved for the Dalits in India is to regain the fuller human self identity, which also means to become the subject of their own history. In fact, the main motive or purpose behind the various efforts including the change of religion from Hinduism to other religion by the Dalits has been too gain their lost identity or to establish a new one. The major problem of the Dalits has always been poverty superimposed by social discrimination Dalits, particularly scheduled castes (untouchables) were denied right to property, right to education and right to bargaining for wages. A good deal of attempt is made in this volume to look into the position of Dalits and their access to education in colonial India and their educational development in the post independence period in the context of more than 53 years of independence. The volume also deals with the access of untouchables to non-farm employment in post-independence period and their identity and the factors coming in the way of their educational development. The scheduled castes in India are considered to be a stigmatised lot and on this they suffer from a number of disabilities that are buttressed by religion.

Now, many a Dalit social reformers have came and made their efforts to give a force lift to the Dalit society. They could define the Dalitness in much impressive way. Dr. Ambedkar was the forerunner among these reformers. Dr. Ambedkar set new guidelines for the Dalit society to follow. According to these modern reformers Dalitness is essentially a means towards achieving a sense of cultural identity. Thus they helped in a great deal to remove the inferiority complex based on to be Dalit. Owing the rapidly changing societal structure the education standard of Dalits invariably going up. However the castes belonged to Dalit society itself. There are variations of social adjustment and educational performance of students of these communities depending up on variations in their socio-economic background, nature of institutions they join, and type of courses they opt for. Hence, it is proposed in this volume to look into variations in socio-economic background of the SC/ST students and their social and academic adjustement in institutions of higher education.

Correlations of Dalits varying socio-economic background and educational performance in particular programmes of study which they pursue is examined very thoroughly. Here, an attempt is made to trace the reason of the present lower status of the so-called untouchables in Indian society.

Bibliography

Ram, Raja : *Education for Scheduled Castes,* Peacock Publications, Chennai, 2003.

Abu Bekar, M. : *Union and the States in Education,* Shabd Sanchar, New Delhi, 2001.

Abha, Neelam: *Scheduled Caste Elite : A Study of Scheduled Caste Elite,* Booklinks Corporation, Hyderabad, 1999.

Addaval, S.B. (ed.) : *The Third India Year Book of Education Educational Research,* NCERT, New Delhi, 1968.

Aggarwal, J.C. : *National Policy on Education,* Arya Book Depot, New Delhi, 1979.

Aggarwal, J.C. : *Development and Planning of Modern Education with Special Reference to Dalits,* Kranti Publishing House, New Delhi, 1992.

Ajay Myrdal : *The Power of Dalits,* in Emmet John Hughs (ed.) *Education in World Perspective,* Lancer Books, New York, 1965.

Anderson, C.A. : *Education and Economic Development,* Frank Cass, London, 1971.

Andrew W. Halping (ed.) : *Administrative Theory in Education,* The MacMillan Company, New York, 1967.

Anmol, Roe : *Psychology of Casteism,* New York, John Wiley and Sons, 1956.

Aparna Basu : *The Growth of Education and Political Development in India,* Oxford University Press, Delhi, 1970.

Arbuckle, D.A. : "Philosophical Issues in Education," *Journal of Counselling Psychology,* 1959.

Biswas, Dutt : *New Educational Pattern in India,* Vikas Publishing House, Delhi, 1916.

Bhatnagar and Gunam Saran : *Education and Social Change,* The Minerva Associates, Calcutta, 1972.

Bhatia, S.C.: *Education and Socio-Cultural Disadvantage,* Xerxes Publications, Delhi, 1982.

Brij Raj Chauhan : *Scheduled Castes and Education,* Anu Publications, Meerut, 1975.

Buch, M.B. (ed.) : *A Survey of Research in Education,* Centre of Advanced Study in Education, M.S. University of Baroda, 1974.

Buch, M.B. (ed.) : *Second Survey of Research in Education,* Society for Educational Research and Development, Baroda, 1979.

Cattell, B.B. : *Abilities: Their Structure, Growth and Action,* Boston, Houghton Mifflin Co., 1971.

Charles Jeffries : *Illiteracy : A World Problem,* Pall Mall Press, London, 1967.

Chourasia, G. : *Challenges and Innovations in Education,* Sterling Publishers, New Delhi, 1977.

Denis, Lawton : *Education and Social Justice,* Sage Publications, London, 1977.

Desai, A.R. : *Rural Sociology in India,* Popular Prakashan, Bombay, 1978.

Desai, A.R. : "Social Change and Educational Policy", in M.S. Gore and Others (ed.), *Papers in the Sociology of Education in India,* NCERT, New Delhi.

Ehsanul Haq : *Education and Political Culture in India,* Sterling Publishers, New Delhi, 1981.

Gandhi, M.K. : *My Views on Education,* Bharatiya Vidya Bhavan, Bombay, 1970.

Gopinathan Nair, P.R. : *Primary Education, Population Growth and Socio-economic Change,* Allied Publishers, New Delhi, 1981.

Gore, M.S. (ed.) : *Sociology of Education,* NCERT, New Delhi, 1967

Inamdar, N.R.: *Educational Administration,* Popular Prakashan, Bombay, 1974.

Iqbal Narain, K.C. Pande : *Panchayati Raj and Educational Administration,* Aalakli Publishers, Jaipur, 1976.

John W., Hanson : *Education and the Development of Nations,* Holt, Rinehart and Winston, New York, 1966.

John Vaizey : *Education for Tomorrow* Penyuin, Landon, 1966

Julian, E. : *The Modern Rural School,* McGraw Hill, New York, 1952.

Kishore Gandhi : *Higher Education: A Sociological Analysis,* B.R. Publishing Corporation, Delhi, 1977.

Kidd, J.R. : *Education for Perspective,* Indian Education Association, New Delhi, 1969.

Kochhar, S.K. : *Pivotal Issues in Education,* Sterling, New Delhi, 1981.

Lakshmana Swamy Mudaliar A.: *Education in India,* Asia Publishing House, Bombay, 1960.

Louis Malassis : *The Rural World : Education and Development,* Croom Helm, London, 1976.

Mukherji, S.N. (ed.) : *Administration of Education in India,* Acharya Book Depot, Baroda, 1962.

Mukherjee, R.K. : *Social Structure of Values,* S. Chand & Company, New Delhi, 1964.

Naik, J.P. : *Educational Planning in India,* Allied Publishers, Bombay, 1965.

Naik, J.P. : *Education of the Scheduled Castes,* Occasional Monograph, ICSSR, New Delhi.

Naik, J.P. : *Elementary Education in India,* Allied Publishers, Bombay, 1975.

Naik, J.P. : *The National Education Policy,* Ministry of Education and Social Welfare, Government of India, New Delhi, 1979.

Naik, J.P. : *Some Perspectives on Non-Fomal Education,* Allied Publishers, New Delhi, 1977.

Niblett, W.R. : *Essential Education,* University of London, London, 1955.

Nural Hasan, S. : *Challenges in Education, Culture and Social Welfare,* Allied Publishers, Bombay, 1977.

Oldhan, J.N. : *Village Education in India,* Oxford University Press, London, 1922.

Pandey, S.N. : *Education and Social Changes,* Motilal Banerasidas, Delhi, 1976.

Premi, M.K. : *Educational Planning in India,* Sterling Publishers, New Delhi, 1972.

Raghunath Safaya : *Innovations and Latest Trends in Education,* The Associated Publishers, Ambala Cantt., 1976.

Rajagopal, M.V. : *Kothari Commission on School Education,* Vidyardhi Prachuranalu, Machilipatnam, 1967.

Ram Reddy, G. (ed.) : *Patterns of Panchayati Raj in India,* MacMillan Company of India, Madras, 1977.

Rao, M.S. : *Education Social Stratification and Mobility,* NCERT, New Delhi, 1997.

Rao, V.K.R.V. : *Education and Human Resource Development,* Allied Publishers, Bombay, 1966.

Ratna, G. Revankar : *The Indian Constitution: A Case Study of Backward Classes,* Associate University Press, Canbury, New Jersey, 1941.

Rudolph & Rudolph (ed.) : *Education and Politics in India,* Harvard University Press, Cambridge, 1972.

Russell, Bertrand : *Education and the Social Order,* Unwin, London, 1977.

Russel, Bertrand : *On Education,* Unwin Books, London, 1971.

Sachidananda : *The Harijan Elite,* Thomson Press, New Delhi, 1977.

Saini, S.K.: *Development of Education,* Cosmo Publications, New Delhi, 1980

Sateswari Saxena : *Education Planning in India,* Sterling Publishers, New Delhi, 1974

Satya, R.N. : *Innovations and Latest Trends in Education,* The Associated Publishers, Ambala Cantt., 1976.

Shri Prakash : *Educational System of India,* Concept Publishing Company, Delhi, 1977.

Shukla, P.D. : *Towards the New Pattern of Education,* Sterling Publishers, New Delhi, 1976.

Siqueira, T.N. : *The Education of India – History and Problems,* Oxford University Press, London, 1952.

Tiwari, D.D. : *Education at the Cross Roads,* Chugh Publications, Allahabad, 1975.

Tiwari, D.D. : *Thoughts on Education,* Chugh Publications, 1972.

Venkatasubramanian, K. : *Education and Learning,* N. Vidyaranya Swamy & Co. Secunderabad, 1979.